Cranbury Public Library
23 North Main St., Cranbury, NJ 08512
(609) 655-0555 f: (609) 655-2858

www.CranburyPublicLibrary.org

D0561193

CITIZEN SPIES

Citizen Spies

The Long Rise of America's Surveillance Society

Joshua Reeves

NEW YORK UNIVERSITY PRESS

New York

NEW YORK UNIVERSITY PRESS
New York
www.nyupress.org

References to Internet websites (URLs) were accurate at the time of writing.
Neither the author nor New York University Press is responsible for URLs that
may have expired or changed since the manuscript was prepared.

ISBN: 978-1-4798-0392-7

For Library of Congress Cataloging-in-Publication data, please contact the
Library of Congress.

New York University Press books are printed on acid-free paper,
and their binding materials are chosen for strength and durability.
We strive to use environmentally responsible suppliers and materials
to the greatest extent possible in publishing our books.

Manufactured in the United States of America

10 9 8 7 6 5 4 3 2 1

Also available as an ebook

CONTENTS

ACKNOWLEDGMENTS

My friend and mentor Hans Kellner once told me that academic debts are many and varied, and over the years I've learned that he was certainly right. Many people have helped me along the path to this book: above all, Jeremy Packer has been a constant source of creativity and guidance. I am also enormously grateful for the generosity displayed by Chris Ingraham, Matt May, and Ethan Stoneman as they endured years of exhausting monologues on surveillance, communication, rhetoric, and violence. I owe special thanks to Mark Andrejevic, Vicki Gallagher, and Hans Kellner for their encouragement and guidance while this project was in its infancy. All of my colleagues at the University of Memphis— especially Tony de Velasco, Patrick Dillon, Leroy Dorsey, Joy Goldsmith, Rika Hudson, Marina Levina, and Camisha Smith—helped keep me sane and happy while this book took shape between 2013 and 2015. The ILL staff at the University of Memphis proved to be tremendous sleuths who repeatedly impressed me with their tenacity and success. I would also like to thank my old pal Adam Chandler of Cornell University Library for tracking down a number of archival documents that were crucial to this project. My anonymous reviewers were incredibly generous and insightful, and I couldn't be more grateful for the challenges they set before me. Thanks, as well, to the staff at NYU Press, especially Alicia Nadkarni; it's been a wild and joyful three years. And to all the friends whose work I learn from and whose company I enjoy—folks like Carole Blair, Jack Bratich, Fernanda Duarte, Rachel Dubrofsky, Dan Faltesek, David Gruber, Rachel Hall, Colin Hesse, Nate Hulsey, Jason Kalin, Ashley Kelly, Kelsy Kretschmer, Kate Maddalena, Torin Monahan, Alex Monea, Ned O'Gorman, Kathy Oswald, Ehren Pflugfelder, Chris Russill, Dawn Shepherd, Dan Sutko, and Ken Zagacki, just to name a few—I look forward to whatever comes next. To my new friends in the College of Liberal Arts at Oregon State University—especially Krystal Canales, Loril Chandler, Sally Gallagher, Lee Ann Garrison, Trischa Goodnow,

Jeff Hale, Robert Iltis, Todd Kesterson, Bill Loges, Katrina Machorro, Elizabeth Root, Kim Rossi, Marion Rossi, and Gregg Walker—I would like to say thanks for making this such an interesting place to be. And finally: thanks to *Surveillance & Society* for providing an outlet for the very earliest iterations of this work. Small parts of the Introduction and Chapter One previously appeared in "If You See Something, Say Something: Lateral Surveillance and the Uses of Responsibility," *Surveillance & Society* 10.3/4 (2012): 235–48.

I should also thank the U.S. Department of Homeland Security, which has trademarked the original title for this book ("If You See Something, Say Something") and thus forced us to come up with a new title at the last minute. I like this one much better. And thanks, above all, for providing such a clear illustration of one of the book's main themes: how the state regulates the communicative conduct of its citizens.

Fortunately, my personal debts are just as many and varied as my academic ones. Although I cannot begin to list them all here, at the very least I should thank all the family and friends who were sidelined during the years I worked on this book. Finally, my wife Leslie deserves the most credit of all. This book—like so many other things I work for and enjoy—would be impossible without her. So it is to Leslie, as well as to Austin, Annelie, Amelia, and Oliver, that I dedicate this book.

Introduction

Seeing, Saying, and Civic Responsibility

When Neighborhood Watch volunteer George Zimmerman was acquitted for the murder of Trayvon Martin, public discourse was flooded with reflections on what the verdict said about America in the twenty-first century. Millions of Americans traced Martin's death—and then, Zimmerman's acquittal—to the nation's enduring legacy of racist violence. Anthea Butler, a professor at the University of Pennsylvania, stirred up controversy by remarking, "When George Zimmerman told Sean Hannity that it was God's will that he shot and killed Trayvon Martin, he was diving right into what most good conservative Christians in America think right now. Whatever makes them protected, safe, and secure is worth it at the expense of the black and brown people they fear."[1] For Butler and many other Americans,[2] the Trayvon affair was an explosive symptom of structural racism in the United States. From their point of view, Zimmerman's appeals to self-defense and neighborhood security simply rationalized interracial suspicion and increased the likelihood of further violence against marginalized groups.

Many Americans, however, had a different take on the Trayvon tragedy. For instance, rightwing activist and southern rock icon Ted Nugent praised the verdict, arguing that Zimmerman simply displayed "the fundamental responsibility of a neighbor who cares."[3] According to Nugent, Zimmerman's brand of neighborhood surveillance and inter-citizen vigilance is as American as apple pie. Offering his own version of the events that led to Trayvon's death, Nugent placed Zimmerman's actions within a context of rising local crime and neighborhood anxiety: "So this guy's neighborhood has been burglarized off and on and the residents are very concerned for their safety and well-being. Neighbors agree to upkick their vigilance and overall level of awareness to watch out for each other and keep an eye out for suspicious individuals and behavior. It could be considered by an official designation such as 'Neighborhood Watch,' but officially labeled or not, it is the purest form of Americans watching out for each other and being good neighbors."[4] For Nugent and other champions of Zimmerman's brand of vigilant citizenship, Trayvon Martin's death was a simple malfunction of the American dream.

This book is grounded in the assumption that Ted Nugent's appraisal of America is basically right. When Nugent identifies George Zimmerman's actions as "the purest form" of American sociality, he hints at a fundamental tension in the myth of the United States.[5] While American society has long nurtured an ethos of rugged, liberal individualism, at the same time it has continuously fostered cultures of vigilance, suspicion, meddling, snooping, and snitching. From its early displays in the witch hysterias and Puritan moral panics of colonial New England; to the vigilante posses of the Wild West and the Ku Klux Klan; to its Brown Scares, Green Scares, and Red Scares; and to the U.S.'s recurrent anxieties about immigrants, political dissidents, rebellious youth, criminals, and religious minorities, vigilance toward neighbors has long been aligned with American ideals of patriotic and moral duty. America's liberal individualism, therefore, has taken a curiously extroverted form, as its citizens have been constantly mobilized against a diverse barrage of enemies within.[6] In this environment, civic responsibility has often devolved into expressions of fear and mutual suspicion, with moral entrepreneurs treating their communities as a proving ground on which they should enact their loyalty to the state or to their personal moral codes. So while Ted Nugent might argue that George Zimmerman was simply acting like a "good neighbor" the night he killed Trayvon Martin, it is obvious that Zimmerman's conception of neighborly conduct was tied up with a volatile mix of suspicion and hostility. Needless to say, this reaction hardly indicates an affirmative sense of community among neighbors. Instead, it points to a potentially explosive sociocultural milieu in which civic duty is affirmed through local rituals of mutual suspicion and surveillance.

Focusing on developments during the twentieth and twenty-first centuries, this book sifts through the American experience in order to develop a genealogy of Neighborhood Watch and other citizen-surveillance programs. In building this account, the book examines how various public and private institutions have worked together to regulate the conduct of American citizens by activating their capacities for surveillance and communication—that is, by cultivating engaged citizens, like George Zimmerman, who feel it is their civic duty to scour their surroundings in order to *see something* and *say something*. I find that we can piece together a provocative portrait of American culture by analyzing how citizen surveillance has been practiced between neighbors; understood by the police, experts, and bureaucrats; promoted by pamphlets, speeches, social media, television, and other cultural programming; facilitated by an evolving participatory media landscape; and rejected or manipulated by everyday citizens, criminal subcultures, and resistance groups. As such, this book will look at how American citizens have been imagined and deployed as crucial—yet unpredictable and potentially dangerous—resources for policing the American experiment.

As the Trayvon Martin affair illustrates quite tragically, violence occasionally threatens to disrupt the liberal dream of peaceful citizen responsibility and self-government. This has been a matter of great concern for institutions like Neighborhood Watch, which takes great care to instruct its volunteers (often unsuccessfully) in the arts of nonviolent citizenship. As a Neighborhood Watch manual distributed by the Bureau of Justice Assistance warns, "Community members only serve as the extra 'eyes and ears' of law enforcement. They should report their observations of suspicious activities to law enforcement; however, citizens should never try to take action on those observations. Trained law enforcement should be the only ones ever to take action based on observations of suspicious activities."[7] Undergirding this policy is the belief that seeing (using carefully trained "eyes and ears") and saying (reporting suspicious activities to law enforcement) provide the practical foundation for citizens to police one another's conduct while still respecting what Max Weber long ago recognized as the state's defining privilege: its monopoly over legitimate violence.[8]

These efforts to cultivate seeing/saying responsibility have had a decisive impact on notions of civic responsibility in the United States. During the Nixon administration, as violent crime levels rose and American cities became increasingly restless, the White House commissioned a report to examine how to best reassert a sense of law and order in urban America. Prepared by politicians, police officials, judges, and prominent clergy, the report declared that one of the best ways to fight crime was to activate the seeing/saying responsibilities of the everyday citizen: according to the report, "the stereotype of the unconcerned, depersonalized *Homo urbanis* blandly watching the misfortunes of others [has] proved inaccurate. Instead, we find a bystander to an emergency is an anguished individual in genuine doubt, concerned to do the right thing but compelled to make complex decisions under pressure of stress and fear. His reactions are shaped by the actions of others—and all too frequently by their inaction."[9] According to the president's commission, the apathy and atomization of American citizens had been overestimated: with proper training and guidance, good Americans would happily fight together to reassert law and order in their communities.

The commission's thesis has proven remarkably accurate: while many Americans still resist the state's call to see something and say something, the law-and-order style of policing that emerged in the 1960s and 1970s has led to the development of a robust range of programs that cultivate seeing/saying citizenship. To take some examples from this book, we might consider National Neighborhood Watch (1972), the development of a nationwide 911 crime-reporting technology apparatus (1968), and Drug Abuse Resistance Education (or D.A.R.E., 1981). These concerted demands on citizens' civic responsibility have been part and parcel of the great liberal policing project, and Americans' cultivated propensity for seeing and saying is at the core of America's participatory political culture. So despite whatever preconceptions we have about Americans' inaction and apathy vis-à-vis their neighbors, these programs and their antecedents have played a vital role in the formation of American social and civic responsibility.

In order to tease out the cultural and political significance of these developments, among the questions addressed in this book are: how have the police and their allies attempted to turn citizens into their "eyes and ears"?[10] How have police authorities attempted to regulate what these citizens see and say? How have media technologies provided citizens with unique opportunities to use surveillance and communication—in all their diversity—to police the conduct of their peers? Because of these demands to see something and say something, in what ways has our civic responsibility been reduced to a sum of policing protocols? How have citizens resisted these pressures to monitor their peers? And finally, to what political effect have certain citizens turned their own capacities for seeing and saying against state authorities, reporting police abuses and political corruption? Ultimately, I hope these concerns prompt my readers to reconsider popular notions about citizen surveillance, civic empowerment, the relationship between communication and social change, and the promise and pitfalls of social responsibility in the digital era.

Why Communication? Surveillance and Communicative Action

This book, therefore, isn't just about surveillance. It's a book about seeing *and* saying, about the political and cultural relationship between surveillance and communication. As an entryway to this problem, I would like to discuss one of the most obvious ways in which today's Americans are being asked to police the conduct of their peers: the "If You See Something, Say Something" campaign, which is an antiterrorism initiative that the U.S. Department of Homeland Security (DHS) launched in 2010. Working with sports stadiums, malls, hotels, local transportation departments, airports, and Wal-Mart, the DHS began using telescreens to repeatedly broadcast a sixty-second video of then DHS secretary Janet Napolitano, encouraging citizens to look out for suspicious activity. As shoppers paid for their goods at Wal-Mart's automated checkout stands, many of them were greeted by Secretary Napolitano urging them to do their part in the fight against terror: "Homeland security begins with hometown security. . . . If you see something suspicious in the parking lot or in the store, say something immediately. Report suspicious activity to your local police or sheriff. If you need help, ask a Wal-Mart manager for assistance. Thank you for doing your part to help keep our hometowns safe."[11] The initiative's video public service announcement campaign warned Americans to be on the lookout for ostensibly "suspicious" activities, such as someone leaving a backpack unattended at a train station, talking on a cell phone, using cash, or frequently checking a wristwatch.

This nationwide campaign, which was first tested after September 11, 2001, by the New York Metropolitan Transportation Authority, has encountered a few setbacks: although the "see something" part of the campaign is gaining technical and cultural momentum—that is, as surveillance has become an increasingly dominant element of our political landscape—the "say something" part ran into a legal roadblock. Under ordinary circumstances, if your neighbor saw you having an angry cell phone conversation and falsely accused you of terrorism, s/he would be vulnerable to libel action. But in the state of legal and cultural exception that has characterized the United States since the September 11 attacks, the civic duty to "say something" has been recognized as an essential weapon in the War on Terror. Republican congressman Peter King made this clear when he introduced the See Something, Say Something Act of 2011, which aimed to protect citizens from libel action if they falsely accused their peers of terrorism. Responding to the controversy caused by this legislation, one of the bill's corporate sponsors explained that it would simply encourage a "vigilant mindset" among citizens.[12] Since September 11, 2001, the sponsor remarked, "elected leaders have repeatedly called on everyday people to be the eyes and ears looking out for the next potential terrorist act. By this Act, Congress will give weight to that request by providing common-sense protections to citizens who do just that."[13] Indeed, with the "If You See Something, Say Something" campaign and its abundant counterparts in the present cultural scene, the Department of Homeland Security and allied authorities are promoting this "vigilant mindset" among citizens, encouraging them to be the "eyes and ears" that surveil their neighbors, family members, and fellow shoppers, travelers, and sports fans.

What is curiously absent from this public discourse, however, is that citizens are not only being asked to use their "eyes and ears," but to use their mouths, as well. As Richard Ericson and Kevin Haggerty have recognized, we now find ourselves in "a knowledge society in which *informing* is promoted not only as legitimate but also as an act of good citizenship."[14] To promote informing as an act of good citizenship, the "If You See Something, Say Something" campaign—which was revived in the early days of 2015 by Napolitano's successor, DHS secretary Jeh Johnson[15]—treats surveillance and communication as two sides of the same coin of responsible citizenship. As Americans are increasingly called on to police themselves and their neighbors, carrying out surveillance is only half the battle. They must also respond to the call of citizenship by dialing the cops, reporting suspicions, filing reports, or resorting to other communicative action in order to prevent or report acts of crime and terrorism.

This oversight in public discourse, in fact, is also present in scholarly discussions of surveillance studies. While academic interest in surveillance is exploding, very little has been said about the political complementarity of communication and surveillance. In 2007, Kelly Gates and Shoshana Magnet introduced a special issue of *The Communication Review* dealing with the relationship between communication and surveillance. Their introduction, which would later be extended in the pair's edited volume *The New Media of Surveillance*,[16] argues: "the relationship between surveillance and communication—especially the media of communication—is an established and growing object of interdisciplinary concern."[17] Gates and Magnet go on to propose a number of potential sites of analysis for studying where surveillance and communication research might intersect. Yet with their focus on the relationships between surveillance and technologies of information and communication—e.g., surveillance cameras, computerized data collection, and mediated representations of surveillance—they have (as they admit) only scratched the surface of this relationship. While increasing numbers of media and communication scholars are taking up research in surveillance, this work, too, tends toward discussions of how media technologies play an indispensable role in the evolving surveillance landscape.

Just as important as this focus on media technologies, however, is an analysis of how public and private institutions work together to cultivate human subjects that enact their civic duty by carrying out regulated acts of speaking citizenship. This book, therefore, gives an answer to Ronald Greene's challenge[18] to theorize the conditions that give rise to diverse modalities of the speaking subject. To better understand the cultural production of this subject, Greene has argued that "we should pay closer attention to the emergence of a more concrete rhetorical subject, a subject that speaks and is spoken to, and the different techniques and technologies organized to transform individuals into a communicating subject."[19] Describing this provocative new path for the study of communication, rhetoric, and culture, Greene takes cues from Michel Foucault, arguing: "The first point to emphasize about a Foucaultian approach to subjectification is a shift from the semiotic to the technological dimensions of rhetoric. . . . Thus, rhetoric can move from its 'typical' location within the terrain of meaning to appear as a technology of the self, using communication and other techniques, to help individuals develop relationships with themselves, as rhetorical subjects."[20] As this book is concerned, Greene's shift from semiotic analysis to subjectification allows us to analyze the cultural processes by which citizenship captures communication power and puts it to work for the state.[21] By learning to carry out regulated acts of communication—that is, by speaking to the right authorities, and by making the right kinds of statements at the appropriate times—subjects can embody ideals of conduct that are associated with moral responsibility and good citizenship. As Greene has argued with his colleague Daryl Hicks, this approach "reveals how power works productively by augmenting the human capacity for speech/communication. . . . [An] under-appreciated aspect of the productive power of cultural governance resides in the generation of subjects who come to understand themselves as speaking subjects willing to regulate and transform their communicative behaviors for the purpose of improving their political, economic, cultural, and affective relationships."[22] While Greene confines his analysis to traditional speaking subjects like orators and debaters, the present book argues that we should broaden our attention to include the processes by which subjects are coaxed into performing more mundane expressions of speaking citizenship—for example, how Americans are convinced to fulfill their civic duty by snitching, witnessing, calling the cops, and carrying out other regulated forms of communicative action that aid in policing their peers. By expanding the focus of critical communication and rhetorical studies to include these mundane, microphysical acts of communication, we can better observe how diverse forms of speaking citizenship are crucial to the ethical self-production of liberal citizens.

The Body as Surveillance Technology

"If you see something, say something," therefore, will serve as this book's key thematic and conceptual backbone. Through five case studies, the book illustrates a number of different ways in which *seeing* and *saying* have functioned as essential and inextricable tools in the self-regulation of the American people, particularly during the twentieth and twenty-first centuries. Following this line of argument, I suggest that while most surveillance scholars are turning their attention to the surveillance potential of various sensors, cameras, and related technologies, the surveilling human subject serves as a crucial yet overlooked cultural phenomenon. In fact, one of the most compelling and provocative claims of recent surveillance research is that, because of the advent of digital technologies, the human subject is being gradually removed from the labor of surveillance.[23] To take a few basic examples, consider that video cameras on street corners and in private buildings capture vast amounts of data—far more than mere humans could store, process, and retrieve. Likewise, web merchants and search engines do not employ swaths of humans to monitor users' web browsing habits or shopping bills in order to customize their advertisements and coupons: these data, on the contrary, are being processed by increasingly complex and autonomous computing systems. Computers, functioning on algorithmic intelligence, sift instantly through that data while they analyze and classify individual and aggregate consumer tendencies.

It is undeniable that in many cases digital surveillance technologies are rendering the observing human subject all but superfluous. Yet there are also good reasons to focus on the human as a subject of surveillance—the most important of which, perhaps, is that we should keep within our analytical purview the full assortment of practices that characterize our current "surveillance society."[24] Ultimately, a purely technical view of surveillance limits what constitutes surveillance as an object of political critique and thus restricts what we as citizens can evaluate, expose, and attempt to resist and change. After all, in our everyday lives we are increasingly called on to carry out surveillance on our peers. While digital technologies might dominate the surveillance landscape, the continuous development of these human-based programs brings up important questions about the current and future state of American culture. Those works that have focused on the surveilling human subject—such as Alexandra Natapoff's *Snitching: Criminal Informants and the Erosion of American Justice*, Jim Redden's *Snitch Culture: How Citizens Are Turned into the Eyes and Ears of the State*, and Steve Hewitt's *Snitch: A History of the Modern Intelligence Informer*—tend to analyze how citizens are coerced or paid to snitch on their fellow citizens. By contrast, this book focuses on how citizen surveillance has been promoted as a civic duty, as well as how that civic duty has been regulated through discourses, technologies, and laws that promote *appropriate* forms of seeing/saying citizenship.

This turn to the human leads us back to our question: if computers make far better surveillance machines than humans, why are we witnessing a rise in the popularity of citizen-surveillance campaigns such as the "If You See Something, Say Something" program? In the following pages, I would like to focus on the two answers that I think are most important. First, the seeing/saying human subject is endowed with unique intelligence-gathering potential that allows it to complement and enrich purely technical forms of data collection and analysis. And second, empowering citizens to police their own geographic, professional, political, and moral communities serves an essential political demand of late liberal government. As to the first point, citizens can serve as mobile, versatile surveillance "technologies" because of their capacities to see something and say something—that is, because of their ability to gather, process, and transmit intelligence, much of which cannot be adequately gathered or interpreted by computers and other media technologies.[25] For example, we might consider that expensive, cutting-edge, and intrusive federal programs like Total Information Awareness and sophisticated technology hubs like the Echelon data-processing center failed to prevent the September 11 attacks. As Armand Mattelart has recognized, such a spectacular failure points out that "the exclusively technological approach to intelligence, at the expense of human intelligence, thus revealed its limitations."[26] Even Michael Hayden, former director of both the CIA and the National Security Agency, emphasizes that human-gathered intelligence still outweighs the value of technical surveillance in the international arena. According to Hayden, "the top twenty percent of American intelligence—that exquisite insight into an enemy's intentions—is generally provided by human sources."[27] So while in many ways we have seen a shift toward technical surveillance in the homeland security and commercial sectors, the limitations of these methods are readily acknowledged by important figures in our political class. Thus as the continued relevance of human-based programs like "If You See Something, Say Something" attests, citizens are still highly valued for their abilities to gather and transmit intelligence.

Due to the citizen's raw epistemological utility, in fact, we are witnessing more comprehensive moves to deploy the seeing/saying human body in the domestic sphere. To the extent that seeing and speaking serve as basic data-processing competencies, they provide an important common ground for the activation of citizen responsibility. While it is readily acknowledged among scholars[28] that "the population" became an *object* of "biopolitical" knowledge and intervention during the nineteenth century—a process that allowed authorities to treat the entire citizenry as a whole biological specimen with collective disease rates, birth and death rates, etc.—the individual human body has likewise become an important *subject* and tool of governmental intervention. We should keep in mind, then, that these human biological capacities serve in many instances as both the target *and the technology* of government. In the words of Barbara Cruikshank, "Democratic citizens . . . are both the effects and the instruments of liberal governance."[29] As I illustrate throughout the book, government is carried out not just *on* the body of individual citizens—for example, via various programs meant to promote general health and welfare, such as vaccination campaigns and food provisions for the poor—government is also carried out *through* these citizens' bodies, particularly through their capacities for surveillance and communication. When the DHS or local authorities ask us to function as the "eyes and ears" of the security apparatus, we are reminded that not only are we the objects of the state's protection, our seeing/saying bodies are also among the essential tools that provide for that protection. Citizens' sight and speech are thus given a *technological* character, in that they are transformed from basic organic faculties into the technical means for scrutinizing and policing the conduct of other citizens. Under various forms of cultural pedagogy—from "If You See Something, Say Something" video promos to Neighborhood Watch training seminars, and from children's D.A.R.E. coloring books to episodes of *America's Most Wanted*—our sight is trained to become surveillance, and our communication is trained to become snitching, witnessing, and reporting.

Seeing, Saying, and Liberal Government

In addition to this cooptation of citizens' sight and speech, citizen-surveillance programs provide for a central function of liberal government: they actively mobilize citizens within their communities, empowering them to provide for crucial aspects of government that the state cannot or will not provide. Following in the footsteps of Michel

Foucault,[30] Toby Miller has characterized this form of liberal "governmentality" as the "means of managing the public by having it manage itself."[31] Born from a rejection of raw, coercive state power, liberal governmentality can be characterized by two primary principles: first, a critique of state intervention into the social and economic spheres, and hence an emphasis on citizens' individual freedom and personal responsibility; and second, an investment in active, entrepreneurial models of citizen engagement. These complementary principles help establish the population as a more or less immanent domain of government, so that citizens not only govern their own behavior but also that of their peers. To get to the bottom of liberal power, then, we cannot think of it in merely negative terms (as simply civic freedom and the *lack* of state intervention); instead, we must consider the ways in which diverse authorities—both public and private, often acting in concert—govern citizens in such a way that they are led to carry out their "freedoms" in very specific ways.

Cultural theorist Tony Bennett has provided an influential expansion on this theme, arguing that liberal governmentality has "aimed to inveigle the general populace into complicity with power by placing them on this side of a power which it represented to it as its own."[32] An essential element of this productive style of social regulation is the promotion of *voluntary* forms of personal and mutual responsibility, so that citizens will choose to improve and protect themselves—and, by extension, often their communities—in the name of security, safety, morality, health, or the common good. This process of "responsibilization,"[33] as Foucault called it, is characterized by two primary types of responsibility: an individualistic self-reliance, and a morally driven (and often moralistic) community engagement. On the one hand, various public and private authorities encourage citizens to make an active effort to improve their hygiene, physical and mental health, and overall productivity. For example, citizens might be provided with moral encouragement and various financial incentives to make basic improvements to their physical well-being: employers might offer to pay for their employees' health club membership fees, and local governments might develop outreach programs that encourage citizens to exercise and to adopt more balanced diets. These programs function by striving to make citizens an object of consistent self-scrutiny and self-improvement, so that they will more or less voluntarily adopt lifestyles that allow them to be more productive members of society without the coercive threat of state punishment. Yet on the other hand, this responsibilization has a centrifugal valence— these citizens learn to care for themselves by caring for a limited set of others to whom they are connected: e.g., their families, their neighborhood blocks, their churches, their political comrades, and so forth. In the words of Nikolas Rose, civic responsibilization entails "the obligation to continuously and repeatedly evidence one's citizenship credentials as one recurrently links oneself into the circuits of civility."[34] As seeing and saying have formed a cornerstone of our civic obligations, active, responsibilized citizens assert their civic value by policing the lives of others in order to promote certain ideals of security, safety, health, cleanliness, and morality.[35] To take some of the examples from this book, these civic entrepreneurs join Neighborhood Watch programs, call the police to report suspicious activities, and otherwise take care to say something when they see something. In doing so, these citizens identify with the rationalities and conduct of the police, forming pockets of inter-citizen vigilance within their geographical, professional, and moral communities.

A crucial element of liberal government, then, is the production of a structured civic environment in which citizens choose to exercise their freedoms in appropriate ways. This is accomplished, in part, by the development of discourses, technologies, and institutions that mediate the ways in which citizens interact with the world around them. To cop the vocabulary of criminologist Les Johnston, this mediating process channels citizens' conduct toward practices of "responsible citizenship" while discouraging them from indulging in acts of unregulated, unapproved, "autonomous citizenship."[36] For Johnston, responsible citizenship is "a form of citizenship that is both sanctioned and sponsored by the state."[37] Today's official Neighborhood Watch, for example, functions as a mediating institution that attempts to channel its volunteers' behavior toward norms of "responsible," legally sanctioned behavior. Through seminars, rules, regulations, slogans, and a hierarchical supervisory structure, Neighborhood Watch trains its citizens in responsible forms of seeing/saying conduct while condemning violent action, concealed weaponry, and other things that threaten the state's monopoly over violence. Seeing and saying are thus promoted as the height of responsible citizenship, while violence and physical engagement are condemned as dangerous forms of "autonomous citizenship." Although autonomous citizens like George Zimmerman will occasionally (and inevitably) break these rules of responsible citizenship, that is simply an accidental hiccup in liberalism's machinery of regulated freedom. To minimize these hiccups, authorities invest considerable resources in diverse forms of institutional, technological, and cultural mediation that promote responsible citizenship while discouraging its autonomous counterparts.

By emphasizing the importance of mediation to this process, therefore, I am emphasizing that citizens are not just asked to see anything and say anything—rather, they are urged to see the right things and say the right things. An important part of this book, therefore, will center on how this mediation between responsible and autonomous citizenship is carried out, as well as how resistance groups and lawbreakers sidestep these attempts to regulate their conduct by seeing and saying things that they shouldn't (or, in some cases, by rejecting seeing/saying dogma altogether). It is thus important to recognize that these attempts to promote seeing/saying citizenship are at different times ignored and even manipulated by members of the public. Surveillance and communication serve as contested sites for citizen engagement, and this book provides a historical look at how programs promoting seeing/saying citizenship have been regulated, rationalized, and oftentimes rejected.

Ultimately, by focusing on how citizens serve as intelligence resources for various authorities, how they play an indispensable role in liberal government by policing the conduct of their peers, and how some of them turn this surveillance power back against authorities, this book recenters attention upon human subjects as agents of surveillance. As the work of Mark Andrejevic[38] has most clearly demonstrated, these forms of "lateral surveillance," which signals the ways in which citizens carry out surveillance on one another, have become defining social practices in the digital era. However, while Andrejevic acknowledges that lateral surveillance is not a new phenomenon,[39] he largely confines his analysis of lateral surveillance to developments of the past two decades. The historical diversity of American lateral surveillance initiatives, therefore, is a story that still needs to be told. By providing a number of case studies of lateral surveillance I hope not only to fill this gap in the historical record, but also to illustrate the importance of contextualizing surveillance alongside its predominant co-conspirator, communication. Through an analysis of how surveillance and communication have been articulated together in various historical moments of governmental reason and practice, this book reveals new possibilities for rethinking the past, present, and future of liberal government. I present "See Something, Say Something," therefore, as more than simply a catchy slogan for a domestic security campaign. While of course it serves as a trope for American citizens' overactive insecurities about criminality and terrorism, "See Something, Say Something" is, just as much, a clear assertion of how two basic biosocial competencies have provided essential resources for the self-regulation of the American public.

Book Overview

This book's chapters each offer a different illustration of how surveillance and communication have been central to citizen-policing projects. While many other important developments in lateral surveillance could be described here—to take just a few examples, American citizens' long history of immigrant surveillance,[40] anticommunist suspicion campaigns during the Cold War,[41] and lateral surveillance initiatives aimed at African Americans,[42] gays and lesbians,[43] the sick and contagious,[44] and other targeted groups throughout the twentieth century—these crucial developments have been described elsewhere in great detail. The case studies in this book, therefore, focus on less-examined lateral surveillance practices that grant unique insight into the rise of what Jack Bratich calls our "democratized spy and snitch culture."[45] While this book does not claim to provide a comprehensive history of American lateral surveillance campaigns, it does aim to illustrate the political versatility of lateral surveillance and communication as they have been practiced together in recent U.S. history.

Chapter One describes how police authorities have used crowdsourcing technologies to distribute seeing/saying responsibilities to the public. From the days of the trumpet in the Middle Ages to the rise of police-affiliated social media accounts, widely scattered police authorities have attempted to extend their surveillance power by using media technologies to tap into the sensory resources of the population. This chapter illustrates how communities are not only the targets of governmental interventions, they are also a means of governing citizens' conduct.[46] From this point of view, "community" is a network of interpersonal relationships that can be nurtured and cultivated in the service of the police apparatus. As surveillance theorist David Lyon has pointed out, "there is evidence that small-scale communities know fairly intimately about each other's lives and that such knowledge may be turned to regulatory purpose."[47] By crowdsourcing community responsibility in this way, police authorities capitalize on civilians' surveillance power by encouraging citizens to be on the lookout for suspects and potential criminality during their everyday lives. Popular shows like *America's Most Wanted* translated these efforts from print and radio to television, and social media like Facebook, Pinterest, and Twitter are rapidly becoming the new frontiers of police crowdsourcing campaigns. Through a historical analysis of these technologies and the rationalities that guide their use— and with close attention to how citizens have used these technologies to crowdsource outrage at police brutality—I describe how crowdsourcing has become an important site of struggle for those wishing to guide others' civic responsibility.

Chapter Two focuses on a different level of responsibilization, describing how 911 technologies have mediated citizens' interactions with the police. Ultimately, this chapter examines how 911 Emergency has helped transform our social responsibility into *civic* responsibility: by encouraging citizens to call 911 rather than take direct local action, 911 Emergency has rechanneled a number of basic social functions through the police station. Analyzing the different media infrastructures that have empowered citizens to contact the police—from the earliest telegraphic "private boxes" of the 1870s, to the development of 911 Emergency, and to the smartphone crime-reporting apps of today—I show how authorities have used technical and communicative protocols to govern what citizens see and say. In this regard, little has changed since the nineteenth century, when a brute standardization of citizen-police telecommunications became standard operating procedure in jurisdictions across the United States. Following this history through to the present day, I analyze the controversial new "See-Hear-Report" program that encourages students at a rural Kentucky high school to use anonymous text messages to report their peers' petty infractions to school and police authorities. Asked to function as anonymized data collection devices for the police apparatus, many citizens prove eager to turn against their peers for the promise of cheap rewards and civic gratification. Yet pranksters have used these anonymizing technologies to their advantage, as "Swatting" and other illegal crime reporting practices have become more prominent in the last decade. While this has given rise to increased police surveillance over 911 and allied crime-reporting technologies, it has also fostered an interesting mix of pranks and other acts of resistance.

This story dovetails with a problem that I describe in further detail in Chapter Three. Although American Neighborhood Watch programs have their roots in the colonial town watch system, I suggest that the crucial developmental moment in community watch history was the taming of vigilante, "autonomous" citizen-policing movements into groups that practiced responsible citizenship. As the U.S. federal government strove to impose centralized sovereign control over its vast territory, it enforced its monopoly on violence by cracking down on autonomous, "Wild West" justice and vigilante movements (particularly in the South and on the western frontier). Local police departments, however, still relied heavily on citizens to provide intelligence and carry out coordinated lateral surveillance. In order to cultivate these civic responsibilities while nevertheless maintaining the state's monopoly on violence, Neighborhood Watch and similar programs emphasized their volunteers' role as the "eyes and ears" of the police force. We might consider this as the gradual and uneven process by which "Wanted Dead or Alive" was transformed into "Dangerous: Do Not Approach—Contact Authorities Immediately." Through this lens, I analyze a wide range of rituals and texts that police departments and allied cultural authorities use to cultivate practices of responsible citizenship among Watch volunteers, including seminars, television commentaries, newspaper editorials, and Neighborhood Watch training materials. While these texts help mediate citizens' social engagement by channeling their conduct toward approved forms of responsible citizenship, I also discuss how laws and police interventions regulate the conduct of citizens' patrols like Cop Block, Copwatch, and the Huey P. Newton Gun Club. These groups, which monitor for police brutality, encounter different challenges than the bourgeois, state-approved groups that watch for the crimes of their fellow citizens.

While previous chapters focus on the adult neoliberal subject, Chapter Four turns its attention to the seeing/saying youth in American history. From the Boy Police and Junior Coppettes in the early years of the twentieth century to Officer Oliver Cowan's Junior Police Corps in the 1940s, American kids have long been trained to exercise their citizenship through responsible practices of seeing and saying. While this tradition has many contemporary counterparts, perhaps its most important legacy lies in D.A.R.E. America (originally Drug Abuse Resistance Education, or simply D.A.R.E.). Emerging in the early years of America's War on Drugs, D.A.R.E. America has used diverse forms of outreach—including seminars, coloring books, school programs, television shows, books, and social media—to train students to police the conduct of their peers and parents. This element of D.A.R.E.'s program—that it encourages kids to spy on their parents—has made it an especially controversial element of the American cultural landscape. Many young D.A.R.E. Kids have told trusted program officers about their parents' casual drug use, only to have their families destroyed and their lives turned upside down when local cops use that information to raid their homes and arrest their parents. Countering this trend in seeing/saying youth culture, however, is a "Stop Snitching" ethos prominent in many urban communities. While the police urge kids and teens to see something and say something, some of their peers remind them that "snitches get stitches." A fight over the speaking subjectivity of these youths is thus waged, as cops launch "Keep Talking" campaigns to counter the rising influence of trends in Stop Snitching youth culture. In this chapter, therefore, "D.A.R.E. America" is analyzed not strictly as a state-sponsored institution, but as an analogy for this social milieu in which youth are beset by these competing claims on their seeing/speaking subjectivities.

Finally, Chapter Five reflects on the lessons of the previous chapters in order to evaluate the controversial lateral surveillance programs that have arisen in the domestic War on Terror. Similar developments, I argue, have repeatedly appeared during times of war. While a number of observers have emphasized the uniqueness of the Department of Homeland Security's domestic programs, this chapter illustrates the genealogical continuity between these initiatives and earlier domestic counterespionage efforts that emphasized citizens' duties to see something and say something. An important element of this continuity is the mobilization of citizens against shadowy, unidentifiable enemies that are potentially lurking around every corner. In fact, the DHS assures us that anyone could be a terrorist, that terrorist attacks could occur anywhere and at anytime, and that the best defense against terrorism is a generalized vigilance in which citizens remain constantly watchful of their neighbors, coworkers, and any other potential homegrown militants. After reviewing precedents during World War One, World War Two, and the Cold War, this chapter analyzes the rise and fall of numerous antiterrorist lateral surveillance initiatives that emerged after September 11, 2001. While the George W. Bush administration never quite developed an energetic, nationwide lateral surveillance initiative, the Obama administration has placed considerable emphasis on seeing, saying, and civic responsibility. While numerous observers have pointed out that this citizen intelligence is of dubious utility in the War on Terror, it is perhaps just as important that the sheer mobilization of citizens within policing roles aids in their identification with the state and its domestic security objectives.

Based upon these observations, in the Conclusion I reflect on the political potential of lateral surveillance in the United States. As with most programs of the liberal present, we could point to a number of more or less positive attributes of current lateral surveillance initiatives. We can be grateful, of course, that some methods of police crowdsourcing have brought violent criminals to justice, and that 911 Emergency allows people to summon help when they are under the threat of attack. Yet as it becomes abundantly clear by my discussion of Neighborhood Watch (Chapter Three), these trends in lateral surveillance have political implications that reverberate far beyond their immediate crime-fighting utility. While it is easy to be critical of the DHS's obtrusive and even "Orwellian" security apparatus[48] (Chapter Five), these diverse efforts simply seem to be individual symptoms of an ongoing tendency to establish civic responsibility as a set of policing procedures. It is unfortunate that, while we could use our eyes and mouths to build solidarity—or even to bring accountability to capital, the police, and a corrupt ruling class—we far too often direct that scrutiny against our friends, families, and neighbors for apparently failing to live up to ideal standards of moral or legal conduct. So while assorted figures from the left and right call on us to discover and police difference among our peers, I urge my readers to recapture their eyes, ears, and mouths from this growing citizen-police apparatus. By learning to see, hear, and speak to one another in new ways, perhaps we can discover creative forms of security that are framed on solidarity, not vigilance, suspicion, and terror.

1

The Power of the Crowd

Police Crowdsourcing

In an electric information environment . . . [t]oo many people know too much about each other. Our new environment
compels commitment and participation. We have become
irrevocably involved with, and responsible for, each other.
—Marshall McLuhan and Quentin Fiore[1]

Now is the time for all good men to come to the aid of their
neighbor! Repeat! Now is the time for all good men to come
to the aid of their neighbor!
—Deputy Barney Fife

On August 24, 1985, a man broke into the home of Bill Carns and Inez
Erickson, a young couple living in Mission Viejo, California. After pull-
ing out a pistol and shooting Bill in the head, the intruder tied up Inez
and raped her repeatedly. Hours later, as her attacker fled the scene, Inez
pulled herself up to the bedroom window just in time to catch a glimpse
of him driving away in an orange Toyota station wagon. Because Inez
was able to provide police with a description of the automobile and a
partial license plate number, the California State Police began scouring the area for the orange Toyota. When the car was found abandoned
four days later, police were able to pull a fingerprint from the car, which
they traced to convicted thief and local drug addict Richard Ramirez.
Ramirez had a mug shot on file with the Los Angeles Police Department,
and detectives confirmed that he fit the physical description that Inez
and other sexual assault survivors in the area had given. On August 30,
Los Angeles County sheriff Sherman Block announced that they had
identified Ramirez as the notorious "Night Stalker" who had carried
out more than a dozen home invasion-murders in the preceding three

months: "All police agencies in California and surrounding states have been notified. . . . You cannot escape. Every law officer and every citizen now knows exactly what you look like and who you are."[2] At the request of the LAPD, Ramirez's mug shot was emblazoned on television screens and newspapers, and radio stations warned listeners to be on the lookout for the lanky, Chicano male with long hair and bad teeth. Unaware that he had suddenly become a local celebrity, that morning Ramirez shot up some cocaine in a public restroom before walking into a liquor store. When the storeowner recognized Ramirez from a photograph on the front page of a newspaper, he repeatedly screamed, "*El matador! El matador!*" ("The killer!") as Ramirez ran out into the street. Surrounded by photographs of himself on newsstands and TV screens, he fled from the neighborhood on foot, trailed by a small mob of citizens who were shouting that he was the Night Stalker. As Ramirez tried to escape, he ran across a highway into an East Los Angeles neighborhood, where he tried to steal a car. But he had no such luck; the mob chased him for several blocks and finally pinned him down until cops arrived on the scene. His photograph had been released to the public only a few hours earlier.

The Richard Ramirez case illustrates the central role that media technologies like newspapers and television play in modern police manhunts. If journalists and the police had not tapped into the crowdsourcing potential of these media, Ramirez might have had the chance to kill again. These crowdsourcing technologies, in fact, have played a central role in policing for hundreds of years. Before the advent of print, citizens used trumpets and rattles to alert their neighbors to the presence of intruders or thieves. Then print technologies like the "hue and cry" declaration, which was an early ancestor of the Wanted poster, pulled citizens into the policing apparatus by alerting them to rewards, crimes, stolen goods, and potential threats. Cultivating what Rachel Hall calls the "vigilant viewer,"[3] throughout American history these crowdsourcing technologies have taken diverse forms, including rogues' galleries, police gazettes, "Missing Child" photographs on milk cartons, popular television shows like *America's Most Wanted*, and now, in the digital age, police-affiliated social media accounts and online community forums.

In a recent public service announcement, John Walsh, the former host of *America's Most Wanted*, provides an important insight into the impetus behind these police crowdsourcing projects: "A police department is only as good as the people it serves. That's why the good cops working the streets . . . need your eyes, your ears, and every ounce of support you can give them. It's a partnership."[4] In this video, Walsh places the responsibility for surveillance squarely on the citizen, who is instructed less in community responsibility than in loyalty to the police apparatus.[5] As neoliberal economic austerity has cut departmental budgets to the bone, police crowdsourcing programs have become a Band-Aid for local authorities who promote civic participation in lieu of tackling the larger structural issues that lead to crime and social alienation. In a process that has grown in intensity since the financial crisis of 2008, many jurisdictions have adopted "technology"—especially crowdsourcing technology—as the answer to crime and countless other social ills, thus forestalling important conversations about the causes and reproduction of crime, violence, and social injustice.

This is a troubling development, even for those of us who are grateful that there are systems in place that allow communities to unite against predators like Richard Ramirez. As criminologist Gary T. Marx has recognized, these efforts "draw on the higher civic tradition of democratic participation, self-help, and community. They may also deter. Yet there is something troubling about them."[6] Indeed, there is a troubling difference between journalists and police agencies collaborating to publicize the I.D. of a serial killer, and, on the other hand, police departments publicizing petty crimes on Facebook and Pinterest in order to increase arrest statistics and generate fine revenues. The disparity between these cases illustrates how police crowdsourcing, despite its democratic, community-friendly veneer, can have questionable social consequences. This chapter will focus on some of these negative effects, because crowdsourcing has enjoyed a rather appreciative reception from scholars and the public at large. Most analysts have accepted crowdsourcing as a more or less new and positive phenomenon that helps businesses and other institutions quickly solve problems.[7] Arguing that it "is just one manifestation of a larger trend toward greater democratization in commerce," Jeff Howe, who coined the term "crowdsourcing" in a 2006 *Wired* magazine article, suggests: "Contrary to the foreboding, dystopian vision that the Internet serves primarily to isolate people from each other, crowdsourcing uses technology to foster unprecedented levels of collaboration and meaningful exchanges."[8] For Howe and other advocates of crowdsourcing and similar social media trends, these technologies naturally give rise to collaboration and democratic participation. However, the history of police crowdsourcing paints a different picture, one that shows how this collaboration is fostered and often manipulated by the police. This chapter, therefore, will call into question much of the received wisdom on crowdsourcing by making three basic assertions: first, that crowdsourcing is anything but new; second, that crowdsourcing is media-dependent; and third, that crowdsourcing can have negative social impacts that go far beyond diminished data quality and exploitive labor arrangements.[9] Thus while Howe, Clay Shirky,[10] and other experts focus on its democratizing potential, it is important to point out, with Daniel Trottier, that these citizen empowerment schemes often serve as simply a distributed expression of raw state power.[11] The current state of police crowdsourcing, I suggest, demonstrates how citizens' bodies and their social relationships are continuously remade into raw resources by a policing apparatus that has come to rely on a vigilant, responsibilized public.

This chapter analyzes several key innovations in crowdsourcing technology that have allowed the police to cultivate and organize this vigilant neighborly conduct.[12] Police agencies have always used "new" media to carry out their work, and these new technologies have inevitably created new relationships between the police and the communities they serve. This brings up a number of questions about lateral surveillance, communication, and the nature of crowdsourced community responsibility, particularly in the digital age. For example, how do new media technologies give rise to new forms of control, state exploitation, and/or democratic access? As crowdsourcing technologies encourage citizens to become more active in policing their communities, does that participation facilitate the construction of a more just social order? Does this form of public participation create more productive and sympathetic relationships between the police and their constituencies, or between the watchers and the watched? However we might answer these questions, one thing is increasingly clear: at the present convergence of digital culture and late liberal politics, community responsibility and self-entrepreneurism have given the police apparatus a rich new social milieu in which to engage, organize, and deploy the seeing/saying bodies of its constituents. And, just as important, they've given citizens and resistance movements new avenues for crowdsourcing their outrage at police brutality and other abuses of the state.

Crowdsourcing in Police History

While exacerbated by recent trends in neoliberal public policy, crowd-sourcing is hardly a new phenomenon in police history. Indeed, we should resist overestimating the uniqueness of neoliberalism and its methods of social regulation, particularly when many historical examples foreshadow neoliberalism's signature synthesis of political economy and individual empowerment. In fact, although today our notions of policing are dominated by its contemporary form as a sovereign institution—complete with salaried officers, specialized technologies, and distinct legal privileges—this brand of professional policing is a historical anomaly that has been prominent for less than two hundred years.[13] In Europe and North America, community-based citizen patrols comprised the dominant form of law enforcement until the rise of the modern police force in the late eighteenth and early nineteenth centuries.[14] And in these early days, policing was coordinated through crowdsourcing initiatives that, in fact, functioned much like *America's Most Wanted* and similar programs of today.

As police historians Robert Trojanowicz and Bonnie Bucqueroux have argued, to understand the emergence of America's community policing tradition requires an excursion into British policing history, particularly into the forms of community-based policing that colonial America inherited from Great Britain.[15] This is an especially good starting place for us, as it illustrates how citizens and sovereign institutions have long struggled over how the population should participate in the policing of its communities. The roots of this community-policing tradition can be found in the days of Anglo-Saxon England. When the Anglo-Saxons conquered and settled Britain between the fifth and seventh centuries, they brought an ancient Germanic system of tribal government and community justice. This system was organized around the local community, the "hundred," each of which comprised a district of roughly one hundred households. The leader of each hundred, its elder, was responsible for judging disputes and pursuing criminal justice. Since court was held only once each season, most parties, too impatient or independent to wait for official justice, would pursue criminals themselves. At this time, community members were still permitted to seek justice without appealing to an elder, so law enforcement was a decidedly local affair.

In lieu of an organized police force, neighbors would frequently band together, pursuing criminals and dispensing punishment without the approval of a sovereign official or written laws.

While we should be careful to avoid mythologizing the communal nature of Anglo-Saxon justice procedures, it is generally accepted that the Norman Conquest introduced a number of important reforms to this system.[16] Upon the Normans' colonization of England in the eleventh century, they introduced new methods of financial extraction into Anglo-Saxon communal arrangements. For example, in the early years of the conquest, William I implemented a community-policing system that manipulated the Anglo-Saxons' structures of community justice.[17] For a number of reasons, among them to prevent the assassination of Norman officials, the Normans—who were heavily outnumbered by the native Anglo-Saxons—levied severe, collective penalties for criminal acts. This new arrangement transformed the traditional rationalities of Anglo-Saxon communal policing, giving rise to two key political innovations: first, the financial and political enrichment of the Norman ruling class, and second—and more importantly, for our purposes— the more or less seamless integration of the conquered Anglo-Saxons into the machinery of their own control. This development signals a long trend in the self-disciplining and responsibilization of local populations via citizen policing, indicating for police historian William Alfred Morris a significant moment in "the union of police and mutual responsibility."[18]

One of the harsher aspects of this responsibilization was the "frankpledge" system, which was a primitive police crowdsourcing arrangement. By imposing collective financial responsibility for the apprehension of criminals and the recovery of stolen goods, the frankpledge effectively conscripted the entire English populace into the policing apparatus. In fact, all members of a village were held financially responsible for the criminal acts of their neighbors, a development that eventually led Anglo-Saxon locals to form ad hoc policing networks. In the thirteenth century Edward I officially sanctioned the verbal "hue and cry" method of crime response and patrol organization, a method that would survive in certain forms well into the nineteenth century. Once an individual witnessed a crime, he was required to chase the perpetrator with a loud, accusatory "hue and cry" that would ring out through the community. (Women would typically produce cries from within their homes.) As these shouts alerted other citizens who would join the manhunt, the crew would chase the criminal and return her or him to a constable for internment, thereby releasing the collective bail imposed upon their community.[19] However, if the criminal eluded the posse and ran to a neighboring village, the inhabitants of both villages— now facing the threat of defaulting on their frankpledge—would strive to apprehend the fleer, forming an ever-larger mob of civilian police.[20]

Eventually, various crowdsourcing media facilitated the hue and cry: horns, rattles, and other technologies were used to deputize local citizens and allow for the organization of their bodies across time and space. Mobile aural technologies transformed oral hue-and-cry and watch-and-ward patrols, allowing for improved communications between households and sometimes even between isolated communities. Sir Frederick Pollock, a nineteenth-century police historian who also served as England and Wales's chief law enforcement officer, described how the horn, which was first introduced into English patrols in the fourteenth century, occupied a central role in citizen policing: when a hue and cry was raised, neighbors would "turn out with the bows, arrows, knives, that they are bound to keep, and besides much shouting, there will be horn-blowing; the 'hue' will be horned from vill to vill."[21] All citizens, as potential deputies, were required to own a variety of weapons that could help them serve in their capacity as the citizen police. As important as the weapons, however, was the medium of the hue: the horn. According to Pollock, the horn allowed for calls to spread "from vill to vill," vastly improving upon the limited range of the human voice. In 1785, English historian and justice of the peace Richard Burn explored the media-related etymologies of *hue* and *cry*, concluding that *hue* originally signified horn blowing while *cry* signified cries of the human voice. Burn traces this distinction as far back as 696 C.E., when Wihtred King of Kent decreed: "if a stranger go out of the road [during a manhunt], and neither shout nor blow a horn, he shall be taken for a thief."[22] Burn suggests that, while in some instances it was fine to summon a constable when a crime is committed, "by the frame of the statutes, it is by no means necessary, nor is it always convenient; for the felon may escape before the warrant be obtained; . . . and hue and cry was part of the law, before justices of the peace were first instituted."[23]

Equipped with these crowdsourcing technologies, early English communities organized their labor into mobile lateral surveillance teams. In the fourteenth century they began to employ what is known as the "watch and ward," which was a civilian surveillance network that deployed groups of day wardens and night watchmen to immediately raise a hue and cry following a criminal act. Watch-and-ward patrols would work in shifts, sometimes occupying watchtowers in order to initiate a hue and cry as soon as an offense was committed. But because the frankpledge indebted all members of a community—not just those who were designated watchmen when the offense occurred—often those who refused to put down their work and follow the criminal were arrested and tried for the fugitive's crimes.[24] The colonialist directives of the frankpledge system thus forced the conquered Anglo-Saxons to remain watchful of their peers, each of whom threatened to disrupt the delicate stability that kept the new Norman elites at bay. In a move that has numerous analogs throughout the history of law enforcement, sovereign authorities were careful to ensure that local citizens, rather than "outsiders" or a specially equipped occupational class, were keeping watch over one another. This early community policing arrangement—which enforced loyalty to the state's security objectives via threats of fines and physical punishment—was a defining expression of English sovereignty in its pre-institutional condition. Unassisted by the institutional competencies that would later characterize sovereign governance, early English elites used crowdsourcing technologies and communal responsibility arrangements to disperse social control throughout their territory.

Crowdsourced Vigilance in Colonial America

Despite the radical changes that have occurred in policing and sovereign power since the Middle Ages, the frankpledge model illustrates the potential for police and other authorities, either intentionally or unintentionally, to use crowdsourcing technologies and "citizen empowerment" schemes as tools of financial extraction and social control. That is not to say, of course, that American crowdsourcing programs have always been as openly repressive as those in the early days of Norman England. Similar to England's watch-and-ward tradition, in the seventeenth and eighteenth centuries American policing operated on a "town watch" system. Participation in these town watches was compulsory for adult males, and until the nineteenth century such watchmen were rarely paid for their services. In New Amsterdam and other seventeenth-century Dutch settlements in the New World, the "rattle watch"—a watch-and-ward arrangement that used rattles as crowdsourcing media—was composed of civilians who would take turns surveilling their communities at nighttime. Many American communities at this time also appointed a "town crier," who would stand in the village square to announce social events and orally crowdsource policing responsibilities.[25]

As the English extended their control over the colonies during the seventeenth and eighteenth centuries, this process evolved: watch-and-ward patrols were typically placed under the supervision of an unpaid constable or sheriff within a loose hierarchy.[26] Yet as we saw with the Norman Conquest, in times of hostility between subjects and their colonial masters this local crowdsourcing system was reconfigured into a more exploitive arrangement. British officials in colonial America, for example, used crowdsourcing methods to tap into community responsibility and stamp out American revolutionary activity. In August 1776, when British troops occupied Long Island, an American patriot reacted by setting several buildings on fire. In response, British colonial authorities instituted a watch-and-ward system aimed at consolidating their occupation and halting the revolution in its tracks. This required, as in earlier days, demanding that locals participate in the policing of their peers, as well as threatening false hue and criers with fines and imprisonment.[27] Reacting to the Long Island fire, Major-General James Robertson, colonial commander of New York, issued the following proclamation:

> Whereas, there is ground to believe that the Rebels, not satisfied with the Destruction of Part of the City, entertain Designs of burning the Rest; And it is thought that a Watch to inspect all Parts of the City, to apprehend Incendiaries, and to Stifle Fires before they rise to a dangerous Height, might be a necessary and proper means to prevent such a calamity. . . . I do therefore require and direct That all Persons may take a Part in this Matter, and turn out to Watch when called for. A sense of duty and Interest will lead all good Subjects and Citizens cheerfully to give their

Figure 1.1. American settlers are given rattles before a night-watch shift. Costello, *Our Police Protectors*, 13.

Attendance; And any who refuse to take Part in preserving the City will be judged unworthy to inhabit it.[28]

Although Robertson asserts that a "sense of duty and interest" would lead citizens to cheerfully participate in his Watch, the political circumstances surrounding his decree illustrate the coercive potential of police crowdsourcing campaigns.

This element of coercion, in fact, can also be seen in the hue and cry declared against American "traitor" Patrick Henry on May 6, 1775. Distributed by the British colonial authorities in town centers throughout Virginia, the printed notices remind the Crown's subjects of their duty to surrender Henry at a moment's notice:

> I have thought proper, with the advice of Sir Majesty's council, and in Sir Majesty's name, to issue this my proclamation, strictly charging all persons, upon their allegiance, not to aid, abet, or give countenance to the said Patrick Henry, or any other persons concerned in such unwarrantable combinations; but on the contrary, to oppose them, and their designs, by every means, which designs must otherwise involve the whole country in the most direful calamity, as they will call for the vengeance of offended majesty, and the insulted laws, to be exerted here, to vindicate the constitutional authority of government.[29]

In this hue and cry, the Crown called on "the whole country" to use "every means" to capture and surrender the wanted patriot. Perhaps most important, Henry's hue and cry also illustrates an important technological evolution in the citizen-policing process: print crowdsourcing allowed crimes to be abstracted from their roots in organic community response. Print-based hue-and-cry declarations like the one in Figure 1.2 were posted in villages, where literate citizens could spread the word about offenders' crimes, whereabouts, and physical characteristics. The tradition of compulsory enlistment was kept alive, at least in theory: once a declaration notice had been posted in high-traffic, public areas, the *entire* male citizenry—not just those who were encountered on an oral hue-and-cry campaign—was shackled with the duties of a police officer. Thus when print hue-and-cry posters began to appear,

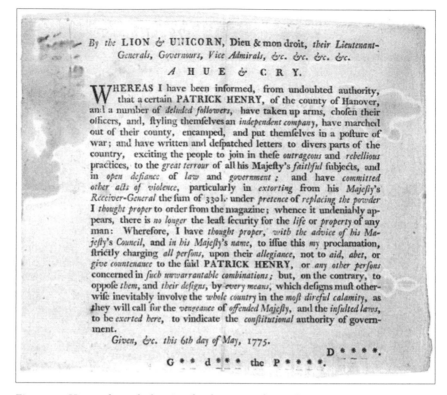

By the LION & UNICORN, Dieu & mon droit, their Lieutenant-Generals, Governours, Vice Admirals, &c. &c. &c. &c.

A HUE & CRY.

WHEREAS I have been informed, from undoubted authority, that a certain PATRICK HENRY, of the county of Hanover, and a number of *deluded followers*, have taken up arms, chosen their officers, and, styling themselves an *independent company*, have marched out of their county, encamped, and put themselves in a posture of war; and have written and despatched letters to divers parts of the country, exciting the people to join in these *outrageous* and *rebellious* practices, to the *great terrour* of all his Majesty's *faithful* subjects, and in *open defiance* of *law* and *government*; and have *committed other acts of violence*, particularly in *extorting* from his Majesty's *Receiver-General* the sum of 330 l. under *pretence* of *replacing the powder* I *thought proper* to order from the magazine; whence it undeniably appears, there is *no longer* the least security for the *life* or *property* of any man: Wherefore, I have *thought proper*, *with the advice of his Majesty's Council*, and *in his Majesty's name*, to issue this *my* proclamation, strictly charging *all persons*, upon their *allegiance*, not to *aid, abet*, or *give countenance* to the said PATRICK HENRY, or *any other persons* concerned in *such unwarrantable combinations*; but, on the contrary, to oppose *them*, and *their designs*, by *every means*, which designs must otherwise inevitably involve the *whole country* in the *most direful calamity*, as they will call for the *vengeance* of *offended Majesty*, and the *insulted laws*, to be *exerted here*, to vindicate the *constitutional* authority of government.

Given, &c. this 6th day of *May*, 1775.

D * * * *.

G * * d * * * the P * * * *.

Figure 1.2. Hue-and-cry declaration for the arrest of Patrick Henry, 1775.

declarations allowed colonial authorities to more easily extract their subjects' loyalty from a distance. In the days of oral hue and cry, criminals were identified by citizens who observed them taking part in a criminal act. However, the durable, print-based dictation of suspects by a state authority—such as in the Wanted poster and the print hue and cry—radically altered the community's jurisdiction and its relationship to the state.

Print hue-and-cry declarations and Wanted posters introduced a new spatiotemporal logic into law enforcement: not only were policing efforts separated from their roots in direct public response, but citizens could be mobilized to respond to alleged crimes that occurred at earlier times and/or outside their communities. Once criminal justice ceased to be a local affair adjudicated between and by neighbors, crime was abstracted from personal or communal experience and reconstituted as an act not against specific citizens, but against the sovereign.[30] This loss of local independence aided the abstraction of criminal justice from its long-standing foundation in communal observation and response, making possible new means for extracting citizen police labor and rechanneling sovereign power through the bodies of its subjects. Thus the written standardization of law, the rise of a print culture, and the growth of transportation networks all served to further implicate citizen policing into the security and revenue objectives of the state.

Crowdsourcing with Mass Media

These technologies took new forms as sovereign police authorities turned to mass-distribution outlets. For example, in the 1770s the *Weekly Hue and Cry*, a police gazette devoted to publicizing the habits, assumed whereabouts, and physical characteristics of criminals, deserters, and the mentally disabled, entered circulation in London; U.S. editions began to appear not long afterward.[31] And of course, the Wanted poster—a direct ancestor of the hue-and-cry declaration—is perhaps the iconic American manifestation of these print-based crowdsourcing police technologies. As Rachel Hall describes in her book *Wanted: The Outlaw in American Visual Culture*, the Wanted genre passed through several print manifestations in the nineteenth century, including fugitive slave notices and the rogue's gallery. These print texts were remediated in diverse forms throughout the twentieth century, and they were eventually used to crowdsource victim identification on milk cartons and community tabloids. This mediated war on crime also extended to narrative genres in the electronic media landscape. With the rise of police radio transmissions in the 1930s, the police had a new instrument for "conquering space and time": according to Kathleen Battles, "the promise of inevitable apprehension" fueled the emergence of radio dragnets that responsibilized police officers and everyday citizens.[32] And also beginning in the 1930s, radio dramas like *Gang Busters* and *Calling All Cars* foreshadowed the rise of realistic television classics like *Cops* and *America's Most Wanted*. Just as commercial print publishers used police gazettes to turn a profit, these radio and television programs solidified formal partnerships between the police and private media industries. Channeling this public/private partnership into televised crowdsourcing, Fox's *America's Most Wanted* was introduced in 1988 to immediate commercial and political success; instantly becoming Fox's most profitable program, it illustrated the immense crowdsourcing potential of "televisual community policing."[33] During its first episode, the show profiled one of the FBI's "Ten Most Wanted" fugitives, a rapist/murderer named David James Roberts who had escaped prison before his trial for triple murder. Following the broadcast, more than seventy-five citizens called *America's Most Wanted* tip lines reporting that Roberts was living a bourgeois life in Staten Island, directing a homeless shelter. Just four days after his profile was featured on the show, on February 11, 1988, Roberts was apprehended and returned to prison to serve the remainder of his life sentence.

One of the longest-running series in television history, *America's Most Wanted* aired for more than twenty-five years until it was canceled in 2013. Because it played such an important role in local and national police crowdsourcing efforts—the show claims to have led to the arrest of 1,185 criminals and the recovery of sixty-one missing children[34]—in its absence, police agencies are scrambling to shore up their own media capacities. Lamenting the show's demise, Geoff Shank, assistant director of investigative operations for the U.S. Marshals Service, reflected: "It was a reciprocal relationship. . . . We provided them cases week in and week out."[35] According to Shank, federal police agencies' investigative procedures have been shaped by the crowdsourcing potential of *America's Most Wanted*. Many agents, Shank argues, will now have to take up work that is more community-oriented: "We can send a thousand FBI agents out to knock on a thousand doors and talk to a thousand people, [or] we can send a couple of FBI agents to do *America's Most Wanted* on a weekend and touch millions of people. . . . The results bear that out. We've had captures come in a matter of minutes after a show was aired."[36] Without the promise of private-funded televisual crowdsourcing, federal agencies are having to turn to other media to fill the gap: "We've got a robust public affairs office," Shank says, "and we're constantly looking to exploit other media outlets."[37]

Current Trends in Crowdsourcing: Social Media

Social media is like community policing on steroids. It's a
force multiplier.
—Lauri Stevens[38]

As the crescendo of neoliberal police reform coincided with the rise of
social media, police officials like Geoff Shank have continued to develop
media strategies for urging citizens to function as corporal extensions
of the police apparatus. The historical outline of this trend can be seen
in the multimedia crowdsourcing campaigns that gained significant cultural steam in the 1990s, especially following the 1996 disappearance of
nine-year-old Amber Hagerman in Arlington, Texas. When Amber's
body was found four days later, members of the Arlington community
devised the AMBER alert system—America's Missing: Broadcasting
Emergency Response—a media crowdsourcing campaign that would
alert local citizens to potential abductions. When a child was reported
missing, the Emergency Alert System would interrupt radio broadcasts
with a description of the child and the suspected abductor, local television channels would loop a small alert across the bottom of the screen,
and electronic highway signs would provide drivers with a description
of the suspect's vehicle. New York, Florida, Nebraska, and West Virginia
took the creative step of printing AMBER alert information on lottery
tickets, and local businesses sometimes use their marquees to assist in
Amber alerts.[39] Now in the digital age, Facebook and Google have got-
ten into the action: Facebook users can sign up for notifications if their
home state releases an AMBER alert, and Google appends a notification
to the top of a page when a user searches for the city in which an alert
has been activated.[40] Describing the potential of these new digital technologies, Colonel Steven Flaherty, superintendent of the Virginia State
Police, remarked, "The social media enables law enforcement to reach
way beyond our normal footprint.... I can only imagine and dream what
we'll be able to accomplish with this new tool in our toolbox."[41] Starting
in February 2013, mobile phone companies, too, have enhanced the "footprint" of AMBER alerts by partnering with the FCC and FEMA (Federal
Emergency Management Agency) to send a standard SMS message to
their customers when an alert has been issued in their communities.[42]

Amid the popularity of the AMBER alert program, a familiar discourse has come to surround its efforts: according to the organization's pamphlet, "when ordinary citizens become the eyes and ears of law enforcement, precious lives can be saved."[43] The AMBER program, therefore, reinscribed the defining biopolitical rhetoric of contemporary police crowdsourcing: as countless PSAs, neighborhood watch brochures, and related policing partnership discourses remind us, we are expected to function as the "eyes and ears" of the police apparatus. And, as social media have provided the police with cost-effective resources for reaching out to and investigating the public, these "eyes and ears of the police" are being recruited to assist with more and more investigations. Since the popular explosion of Facebook, Twitter, and other social media between 2006 and 2009, police agencies have developed various strategies for exploiting online social networks.[44] In the fall of 2015, a national survey conducted by the International Association of Chiefs of Police found that more than ninety-six percent of American police agencies use some sort of social media;[45] and many of these agencies, unsurprisingly, use social media to conduct warrantless investigations.[46] In a growing number of cases, police officers are assigned to monitor suspects' social media accounts and infiltrate their networks. Detectives have been known to create fake Facebook profiles in order to gain access to a suspect's personal information, and they have also applied pressure to existing "friends" of Facebook users in order to gain information about the contents of suspects' profiles.[47] This invasion of privacy in the legally ambiguous frontier of social media has reached staggering proportions in the United States. In 2012, Twitter released a report showing that the U.S. leads the world in official requests for information on citizens; the report states that in the first half of 2012, U.S. law enforcement agencies made more information requests than they did in all of 2011.[48] Some police departments, like those in Montgomery County, Texas, have even begun tweeting the names of DUI *suspects*—not convicts—in a spectacle of crowdsourced public shaming. As the assistant district attorney for Montgomery County, Warren Diepraam, put it: "[District Attorney Brett] Ligon has recognized that DWI is our most frequently committed crime in Montgomery County. . . . The message he's sending is: 'If you're going to commit an offense of DWI in Montgomery County, we're coming after you.' We're hoping it has a deterrent effect on individuals."[49]

THE POWER OF THE CROWD | 37

While these cases are certainly alarming, we should also be concerned that these technologies are becoming the next frontier of mass-responsibilization efforts, as police agencies use social media to crowdsource the fight against crime. For example, the Philadelphia Police Department (PPD) prides itself on its social media presence, which is primarily invested in Twitter, Facebook, and YouTube. The push to update the PPD's web presence began on Halloween 2007, when PPD officer Charles Cassidy was shot during a robbery at a Dunkin' Donuts. Even though the murder was caught on the store's video camera in DVR format, the PPD was not equipped to access or share that data: they had to send the disc via postal mail to FBI headquarters, where it was then processed and sent back to the PPD in an accessible and transmissible format. Following the debacle, PPD lieutenant Raymond J. Evers reflected, "We had to waste 36 hours to process a video. It showed a glaring problem. It should not take 36 hours to get info from a DVR. That was the impetus."[50] Armed with grants from the federal government, the PPD launched websites, purchased hardware and software, and hired media strategists. Remarking on these developments in its crowdsourcing arsenal, PPD commissioner Charles H. Ramsey asserted that the department's top priority became "making it easy and as comfortable as possible for people to reach out to us."[51]

But the PPD didn't stop there. In 2010 it launched a Facebook page, which now has over 160,000 likes and is one of the most popular police profiles in the United States. Peppered with pictures of police officers reaching out to the community, the page is updated several times a day with photographs and videos of criminal suspects. The PPD also uses Facebook to announce rewards—such as "Reward Increased to $80,000 in Abduction Case," which will be followed by a video or photograph of the crime or wanted criminal—and to feature missing person cases. Citizen participation, however, is strictly limited: the only input from users is the occasional "Now we just need to get more of these scumbags off the streets!" as they cheer on the police and express their solidarity with local policing efforts. Citizens are forbidden from announcing crimes or adding additional details about suspects. The PPD's Twitter account functions in a similar way: since 2009, @PhillyPolice has posted more than nine thousand tweets aimed at recruiting its more than ninety thousand followers into the fight against crime. In 2010, the department began turning to YouTube to crowdsource policing responsibilities: with more than four million views and hundreds of videos, the PPD's YouTube page has been credited with increasing the city's violent crime clearance rate (although *not* reducing its violent crime). Amid this success in capturing suspects, the department has developed a Digital Imaging Video Response Team (DIVRT) equipped with officers who have been specially trained to extract video from crime scenes and rapidly disseminate it through social media channels.[52] As Commissioner Ramsey remarked, "It's absolutely amazing that since we began posting video online, people watch it. . . . Not only do they watch it. If they recognize someone, they pass along the tip."[53]

Although social media seem to have brought the PPD a degree of success in catching suspects, their impact has not been entirely positive. First, these media have shown little ability to halt violent crime: in Philadelphia in 2012, despite the growing presence of surveillance cameras, police social media, and responsibilized citizen-officers who scrutinize their communities for suspects, murders rose for the third straight year.[54] After small dips in 2013 and 2014, Philadelphia's murder rate rose a dramatic twelve percent in 2015; and, despite the PPD's increasingly energetic use of social media, the arrest rate for murders dropped from seventy-one percent in 2013 to fifty-two percent in 2015.[55] With these unimpressive statistics in mind, we should recall that social media are not primarily useful in capturing murderers and rapists, but are most often employed to publicize petty crimes and misdemeanors such as drug possession, driving under the influence, and probation violation. Outside high-crime urban environments like Philadelphia, where social media encourage the citizen policing of serious *violent* crime, police departments have a tendency to put these media in the service of collecting fines and enforcing petty violations. A good case in point is Pottstown, Pennsylvania, which is a small town of about twenty-two thousand located thirty miles northwest of Philadelphia. Without the technological resources of the Philadelphia Police Department, Pottstown police officials—working in concert with the local newspaper, the Pottstown *Mercury*—employ Pinterest as their social networking site of choice.[56] Seen as a gendered medium—as of 2014, more than eighty percent of active Pinterest users are women[57]—the site allegedly offers an innovative way to involve women in lateral surveillance. Lauri Stevens, a social media consultant for law enforcement, lauds Pinterest as the hottest new method of police crowdsourcing: "Facebook is awesome because there are a billion people on it. There aren't a billion people on Pinterest yet, but there are a lot. And the people on there are mostly women, who just really want to put bad guys behind bars."[58] As Stevens puts it, "This is a way to get all of those people out there all the time in front of more people."[59] Because full responsibilization is the telos crowdsourcing policing programs, Pinterest is seen as a key piece of the citizen-policing puzzle. By targeting this gendered medium, police agencies are striving to responsibilize an untapped and apparently vigilant population resource which, without the site, might not get into the lateral surveillance game.

On its Pinterest page, the Pottstown PD posts mug shots of suspects who have been arrested and have missed court dates—or, alternatively, of individuals suspected of crimes—in addition to listing suspects' last known addresses. Citizens, of course, are urged to contact the department with any information about their whereabouts. The Pinterest page, which is updated weekly or biweekly, typically posts about twenty-five suspects at a time; the most prominent offense advertised by the page is, unsurprisingly, drug possession. Retail theft, conspiracy to theft, forgery, petty theft, simple assault, receiving stolen property, driving under the influence, unauthorized use of a motor vehicle, and other misdemeanors dominate the profiles; violent felonies are nowhere to be seen. Still, the Pottstown PD has received national recognition and media attention for its Pinterest crowdsourcing program. Remarking on what he finds to be the program's success, Pottstown police captain Richard Drumheller reported, "We've actually seen a fifty-seven percent increase in our warrant services, and we actually got more people based on our tips and our calls. . . . For us it's like, 'Yes,' because it's very enjoyable in police work when the public helps you."[60] One should notice in Captain Drumheller's statement that, while Philadelphia police officials are struggling to contain violence in their neighborhoods, Pinterest is most helpful in Pottstown as a way to improve the statistics of the township's "warrant services" (i.e., arrests). When violent crime is not at stake, social media threaten to become technologies for revenue generation as police implicate community bonds in networks of surveillance power. Citizens—whether idle, female, or otherwise—are transformed into surveillance devices for a policing apparatus that has come to thrive on this cost-effective method for increasing revenue, improving arrest statistics, and identifying with the public through coordinated action.

In addition to using established social media sites like Facebook and Pinterest, some police departments have infiltrated and promoted local social networking services to recruit and responsibilize citizens. Nextdoor, which is a geographically restricted social networking app, empowers cops to cultivate a "virtual neighborhood watch" in the communities they police. While Facebook and Pinterest are profile-driven networks, Nextdoor allows cops and citizens to post want ads, messages, and crime alerts to community networks. According to Sacramento police chief Sam Somers, who adopted Nextdoor in 2013, the site provides a unique opportunity for the police to crowdsource policing responsibilities to the public. In a familiar neoliberal tone, Chief Somers offers up digital technology and citizen empowerment as the ideal solutions to local crime: "We have to have the community support. We have to have the community involved. We have to have their eyes and ears. Because, if we don't have that, there's not enough of us to be able to police this city to make it the safest."[61] Like other police crowdsourcing enthusiasts, Somer approaches digital technology as an idealized, cost-effective solution for communities plagued by poverty and crime. Many cops, in fact, display a strange naïveté about the potential of Nextdoor and similar apps to rebuild community bonds and social cohesion. A police officer in Mobile, Alabama, for example, dreams of a return to the idyllic community solidarity that characterizes his vision of 1970s America: "I think this app here for the city is going to be a great opportunity to maybe go back to the 70s where the neighbors know each other."[62] As with Facebook, Pinterest, and other social media, the police tend to impose classical narratives of community solidarity onto the contemporary digital milieu. The connectivity delivered by these media, however, hardly delivers the kind of friendly, 1970s-style sociality idealized by crowdsourcing advocates. On the contrary, these technologies allow the police and their community allies to foster digital forms of participation and cooperation that do little or nothing to address poverty, social alienation, and the other systemic problems that give rise to local crime. As in other cultural settings, the promise of digital democracy leads community leaders to make the mistake of using new technology as a quick and inexpensive—but largely ineffective—"solution" for deep-seated social problems.

Misidentifications, Misinformation

Indeed, as this chapter has shown, crowdsourcing technologies often fuel these larger injustices. These technologies' success in generating vigilance and social suspicion, in particular, hints at the larger political dangers of our seeing/saying culture. Take *America's Most Wanted*, for example. While the show was quick to promote its success in facilitating the capture of fugitives, it was more hesitant to discuss how its vigilant programming gave rise to increased social suspicion and even false arrests. In September 1993, for example, a number of *America's Most Wanted* viewers reported that their neighbor, Edward Fisher, was the man appearing on their television screens. Although Fisher had for years lived in a small town in northern Pennsylvania, one of his neighbors reported to the police that she was "ninety-nine percent sure" that Fisher was the man in question. Acting on this information, the police arrested Fisher for murder, detaining him until he was eventually released when fingerprint evidence exonerated him of the crime.[63] While this case illustrates the danger of mistaken identities, it also demonstrates the intense vigilance and suspicion that crowdsourcing media can stir: despite the tremendous unlikelihood that Fisher would be the perpetrator of murders more than a thousand miles away from his home, his neighbors called the *America's Most Wanted* tip line to accuse him of being the killer. This unfortunate scenario calls to mind the stark assessment of urban suspicion and alienation put forward by criminologists Jerome H. Skolnick and David H. Bayley: "In our often anomic urban society the transcendent identity of many city dwellers is that of crime victim. Their neighbors may be the very people they fear."[64]

As a symptom of these technologies' tendency to uproot crime response from its immediate environment, social media can easily lend to mistakes of identification and false arrests. For example, after a riot following the San Francisco Giants' World Series win in October 2012, a group of concerned citizens posted to Facebook a photograph of a man hurling a street sign into a bus window. This responsibilization effort went viral as the photo was retweeted thousands of times among San Francisco residents. A thread devoted to finding the culprit quickly appeared on Reddit, the popular international social media network. Amid all this buzz, local San Franciscan Tony Lukewicz thought that the bus vandal looked like himself, so he made the by-then notorious image his Facebook photo. Not getting the joke, someone took a screenshot of Lukewicz's profile photograph and posted it to Twitter along with his name. A few hours later the photograph ended up on the Facebook page of a local nightclub, where commenters began posting Lukewicz's phone number, address, and other personal details about him and even his family. Soon Lukewicz was receiving text messages threatening his life.[65]

In an interview with *Wired* magazine, Lukewicz made a telling remark about his misfortune: "Anyone who knows me knows I'm not even like that."[66] This, of course, is a primary danger with crowdsourcing technologies: they can easily lead vigilant citizens to mobilize against false or even imagined enemies. One such social media hoax almost resulted in the murder of a Philadelphia man who was falsely accused of killing a number of local girls. When a Philadelphia neighborhood was stricken with a series of murders and sexual assaults in the fall of 2010, a Facebook page emerged identifying local man Triz Jefferies as the "Kensington Strangler." The Facebook group page, titled "Catch the Kensington Strangler, Before He Catches Someone You Love," featured the twenty-four-year-old's name, photograph, address, and phone number. A group of vigilantes converged on his home, where he had to be rescued by police officers who took him to a police station and conducted DNA tests that exonerated him of the crime. Police sergeant Ray Evers pinpointed the danger behind this method of responsibilization: "It's very unfortunate. . . . What if we didn't get to this guy first . . . and he was just walking down the street? It could have been a whole different story."[67] When community vigilance is plugged into the network—as it frequently is in the age of Facebook and other social media—all it takes is one malicious or faulty node to reorient the community's outrage around an innocent target.

Crowdsourcing the Boston Marathon Bombing Investigation

Perhaps the most intensely crowdsourced manhunt in recent U.S. history was the FBI's attempt to locate the 2013 Boston Marathon bombing suspects, Dzhokhar and Tamerlan Tsarnaev. The Boston case is especially interesting because it illustrates how crowdsourcing has become a contested site of seeing/saying citizenship as digital technologies have complicated the state's monopoly over police crowdsourcing. On April 18, three days after the attack, the FBI released the suspects' photos to the public. Reminding citizens to demonstrate their civic loyalty by seeing and saying, the case's lead investigator, Special Agent Richard DesLauriers, announced: "Today, we are enlisting the public's help to identify the two suspects. . . . For more than 100 years, the FBI has relied on the public to be its eyes and ears. With the media's help, in an instant, these images will be delivered directly into the hands of millions around the world. We know the public will play a critical role in identifying and locating them. . . . Somebody out there knows these individuals as friends, neighbors, co-workers, or family members of the suspects. Though it may be difficult, the nation is counting on those with information to come forward."[68] Immediately deluged with more than two thousand tips from citizens, the FBI was able to locate the suspects within twenty-four hours. By 9:00 p.m. on April 19, Tamerlan Tsarnaev had been killed in a police shootout, and his brother, Dzokhar, was in police custody. To all appearances, the FBI's crowdsourced investigation had been a remarkable success.

Yet this version of events glosses over the deeply controversial role that crowdsourcing played in the investigation.[69] In the days immediately following the attack, the FBI and local police agencies failed to maintain control over the flow and interpretation of video and photographic evidence. For example, on April 18, the front page of the *New York Post* featured an amateur photograph of two suspicious "bag men" that the paper identified as official police suspects. But the two men— who settled a lawsuit with the *Post* in 2014—were quickly cleared in the attacks, and the FBI scrambled to redirect the public's attention to its official suspects. But legacy media were not the only sites of media controversy surrounding the case. In the immediate aftermath of the attack, citizens opened an investigative forum on Reddit—r/Findthebostonbombers—where users could upload their own privately gathered intelligence.[70] At the behest of the forum's moderator, users uploaded their own private videos and photographs of the moments leading up to the attack. Asking users to post footage of suspicious persons, the moderator argued that the collective intelligence of citizen networks could trump the work of merely a few professional investigators: "it's been proven that a crowd of thousands can do things like this much quicker and better. . . . I'd take thousands of people over a select few very smart investigators any day."[71] Immediately, citizens began using this crowdsourced intelligence to develop elaborate theories of who was responsible for the attack. In addition to the "bag men" that the *New York Post* wrongly identified, a troupe of amateur media activists set their sights on a twenty-two-year-old student at Brown University, Sunil Tripathi. Acquaintances of Tripathi posted on social media like Reddit, 4chan, and Twitter that he looked like "the suspect in the white hat"—the then-unidentified suspect who was later identified as Dzokhar Tsarnaev. Because Tripathi had gone missing several days earlier, social media were abuzz in speculation about his involvement. News stations sent reporters to his family home in Bryn Mawr, Pennsylvania, where his parents and neighbors were harassed, interrogated, and even threatened. This media circus was soon disrupted, however, when the FBI officially released the identity of "the suspect in the white hat." It turned out that Sunil Tripathi was "missing" because he had committed suicide several days earlier, and his body was soon found in the Providence River.[72]

Needless to say, this kind of crowdsourced intelligence was not what the FBI had in mind. While the FBI is happy to enlist citizens' eyes and ears in official investigations, the Boston Marathon investigation illustrates how police agencies struggled to assert control over how crowdsourced evidence was publicized and interpreted. In fact, the FBI admitted that it strategically released the Tsarnaev brothers' photographs to the public in order to reassert control over the investigation. At that stage of the investigation, crowdsourcing was not a way to tap into the collective intelligence of the public. Rather, it was a way to impose an official narrative onto the chaos of citizen-generated theories about the attack. According to the *Washington Post*, "Investigators were concerned that if they didn't assert control over the release of the Tsarnaevs' photos, their manhunt would become a chaotic free-for-all, with news media cars and helicopters, as well as online vigilante detectives, competing with police in the chase to find the suspects. By stressing that all information had to flow to 911 and official investigators, the FBI hoped to cut off that freelance sleuthing and attend to public safety even as they searched for the brothers."[73] The Boston Police Department—

which has a highly active Twitter presence with more than 375,000 followers—urged citizens to stop tweeting tips and sharing intelligence over social media. Soon, investigators like Special Agent DesLauriers began to emphasize that the FBI's officially released images "should be the only ones—the only ones—that the public should view to assist us. Other photos should not be deemed credible and unnecessarily divert the public's attention in the wrong direction and create undue work for vital law enforcement resources."[74] Federal police agencies quickly assailed the amateur investigations fueled by Reddit and other social media, taking care to dismiss and marginalize any narratives that contradicted the official federal version of events. Even President Obama warned against citizens developing "theories" of their own: "In this age of instant reporting, tweets and blogs, there's a temptation to latch on to any bit of information, sometimes to jump to conclusions. . . . But when a tragedy like this happens, with public safety at risk and the stakes so high, it's important we do this right."[75]

Amid these calls to more tightly regulate citizen crowdsourcing, in 2014 large urban police departments began collaborating with Amazon Web Services to develop a tip aggregation program called the Large Emergency Event Digital Information Repository (LEEDIR). Armed with Amazon's massive bandwidth capabilities, the LEEDIR app allows citizens to upload photos, videos, and other information that can aid in ongoing police investigations. But unlike the amateur investigative forums at Reddit, citizens cannot access this information from a public database. While police authorities recognize the potential value of collective intelligence, they are also developing measures to limit citizens' capacity to access and use that information.[76] Like how the Philadelphia Police Department selectively allows citizens to comment on its Facebook posts while forbidding them to post original intelligence, other police agencies take care to restrict how the public participates in their crowdsourcing programs. Many departments have begun to routinely ask users to refrain from using social media to speculate about investigations—such as in Los Angeles in 2013, during the manhunt for mass murderer and ex-cop Christopher Dorner.[77] While the police are happy to engage the eyes and ears of the public, they are beginning to realize just how volatile citizen engagement can be in the digital age.

Crowdsourcing the Resistance

One reason why the state is so motivated to regulate citizen participation in police crowdsourcing is that resistance groups are using these technologies to fight police power. While these platforms allow for the organization of protesting bodies across time and space,[78] they also allow for police brutality to be captured and disseminated through networks of scrutiny and outrage. The synergistic spread of social media and mobile technologies has significantly altered the climate of police resistance—much has changed, indeed, since the days when George Holliday shot a crude film of police officers assaulting Rodney King in March 1991. As Christopher J. Schneider has argued, ubiquitous connectivity has ushered in a new era of crowdsourced police resistance: "Police authority has been directly challenged in the past in the form of public protests and demonstrations; however, a key contemporary difference concerns the manner in which social media platforms allow users to mobilize en masse much more quickly, and often around some form of publicly accessible empirical evidence (e.g., videos of police brutality)."[79] While protests hardly need social media in order to succeed, the rise of smartphones and kindred technologies can galvanize public resistance with shareable visual representations of state violence. In fact, there is a long tradition of citizens using social media to document police abuses; since at least 2006, YouTube has been a popular avenue for publicizing police brutality.[80]

The Occupy movement, in particular, has been successful at using crowdsourcing technologies to direct popular outrage at the police. On November 9, 2011, Occupy UC Davis, which was based on the Davis campus of the University of California, staged a campus protest against staff furloughs, tuition increases, and administrator salary raises in the UC system. When university cops showed up and began harassing the protestors, students used Twitter, Facebook, and live video streams to stir up a mass protest. When more than one thousand students, faculty, and local residents quickly converged on UC Davis and occupied swaths of the campus, the cops responded by donning riot gear and ripping up the protestors' tents. Amid the ensuing struggle, several cops beat protestors with batons, and thirty-nine Occupiers were arrested. The cops, however, did not stop there: while dozens of spectators looked on, Lieutenant John Pike of the UC Davis Police Department sprayed military-grade pepper spray into the faces of eleven protestors who refused to disperse from the university quad. Armed with smartphones, several protestors captured video footage of Lieutenant Pike spraying the students, two of whom had to be hospitalized for their injuries. Within several minutes, videos of the attack were uploaded to YouTube. Five days later, the videos had received more than three million views.[81]

As a direct result of the ensuing public outcry, two of the police officers—as well as their supervisor, UC Davis police chief Annette Spicuzzi—were placed on administrative leave. Following a six-month investigation, the UC Davis Academic Senate Executive Council censured UC Davis's chancellor, Linda P. B. Katehi, and she publicly apologized at a rally attended by more than five thousand students, faculty, and local citizens. While Chancellor Katahi was able to keep her job following the incident, Lieutenant Pike, who had gained national notoriety, was eventually let go by the UC Davis Police Department. For University of Detroit law professor Richard Broughton, the sanctioning and marginalization of these protest-busting cops proved that social media and ubiquitous connectivity can be a useful tool in the fight against police brutality: "Everyone carries something on their person now that allows them to record police action, and that has given the police less of a place to hide."[82]

While in theory Broughton is right, the matter is certainly more complicated. Smartphones and social media allow everyday citizens to capture police brutality and to crowdsource political responses to an outraged public. Yet, as Lieutenant Pike's story illustrates, police power is so deeply entrenched in the U.S. that cops are often able to escape punishment for their crimes. Little has changed, indeed, since Rodney King's attackers were acquitted in a Simi Valley courtroom in April 1992. Resistance crowdsourcing can lead to popular outrage, but it does not necessarily lead to justice. So while Pike has failed to regain his job with the UC Davis Police Department, in October 2013 he successfully settled a worker's compensation claim in which California taxpayers were forced to dole out $38,000 for the psychiatric distress he suffered after he attacked the students.[83]

In addition to skirting criminal penalties for recorded instances of police brutality, the police have shown a talent for turning protestors' media devices against them. For example, in order to increase police surveillance of volatile areas, cops have begun watching Occupy protestors' social media sites in order to find video clips and images that could aid them in infiltrating and disrupting camps of resistance.[84] And in an even more important development, to prevent citizens from recording their behavior, police officers frequently order citizens to turn off recording equipment at protests and crime scenes. In states like Texas, legislatures are even debating new laws that would prohibit recording the police.[85] A more extreme example of this tendency, however, is "kill switch" technology, which allows authorities to power off any phones in a given geographic area. Some police agencies have even supported legislation which demands that all new smartphones be equipped with kill switch capacities. The first of these kill switch bills was passed by Minnesota in March 2014, and California governor Jerry Brown signed similar legislation in August of that year. The decisive influence of the Minnesota and California markets persuaded Google, Apple, and other top phone manufacturers to include kill switch technologies in their new phones in order to comply with the mandates, which went into effect in 2015. It was estimated that, by the end of 2015, ninety-seven percent of the phones used in the United States would have a kill switch.[86] And while these technologies are often justified in the terms of theft prevention, kill switches are already being used to prevent protestors and bystanders from recording and publicizing police brutality. Invoking public safety concerns, authorities of the BART subway system in the San Francisco Bay Area used emergency kill switch technology in 2011, and some activists allege that the Ferguson Police Department in Missouri used the technology to disrupt Livestream webcasts of police brutality during the Michael Brown protests in 2014.[87]

Conclusion

The bottom line, then, is that the police realize the power of the crowd: they exercise this power by using media technologies to energize citizens and tap into social networks. While the police develop their own capacities for crowdsourcing, they are also collaborating with tech companies and state legislatures to develop legal and technological strategies that prevent citizens from turning that crowd power against them. These technologies are becoming a popular site of contestation as cops and resistance groups struggle over the political potential of digital crowd-sourcing. Citizens' technological ingenuity, however, is constantly providing new opportunities for police surveillance and accountability. Apps like iCitizen, Five-O, and Driving While Black allow citizens to record police stops, report police abuses, give feedback on cops, and inform their social networks that they have had an encounter with the police. While cops prefer to limit citizens' seeing/saying participation to media they can control (such as official police-affiliated social media profiles), private apps and alternative social networking sites provide citizens with promising, if abusable, alternatives to official police media.

When we analyze the social and political impact of digital media, it is natural to follow Henry Jenkins in emphasizing their democratic potential: "The new media operate with different principles than the broadcast media that dominated American politics for so long: access, participation, reciprocity, and peer-to-peer rather than one-to-many communication."[88] Yet as Jenkins notes, in practice the picture is not quite so rosy. We must examine how traditional logics of control are being remediated into the digital age, as powerful actors develop new means for harnessing and redirecting this participatory potential. Just as the Philadelphia Police Department prevents citizens from posting crime details on their popular Facebook page—and as kill switch technologies have been deployed to prevent citizens from publicizing police brutality—police agencies struggle to ensure that digital citizens are empowered to participate in only approved ways. As these battles over police crowdsourcing illustrate, "participation" in the digital age should not be conflated with collaborative democracy and civic cooperation; rather, digital participation is a conceptual locus of struggle where cops and resistance groups fight over the boundaries of responsible citizenship. And despite citizen-driven innovation in apps and other cop-watching technologies, the courts, the cops, and their allies will fight to ensure that the police keep the upper hand in this struggle.

This chapter has shown that the technologization of the citizen and the capture of its corporal and social resources is an old process that has undergone many changes. Crowdsourcing media—when combined with the punitive threats of colonial power, or with neoliberal discourses of participatory democracy and self-empowerment—have enabled police agencies to convert citizens into resources for the expansion of their surveillance networks. While the periodic success of these responsibilization efforts cannot be denied—one might consider the Richard Ramirez case with which this chapter began, or the accomplishments claimed by *America's Most Wanted*—the capacity for this power to be abused and misapplied should not be overlooked, especially as emerging digital technologies such as crime mapping[89] and electronic crime notifications[90] proliferate throughout urban and rural communities. In the digital age we've seen that the "democratizing" promise of new media allows for a broader extension of the policing apparatus into our habits, responsibilities, communities, and bodies, as crowdsourcing technologies capture and redeploy the sensory resources of the public. Today, as neoliberal social reforms are slashing public expenditures across the board—and while social media crowdsourcing programs appear to provide a cost-effective solution to cash-strapped police departments—two especially alarming trends in police crowdsourcing beg for further critical attention: first, many small town police agencies are using platforms like Twitter and Pinterest to technologize their constituencies in order to help the state enforce petty fines and track nonviolent offenders; and second, in high-crime cities like Philadelphia, social media are being used as a Band-Aid to cover up the spectacular failure of neoliberal urban police reforms. However, as this chapter has shown, these trends are simply on the cutting edge of developments that have been long underway. They do not, in any case, bode well for our digital future.

2

Citizen Equipment

The Rise of 911 Emergency

At 2:00 a.m. in a southwest Denver neighborhood, forty-four-year-old Loretta Barella Rosa ran across the street to her neighbor's house, banging on the door and screaming for help. Loretta's husband, Christopher Alex Parea, was following at her heels, demanding that she return to their house. When Loretta's neighbor came to the door and saw the terror in Loretta's face, instead of opening the door she grabbed a telephone and called the police. While the neighbor watched Parea drag Loretta off the porch and pull her across the street, the 911 operator assured her that help was on the way. Yet as the neighbor waited, the police failed to arrive. Forty minutes later, the neighbor called 911 again. The dispatcher assured her, "We're trying to get somebody there."[1] When a police officer finally arrived on the scene at 3:10 a.m.—seventy minutes after the initial 911 call—the neighbor stayed inside her house because she wanted to remain anonymous. The officer shined a flashlight into a window of the home that Loretta and Parea shared before retreating to his car and leaving the scene. Five hours later, at 8:15 a.m., Parea himself called 911, informing the police that he might have killed his wife. This time the officers promptly embarked to the house, where they found Loretta's dead body lying in a pool of blood. At about 9:00 a.m., Parea was finally taken into police custody, where he was held on suspicion of Loretta's murder.[2]

The sad story of Loretta's death points to a number of social challenges in contemporary American life. Most clearly it touches on the lack of accountability that many urban police departments have to their constituents, particularly in neighborhoods filled with immigrants and the poor. Yet Loretta's death also presents a unique perspective on the relationship between media and police power, particularly how communication technologies introduce a tightly constrained field of action into citizens' social responsibility. Once the neighbor called the cops, she trusted them to fully assume the burden of protecting Loretta. So when Loretta's neighbor informed the operator, "I've never seen anything like it. . . . She needs somebody out here,"[3] she followed through on her end of the social compact: when it comes to policing, seeing and saying—surveillance and communication—are supposed to be citizens' sole responsibilities. Although the dying woman really "needed somebody," Loretta's neighbor obediently stayed inside and waited for the cops.

Because the telephone and other media technologies have allowed the police apparatus to "govern at a distance"[4]—that is, they have provided the technical capacity for citizens to take personal responsibility for local governance and, when necessary, to summon authorities from afar—the police apparatus has been inserted into the very center of communal structures of responsibility, often alienating citizens from their neighbors and discouraging direct social action. Ultimately, this technological mediation has played an important role in transforming social responsibility into *civic* responsibility. For Peter Moskos, a criminologist and former Baltimore police officer, the telephone and kindred technologies gave rise to this rift in local solidarity: "Citizens, rather than being encouraged to maintain community standards, were urged to stay behind locked doors and call 911."[5] While in the best of circumstances this deference to the police might not be a cause for serious concern, today, when police agencies are financially drained and increasingly unaccountable to their constituents, neighbors are often left to rely on one another for direct local action. In this regard, although the Denver Police Department has refused to comment on their deplorable failure to save Loretta's life, her neighbor gave a plausible reason for the police's response delay: she called 911 right when the bars were closing on a Saturday night, so the cops were probably busy handing out disorderly conduct violations and underage drinking tickets.[6] At a time when public agencies are under the gun to justify and sustain themselves financially, it is tragic, although not especially surprising, that police departments will carry out revenue-generating activities at the expense of responding to potentially deadly domestic disturbances. So while it is difficult to fault Loretta's neighbor for staying inside while her friend was being beaten to death across the street, we *should* begin to think in creative ways about local solidarity in these neoliberal times.

This chapter reviews how police telecommunications systems—such as the telegraphic private box, the telephone callbox, 911 Emergency, and crime-reporting smartphone apps—have helped the police monitor and guide how citizens recognize and report crime in their communities. Throughout their history, these technologies have performed a number of mediating functions that have allowed police agencies to recruit ideal informants, surveil and track witnesses, prevent the reporting of low-priority crimes (such as sexual assault and other offenses against women), and discourage certain populations from contacting the police. Thus while a number of scholars have focused on how media representations instruct their audiences how to live in accordance with liberal ideals,[7] in this chapter I will focus on how technologies like the telegraph private box and 911 Emergency have provided the technical infrastructure that makes possible the very formation of liberal governance. Advances in telecommunication technologies have allowed sparse police patrols to extend their surveillance reach by opening up communications between select citizens, police headquarters, and officers on the ground.[8] By empowering these citizens to contact the police, the advent of citizen-police telecommunications demonstrates what Jeremy Packer has identified as the fundamental role of communication technologies in liberal government: to "activate subjects without being overly intrusive or coercive. . . . [Liberalism] is a form of governance built upon allowing and encouraging—one might even say fostering—very particular forms of freedom that lead to, and are derived by, the maxim that government rules best when ruling least."[9] While the telegraph and telephone did not teach citizens how to care for themselves and their communities in accordance with liberal ideals, they did make possible new forms of civic participation and new relational norms between citizens and the police.[10] Thus media technologies—from the earliest police telegraph to today's chicest smartphone—have introduced spatial and temporal versatility into liberal systems of social control, providing loci of regulation by which citizens' behavior can be channeled into productive, monitored forms of seeing/saying citizenship. As Andrew Barry has emphasized in his work on the telegraph, telecommunication technologies "have come to provide the perfect material base for liberal government."[11] Indeed: the long history of 911 Emergency illustrates how technologically mediated lateral surveillance and communication have provided crucial tools for the formation and maintenance of American liberalism.

Telecommunications and the "Reactive" Police Force

Every citizen . . . must feel an interest in the institution and development of the system that protects his person and property.
—Howard Sprogle[12]

As I detailed in the previous chapter, a number of media technologies have been used to locally responsibilize citizens and secure their loyalty to the police apparatus. Crowdsourcing, however, is not the only way that media have been deployed to secure citizen participation. Describing how early citizen crowdsourcing efforts like the hue and cry were transformed into a sanitized "reporting" process, Ann DeWindt and Edwin DeWindt observe: "A once vigorous, boisterous, sometimes reckless and potentially dangerous, fundamentally oral and face-to-face institution, with collective responsibility assumed for its success, had . . . been tamed, bureaucratized, depersonalized, and reduced to a routine of composing and filing a memorandum."[13] This development of a media-driven crime reporting process reached a crucial stage with the rise of telecommunication technologies in the nineteenth century, as "reporting" became a mechanism of patrol activation as well as record-keeping. By constructing a system of citizen-police telecommunications, police agencies provided citizens with the necessary technical equipment to see something and say something: to report their fellow citizens' misdeeds and summon police from a distance.

The modern police apparatus, in fact, has been molded by the way in which these technologies empower citizens to witness and report crime. In his classic analysis of American policing in the 1970s, Albert J. Reiss declared that the modern police force is fundamentally a "reactive organization."[14] Given its institutional and technological structure, the modern police force has been designed to *react* to citizen-generated tips and complaints.[15] Recent research, in fact, has shown that citizens' phone calls determine the majority of police activities, even outweighing the demands of tactical strategy and mandates from police administration.[16] In fact, in major urban jurisdictions like Washington, D.C., police routinely spend seventy percent of their time fielding constituents' 911 calls.[17] And in some parts of the country, 911 calls consume as much as ninety percent of officers' time.[18] While the spread of 911 in the 1970s and 1980s energized this transformation of the police force, citizen tips have long provided the very organizational conditions of the modern police patrol. In fact, one hundred years before the rise of 911, police agencies were already experimenting with how media technologies could cultivate and control active modes of citizen participation.[19]

While the telegraph had an enormous impact on diverse sectors of public and professional life, it had a particularly decisive effect on the labor of policing. In fact, one of the earliest experiments in electric telegraphy was in 1845, when police from the south of England used a telegraph to nab a murderer en route to London. John Tawell, who had murdered his mistress before boarding a train to London's Paddington Station, was outrun by this new technology: after disembarking he was followed, apprehended, and eventually hanged for his crime.[20] Tawell's case, like many others that would follow, demonstrated the extraordinary impact that telecommunications technologies could have on police work. For early police historian Howard Sprogle, telegraph systems gave the police a radical boost in reach and efficiency: "By making a comparatively small force extremely efficient, and therefore a large force unnecessary, it saves a large annual expenditure for the maintenance of the department. Its introduction is in the line of real economy."[21] The advantages of the police telegraph, therefore, were often described in the terms of political economy: the police could extend their gaze deep into the lives of the public without having to employ a massive force. As a journalist with the New Jersey *Ledger* observed in 1856, the police telegraph

> operates as a great labor saving machine . . . [It] makes the Central Police Station an intelligence office of the most extended character. . . . Extending its ramifications to every part of the city, it, in conjunction with the police force, renders the head of that department almost ubiquitous. . . . The entire police force on duty may all be aroused to vigilance in a moment, and the whole city be put instantly under surveillance for the de-

tection of crime. It in effect greatly multiplies the police force, without the cost of maintaining a larger number of officers in the service, for it makes every man's labor available just at the period and place where it is needed.[22]

Reminiscent of the "eyes and ears" rhetoric explored in the previous chapter, the rhetoric of sensory extension is given new life with the rise of the telegraph. And just as with crowdsourcing media, the seeing/saying public was not given unconditional access to this new communications system. As soon as police agencies began distributing telegraph booths to public areas, they devised means to monitor, restrict, and guide citizens' access. An extensive technological apparatus—comprised of highly regulated callboxes, rigid media interfaces, highly trained operators and dispatchers, and diverse mechanisms of data gathering and surveillance—have mediated citizens' relationships with the police, cultivating very particular habits of seeing, saying, and related public support.

In their earliest days, police callboxes were locked and accessible only to cops. But by the 1860s and 1870s, a few select residents of large cities like Chicago, New York, and Baltimore were allowed to use these telegraph machines in the event of an emergency.[23] By restricting access to only the most trusted citizens, officials sought to tightly control the flow of information from the streets to police headquarters. In 1884 George Bartlett Prescott, an electrical engineer who wrote several books on early telecommunication technologies, described the process by which the police used these new media to facilitate very particular modes of seeing and saying:

[The telephone boxes] are opened by means of keys, which are given to all the principal people of the city, as well as to the police. In order to prevent their abuse, the locks of the alarm stations are made in such a manner that the key cannot be removed, when once placed in the lock, except by a policeman. As each key is numbered, and cannot be removed except by the co-operation of the police, the person who has given the alarm, on opening the sentry box, cannot prevent himself from being known. By this means all annoyance from unnecessary alarms are avoided, because the possessor of a key opens the box only when assistance is necessary, and is not lavish of his calls for fear of having to give up his key. It will thus be seen that each citizen co-operates by this means in the general surveillance.[24]

While a few trusted citizens were empowered to directly contact the police, the citizen's telegraph key would remain locked in the box until an officer responded, thus allowing the police to identify who made the call. Submitting to surveillance, therefore, was a condition of citizens' participation, placing early 911 technologies among the first efforts at the technical police surveillance of law-abiding American citizens.

Police agencies also regulated citizens' participation by determining what criminal acts were reportable. For instance, one of the reasons the telegraph was so useful to the police was that it tightly controlled its users' communicative output. As James Carey has observed, because electric transmissions were so expensive in the nineteenth century, the telegraph "demanded something closer to a 'scientific' language, a language of strict denotation in which the connotative features of utterance were under rigid control."[25] In fact, the telegraph industry attempted to woo police officials with the telegraph's promise of precise, rapid communication. An 1872 advertisement for Gamewell & Co.'s police telegraphs declared that their machine allowed for "perfect, complete, and reliable" communication: "it shall be absolutely perfect."[26] The telegraph's technical constraints, therefore, allowed the police to enforce a normalized, "perfect" ideal of civic participation by regulating the communicative behavior of crime witnesses. As in other highly regulated communicative situations, uniformity and simplicity were the hallmark of this normalization.[27] For instance, when citizens approached a telegraphic "private box"—a forerunner of the phone booth that was about eight feet tall and twenty-eight inches in diameter—they were forced to manage the box's system of dials, levers, and kinetic procedures in a way that minimized the possibility of any ambiguity, distortion, imprecision, fraud, or other forms of "noise"[28] in their interactions with the police. Once a citizen unlocked the box, s/he was confronted with a strange device outfitted with a pointer that could be aligned with any one of eleven choices: arson, theft, forgery, rioting, drunkenness, murder, accidents, ordinance violation, fighting, test line, and fire. The citizen would then pigeonhole the report into one of these categories, align the pointer, and

pull a handle, thus relaying to police headquarters Morse-coded data
about the report and the box's location. Thus when citizens were confronted with the telegraph's interface, they were forced to act in accordance with the promise of the new medium: as the telegraph required
precise, rapid communication, the citizen in the street could be made to
act in kind. By forcing witnesses to adopt this artificial linguistic economy, the police imposed a language of witnessing that was, in the words
of Philadelphia's fire chief in 1856, "beautifully simple."[29]

In effect, the telegraph box's interface established a narrow, highly
regulated domain of citizen action by determining where citizens com-
municated with the police, how they carried out that communication,
whom they could communicate with, and what acts were reportable.
Even when boxes were placed in more affluent areas, only trusted citizens were empowered to use them, thereby cutting off the vast majority
of citizens from this citizen-police communications apparatus. Also, by
tightly controlling the domain of the sayable through the means of the
eleven-point interface, police agencies determined which crimes were
reportable—and thus, which acts were publicly intelligible as being
criminal offenses. For instance, although drunkenness and fighting are
listed—thereby singling out the working class—rape and sexual assault
are not, and thus they could not be directly reported via the callbox system. And perhaps of most importance, these boxes literally rerouted social responsibility through police headquarters. Whereas citizens would
traditionally respond to violence and protect one another at the communal level, the telegraph box had only one output channel: the police department. The police telegraph and kindred media devices thus played
an essential part in solidifying the modern police force's role as the community's sole arbiter of justice and protection, "empowering" citizens by
short-circuiting their communal solidarity and channeling their social
action toward highly regulated communications with the police.

Calling the Cops

The telegraph's beautiful simplicity proved attractive to police agencies
across the United States. In 1858, the firm of Charles T. and J. N. Chester
outfitted New York City with a public police telegraph system, and Philadelphia followed soon after.[30] Telegraphic boxes remained a popular

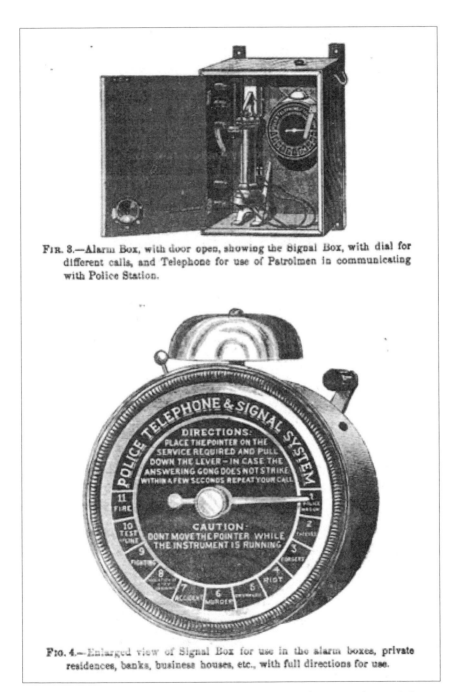

FIG. 3.—Alarm Box, with door open, showing the Signal Box, with dial for different calls, and Telephone for use of Patrolmen in communicating with Police Station.

FIG. 4.—Enlarged view of Signal Box for use in the alarm boxes, private residences, banks, business houses, etc., with full directions for use.

Figure 2.1. Police telegraph system used in Chicago during the 1880s. Chicago Police Department, *Report of the General Superintendent*, 49.

citizen-police communications tool until a new innovation came along in 1877: the telephonic callbox, which allowed police officers and trusted citizens to carry on conversations with call takers at police headquarters. That year the city of Albany, New York, installed the first police telephone callbox, and urban jurisdictions like Brooklyn, Boston, Chicago, and Milwaukee soon followed. The public boxes, which were topped with lights that would flash upon activation, encouraged citizens to contact headquarters when they witnessed crimes in the area. By the 1890s, most jurisdictions had adopted telephonic communications, and hundreds of thousands of police calls were being made each year.[31] In fact, in 1884 George Bartlett Prescott expressed excitement at how callboxes allowed citizens to take an active part in the security of their communities. According to Prescott, the new police telephones empowered citizens to "call for assistance in a few moments, and thus secure from a small number of policemen the same amount of practical service that they would ordinarily get only from a numerous force. We thus see . . . that each individual plays a part in the general security, and that every one contributes to the repose of all."[32]

To ensure that everyone contributed to this "general security," however, the behavior of telephone users—just like that of telegraph users— would have to be carefully monitored and governed. Just as with the telegraph boxes of earlier decades, police agencies permitted some trusted citizens to speak directly to headquarters from callboxes and even home telephones. Among the diverse strategies for monitoring these calls, when the Chicago Police Department installed telephone machines in select households it ensured that metadata about the location and time of each call were collected at headquarters. In these early days, the department would even keep house keys for those homes with direct-to-police telephones, allowing officers to enter the premises whenever a call was made.[33] So while the emergence of the telephone allowed the police to responsibilize broader sectors of the population, police agencies were careful to monitor, regulate, and guide this new freedom.

To ensure that the precision of the locked telegraphic private box was remediated into the new open system of unlocked public call boxes, federal investigators began regularly convening to study how to best use the biosocial resources of the seeing/saying public. In 1902, for example, Congress ordered the Department of Commerce and Labor to gather statistics on how police and fire agencies used telephones and telegraphs. In the department's published findings, the authors waxed ambivalently on the advantages of the telephone: "Notwithstanding the advantage of being able to carry on a conversation by telephone, there is a certain advantage in automatic signaling, as there can be no variation, and no wrong idea can be conveyed by an excited dispatcher to a confused operator at central who can not understand what is being said."[34] While telegraphic signals required many levels of mediation and translation, telephonic communication threatened to introduce other forms of feedback and noise into the citizen-police communications system. Despite these concerns, however, the 1906 congressional report suggested adding the volatile element of citizen conversation into the mix. However, certain elements of this process would have to be prioritized; as this and future congressional reports would repeatedly emphasize, operators needed to be trained to serve very specific, technical functions in mediating the process of citizen crime reporting.

In the early decades of the twentieth century, this was accomplished by translating the telegraph's technical constraints into the conversation protocols between citizens and telephone switchboard operators. For the first fifty years of the phone's existence, all civilian calls were routed through operators who would manually connect callers. Yet police calls were subjected to an additional layer of mediation: police dispatchers were trained to extract very specific information in order to discern a caller's location and determine the call's level of emergency. As a 1942 manual for switchboard operating procedure reveals, these dispatchers functioned as a screen for citizen-generated knowledge. Dispatchers not only screened calls for certain information, they also took an active role in coproducing a particular kind of discourse: "The primary responsibility of a telephone switchboard operator is to provide telephone service of a uniformly high standard, with the least possible delay, confusion, or annoyance to telephone users. The competent operator . . . performs his functions with courtesy, accuracy, and speed."[35] Mistakes, the operator is assured, "are usually due either to misunderstanding or to carelessness."[36] And speed, of course, was essential: "Speed . . . depends largely upon the operator's skill and accuracy in making connections. Speed can be acquired only by practice and a systematic effort to eliminate all unnecessary movements."[37] These demands for accuracy and speed, of course, were not passive responsibilities: the operator's role was to guide the conversation along very specific lines. With these protocols operators were able to cultivate a very particular form of speaking subject, helping callers domesticate their sensory experience into actionable data that could be best used in investigations and trials. With the rise of telephonic citizen-police communications, therefore, a new strategy of communication governance emerges: although flawless communication was at first a problem of ensuring that only trusted citizens could communicate with the police, it soon became a problem of ensuring that all citizens could function as flawless communicators.

Although rotary telephones had been invented in the late nineteenth century, they were slow to revolutionize the operator-assisted model of telephonic communications. In the 1950s and 1960s, rotary phones empowered citizens to bypass operators and connect their own calls—including, of course, their calls to the police. Aiding the police's priorities of "speed" and "accuracy," the gradual displacement of switchboard operators in the 1950s and 1960s granted police agencies a new opportunity and a new problem: how could they harness this new direct communications capacity in order to boost police response times and assist investigations? The most significant attempt to address this problem can be traced to President Lyndon Johnson's "war against crime." Amid the rising crime rates of the 1960s, Johnson appointed a nineteen-member team to assess the American criminal justice system. This team, which was headed by Attorney General Nicholas Katzenbach and Harvard law professor James Vorenberg, made a number of policy recommendations related to emergency services and citizen-police communications. Emphasizing the role of the seeing/saying citizen in fighting crime, the commission announced a renewed shift toward empowering citizens through communication technologies: "Because the members of a police force are so widely dispersed when they are at work the efficiency of police communications systems is crucial. Rapid response to emergency calls, which . . . has shown to be an important factor in crime solution, depends on good communications [with the public]."[38] This was particularly important, they argued, because police response time was an essential factor in crime suppression. The commission found that for crimes that went unsolved, the police's average response time was 6.3

minutes; for cases that the police eventually solved, the average was 4.1 minutes.[39]

To decrease response times, the commission recommended a number of communications policy changes. Perhaps their most significant suggestion was to establish a nationwide emergency number, 911.[40] The president's commission found that Los Angeles had fifty different numbers that reached different local police jurisdictions, making it difficult for victims and witnesses to know which number to call during an emergency. Empowering citizens to more easily contact the authorities, the commission decided, was preferable to adopting the alternative: a panoptic surveillance apparatus. Although the commission considered the possibilities of introducing strategically placed microphones and closed-circuit television surveillance, they concluded that these devices were too intrusive, costly, and error prone.[41] Rather, the commission suggested that telecommunications could be utilized in such a way that the state could get maximum value from its citizens. As the report concluded, "The apprehension process can respond only after it gets a call, and a number of things can be done to modify existing street communications equipment to make it easier for a victim or a witness to reach the police."[42] Continuing, the report lamented that a lack of money might prevent citizens from reporting crimes: "The victim of a robber careful enough to steal the last dime cannot now use the public telephone. Public telephones can be adapted so that the operator can be reached without using money."[43] According to the president's commission, many urban jurisdictions had extensive networks of callboxes that were essentially useless because, as they were difficult to locate and were often locked, they didn't tap into the immense surveillance power of the general public. The report even suggested that the boxes be painted in red, white, and blue in order to draw the public's attention and to associate witnessing with patriotic duty.[44]

During the life of the telephone, therefore, the U.S. has witnessed a remarkable shift in the way that the population is allowed to participate in the policing process. In the early days of locked callboxes, very few citizens were trusted to participate. However, the spread of residential telephones opened the possibility for a new emphasis on citizens' seeing/saying responsibility to the state. As the report of President Johnson's commission made clear, now that the majority of citizens were proficient telephone users, law enforcement could use this proficiency to their advantage. The private innovation of the domestic rotary phone, therefore, was repurposed for the public domain: phone booths—once the only way to call the cops—exploded in popularity and, as the call for them to be painted in red, white, and blue suggests, they even became a sign of public service and social responsibility. When the possibility was raised about the public misusing this new responsibility to generate false alarms, the commission concluded that criminals would be dissuaded because they had to use their voices and could thus be identified. For this reason, the false alarm rate for telephone systems, they claimed, was less than three percent.[45]

Open Participation and Next-Generation 911

This unprecedented distribution of communicative access, however, gave rise to a number of problems. As I noted earlier in this chapter, Albert J. Reiss has illustrated how these technocultural developments led to the restructuring of the police department as a "reactive force." This shift toward "demand-led policing," which was made possible by the emergence of the private telephone and strategically placed urban telephone booths, helped produce a skewed public image of the police's role in society. As Peter K. Manning has pointed out, "the police were perhaps overly successful in 'selling' the idea of demand-led policing."[46] Manning argues that by promoting the police as an organization that provides citizens with "services," police agencies convinced the public that "response-to-calls-based policing was both a service and an effective means of controlling crime and criminals. The American version of this persuasion is perhaps seen most clearly and visibly in the way people are encouraged to call 911 via advertising on billboards, television, radio, and other mass media, and on police cars themselves. . . . What is central is the power of the idea—that police serve best by rapid responses to calls for service—in the mind of the public, the politicians, and the police."[47] Thus the figure of the seeing/saying citizen, in partnership with call-and-respond-oriented police agencies, gave rise to a reactive form of policing that took cops off their beats and placed them in patrol cars.[48]

This development coincided with a period of intense technologization in the policing profession, a key feature of what has come to be known as "law-and-order policing."[49] Many of the problems faced by urban police departments were seen to be answerable through technology-driven modernization, and the National Science Foundation and other agencies began pouring substantial funds into projects that studied policing technologies.[50] Yet as this new policing paradigm gained momentum in the 1970s and 1980s, the federal government realized that many of its key "law-and-order" initiatives were not bearing fruit. Despite the near ubiquity of public and private telephones, and despite national efforts to establish crime reporting as an act of responsible citizenship, police agencies were still struggling to contain rising crime rates. According to authorities, citizens were simply not using 911 like they should. In 1984, when the Department of Justice (DOJ) was urged to publish a report on the state of 911 Emergency, it found that citizens' hesitance to dial 911 was one of the biggest obstacles in the war on crime. The report recommended a number of interesting solutions to this problem, emphasizing that local police departments would have to do more to understand the challenges of 911 citizenship in the urban crime environment: "To understand . . . citizen-police communications, one must look at what citizens attempting to call the police go through."[51] The report found that citizens fail to report crimes for a number of valid reasons, the most important of which were inconvenience, fear of reprisal, embarrassment, and fear of culpability.[52] Predictably, the DOJ report argued that these problems could be solved by adopting technical systems that provided citizens with even greater convenience and anonymity.

The DOJ also proposed that operators, dispatchers, and police departments adopt strict new call screening practices. For example, while in the 1970s most police departments restricted 911 calls to only the most life-threatening and emergent situations—ordering that citizens direct other calls through the department's non-emergency number—the 1984 DOJ report recommended routing *all* police calls through 911, "leaving it to a trained, experienced professional to distinguish between urgent and non-urgent calls."[53] In other words, this important innovation signals a shift from trusted citizen authority to call-screening by "trained, experienced professionals." The experiment in democratic urban citizen-police communications—by which every call for service was answered with a police dispatch—had proven too costly and inefficient. New screening mechanisms were in order: to make citizen reporting more efficient, and not to waste cops' time, the report argued for a form of "differential response" that divided call urgency into "immediate mobile response," "expedited mobile response," or "routine mobile response."[54] To best allocate officers' time, these screening strategies could also include "a variety of police response mechanisms, both mobile and non-mobile, by either sworn officers or civilian employees, in person or by telephone or mail, using walk-in reporting or report-taking by appointment—a wide range of nontraditional responses depending on the urgency and nature of the call."[55] Citizens, therefore, would be urged to report any and all suspicions and problems through a central number, and police agencies would filter through these reports in order to devise which response, if any, would be most appropriate.

This heavily screened democratization gained steam in the 1990s, and it has received a considerable boost in the digital age as "Next-Generation 911" uses new technologies to give citizens as many opportunities as possible to see something and say something. As Gordon Gow and Mark Ihnat have shown, these "E-911" services arise out of the same impulse that fueled the adoption of a national emergency number. While the gradual implementation of 911 as a universal police number allowed citizens to more effortlessly join the war on crime, E-911 has been used to address emergency services to the digital/mobile world.[56] Services like text-to-911, GPS-enabled reporting, online tip submission, and crime-reporting smartphone apps have come to dominate the 911 media landscape. In 2007, for example, the Boston PD became the first major American police department to encourage citizens to submit crime tips via text.[57] Capitalizing on these trends, the Federal Communications Commission reports that its text-to-911 program, which allows for a similar routing of text messages to appropriate police agencies, has been available to select jurisdictions since 2015.[58]

Perhaps the most interesting development in Next-Generation 911 technologies is the crime-reporting smartphone app. A new iPhone app, iWitness, is a good case in point. Greg Heuss, the app's designer, promotes his product by lauding the mechanical ease with which consumers can capture and transmit data: "Any time the user feels endangered, the user simply touches the screen of their phone. At that point, the phone begins capturing video and audio of the scene . . . a steady light is emitted from the phone, and the user's GPS coordinates are recorded. If a

Figure 2.2. CrimePush app. Note the interface similarities to the telegraph box in Figure 2.1. Photo retrieved from Brendan Hugo, "CrimePush Provides a More Modern Way to Report Crimes," *ABI*, February 1, 2012. http://anythingbutiphone.com.

'threat' feels imminent, the user touches the screen again, [and] 911 is called."[59] One touch of the screen activates the phone's video and audio recording software, and another touch dials 911. Importantly, these multimodal data streamline the messy witnessing process: "[Heuss] added that law enforcement like the fact that the app records [a] video and audio file of the perpetrator—something he said was 'much better than a vague description that most victims give to the police now.'"[60] In a similar smartphone application, CrimePush, users are given a touchscreen with small icons depicting nine basic categories of crime. With an interface eerily reminiscent of the private box featured in Figure 2.1, users push the icon that represents the appropriate crime, and a bundle of data—including photo, video, audio, and location of the call—is sent to local law enforcement agencies. A *Forbes* report observed that Crime-Push allows users to report crime effortlessly so that they "may continue with their busy lives knowing that with a push of a button, police will know and have everything to pursue the criminal. Ordinary users become the eyes and ears of authorities."[61]

This familiar goal of converting the public into the "eyes and ears" of authorities is being fueled by the emergence of iWitness, CrimePush, and other digital applications that allow citizens to transmit video and audio data to law enforcement authorities. In fact, these efforts are becoming increasingly localized, as police agencies reach out to different sectors of the population in order to tie digital witnessing to an ethos of community responsibility. In Somerset, Kentucky, for example, the local police department has initiated the aptly named "See-Hear-Report" program, an initiative that calls on primary and secondary school students to use anonymous text messages to report their peers for criminal or delinquent behavior.[62] Somerset police chief Doug Nelson says these initiatives are the natural next-step of law enforcement in a digital culture: "Students today are growing up in a digital age. . . . Therefore, it's important for the law enforcement community and our police department to offer different ways to interact with our youth."[63] Yet in lieu of "interacting" with the local youth, the Somerset Police Department has simply provided them with the technical resources to effortlessly police their peers. According to Chief Nelson, "Text messaging is a common communication method for them these days and we want to make it easy for them to pass information to us that could save lives"[64] This small town "See-Hear-Report" program, as Chief Nelson claims, might occasionally "save lives." Yet it is certain to encourage petty snitching practices among students living in this low-crime recreational community of eleven thousand residents, particularly with the introduction of cash rewards.

Policing the Callers, Pranking the Police

In addition to providing important technical infrastructure for our current spy-and-snitch culture, the growth in Next-Generation 911 technologies has opened up the possibility of a more generalized climate of surveillance. As David Lyon reminds us, if our cell phones can be tracked by cops in an emergency, they can be tracked by cops in non-emergencies, too.[65] Putting a finer point on the inherent dangers of geolocative 911, media theorist David Phillips warns: "despite the special purpose to which the 911 system is dedicated, the wireless 911 initiative has created the infrastructure for a general purpose locational surveillance infrastructure capable both of surveilling broad patterns of activities and of responding to particular individuals. Moreover, the infrastructure is more available to police agencies and to well-established and well-funded corporate entities than to grassroots organizations."[66]

While it is difficult to disagree with Phillips's critique of 911 technologies, it is also important to recognize how citizens have renegotiated this technical infrastructure in order to resist traditional forms of 911 citizenship.

Police departments have long exploited the surveillance potential of 911 technologies. As Richard Lindberg notes in his history of the Chicago Police Department, many police officials envisioned the early telegraph box as a way to ensure that lazy cops were walking their beats. Requiring cops to send telegraphs from specific locations at specified times allowed police administrations to keep an eye on their officers' activities.[67] Yet police agencies also used these technologies to track and identify civilians that reported crimes to the police. While the telegraph empowered trustworthy citizens to support police investigations and increase the department's sensory reach, at the same time it allowed criminals and careless citizens to manipulate officers and waste police resources. So while the police wanted to open the lines of communication with citizens, they also strove to ensure that their own time wasn't wasted by frivolous requests or bogus tips. A recurring trend in citizen-police communications, therefore, has been the development of surveillance mechanisms whereby police departments gather as much data as possible on 911 callers. In the early days of the telegraphic private box, for example, users had no expectation of anonymity because they could not remove their personally customized keys from the box's lock. This tendency to carry out preventive surveillance on citizens who called the police has taken many forms: from the earliest days of the telephone, call takers have been under strict orders to gather as much information as possible about callers,[68] and in most cases emergency calls have been geographically traceable. This surveillance has gradually reached a reflexive level of intensity: since the 1970s, when the telecommunications industry began to automatically determine the location of incoming calls to 911 (what is called "automatic location identification"), vocal speech has not even been required to set in motion a police response. Operational protocols require dispatchers to send officers to a home or business that has dialed 911, even if no human on the other end speaks (or even if they admit that they dialed 911 by mistake). This has been the case with cell phones since 1996, when providers were required to grant direct-access 911 capabilities along with GPS tracking of all incoming 911 calls. Now that more than ninety percent of American adults own cell phones,[69] all callers need to do is dial 911 and push "Send" in order to initiate a GPS-coordinated police response. Yet even with all of these geolocative surveillance capabilities, 911 call takers are still drilled in conversation-based methods of personal data gathering: the NYPD, for example, requires 911 operators to ask callers as many as a dozen questions. They are required to ask about the caller's exact location—including borough, cross streets, and apartment number—as well as her or his name and phone number. Operators are then required to verify all information before they are allowed to ask the nature of the emergency.[70] Thus while 911 response times are still important to urban police departments, enforcing surveillance-oriented conversational protocols tops the police's list of priorities.

In the eyes of the police, there are good reasons for all this preventive surveillance. Instead of using 911 Emergency like responsible citizens, many callers violate the protocols and responsibilities that have long characterized citizen-police communications. For example, because 911 calls from public booths cannot be easily tracked, they are popular tools for prank callers. Cop Block, one of the police resistance organizations discussed in the previous chapter, encourages citizens to exploit anonymous 911 technologies in order to discredit them as a tool of police power. According to a Cop Block activist, "Anonymous tips by telephone are a real danger for cannabis users, and they have to be stopped. The best way to stop anonymous tips is by calling in bogus or phony anonymous tips, and often. But doing this is not danger-free, and can lead to your incarceration. The idea is to have the cops go on so many fruitless phony tips calls that such calls will no longer be trusted, especially by judges issuing search warrants."[71] Cop Block then lists a number of steps that activists can take—such as always using a pay phone, spending as little time on the phone as possible, and informing the call taker that illegal activity is taking place at the house or business of a political enemy—to exasperate cops into ignoring anonymous tips.

These kinds of pranks, of course, are not the first of their kind. In the 1990s, when Sarah J. Tracy and Karen Tracy carried out their landmark ethnographic research on 911 communications, they reported that call takers receive a staggering proportion of prank calls from phone booths. As Tracy and Tracy document, many of these callers lash out at the police under the cover of anonymity, such as one caller who remarked: "Pigs . . . fuckin' pieces of shit."[72] The caller immediately called back and shouted, "Fuckin' pigs," before once again hanging up the phone.[73] The DOJ, however, doesn't find such pranks very funny: these kinds of antics have led the department to classify the misuse and abuse of 911 "an urgent problem."[74] To respond to this problem, many local jurisdictions have used public service announcements and other outreach methods to educate citizens about improper uses of 911. A Franklin, Ohio, public service announcement, for example, warned children that "we know where you are" when you call 911, a campaign that, according to the Department of Justice, reduced the frequency of prank 911 calls.[75]

While these campaigns might reduce prank 911 calls, many people still use the citizen-police communications infrastructure to violate the norms and etiquettes of 911 citizenship. These trends illustrate not only how pranksters and resistance movements use 911 technologies to manipulate the state, but also how police agencies respond to these attacks by demanding enhanced powers to carry out surveillance on the population at large. For example, in June 2012 the North Hollywood Police Department received a call that a violent kidnapping was underway at pop star Miley Cyrus's house, and that shots had been fired. A police helicopter and a dozen heavily armed officers converged on Cyrus's multimillion-dollar compound, drawing their guns and creating a perimeter around the house.[76] Yet they soon found out that Cyrus was not home, and that she had been "Swatted" (or "SWAT-ted"): that is, someone had used 911 technologies to dispatch a SWAT team to her house when no crime was actually taking place. Cyrus, they realized, was simply the latest celebrity target in a growing prank trend: Ashton Kutcher, Russell Brand, Magic Johnson, Selena Gomez, Paris Hilton, Ryan Seacrest, Justin Timberlake, Khloe Kardashian, and other Los Angeles pop culture favorites have also been Swatted by pranksters using 911 technologies.[77] In 2012, the FBI estimated that there were about four hundred Swatting incidents in the United States annually, and that their numbers were on the rise.[78]

Sometimes Swatting pranks take on a more political bent, however. Erick Erickson, a neoconservative blogger and CNN contributor, was Swatted in May 2012. That night a caller contacted the sheriff's office, claiming to be Erickson and informing the operator that he had just murdered his wife. After the operator asked for his phone number, the prankster said: "I don't know. I guess you're going to have to find out. I'm gonna—going to shoot someone else soon."[79] After the Swatter hung up the phone, the police used caller ID to trace the call to Erickson's house, where an unknown number of officers proceeded to "take the house," blocking off all exits and rushing the residence. Following the incident, some of Erickson's friends in Congress decided that Swatting was a growing problem that deserved the special attention of the DOJ. In a letter to Attorney General Eric Holder, a group of eighty GOP congresspersons urged the Obama administration to crack down on "these hate filled ploys." According to the letter, which was penned by U.S. Representative Sandy Adams of Florida, "The use of SWAT-ting as a harassment tool is apparently not new, but its use as a tool for targeting political speech appears to be a more recent development. . . . During the last year, some of the more widely reported cases of SWAT-ting have taken place against blog operators across the country. . . . The emerging pattern is both disturbing and dangerous."[80] As Adams's letter reveals, one of the reasons Swatting is so dangerous to the police and the political class is that Swatting technologies are notoriously difficult to trace. Many Swatters use Skype,[81] the Internet-based telecom software that allows users to make video and audio calls, while others use Internet-based telephone hardware like magicJacks.[82] These calls are highly difficult to track to specific users, as are other popular Swatting technologies that deploy Voice Over Internet Protocol programs (VOIPs). VOIPs allow users to coopt distant telephone networks, thus disguising their own telephone numbers and addresses and making a call's origin virtually impossible to ascertain.[83] Other popular Swatting technologies including teletype systems designed for deaf callers, as well as SpoofCards, which allow users to determined which phone number is displayed on the target's Caller ID system.

These surveillance-busting measures have proven quite successful in throwing the police off the scent of cautious Swatters and other pranksters. In response, the police have taken defensive measures that illustrate just how important 911 is to the liberal policing project. Since its earliest days, 911 Emergency has been a tool *by* the state, *for* the state. In order for the police apparatus to function in its present form, citizens must see and say according to the strict protocols of the American social compact. To maintain a sparse, reactive police force based upon a model of liberal political economy, citizens must operate as reliable participants in the policing of the social order. If citizens fail in this essential civic responsibility of seeing and saying—if they withhold or manipulate intelligence, or if they mislead the police by providing false information— then the state will have to gradually abandon its own liberal rules of engagement, turning instead to enhanced police power and invasive surveillance, an excellent illustration of what David Lyon calls "surveillance creep."[84] As a response to Swatting, for example, police agencies and legislators have called for the intensified surveillance and tracking of popular communication channels, as well as a crackdown on "spoofing" technologies and other identification shielding products. These responses have included increased surveillance of IP Relay services,[85] expansive new definitions of IP Relay fraud,[86] enhanced civil and criminal penalties,[87] as well as calls for making Swatting a federal offense.[88] As Representative Adams demanded in her letter to Eric Holder, "These crimes are not to be tolerated and necessitate thorough examination at every level."[89]

Finally, there is one more important site of 911 resistance that deserves our attention. One of the more provocative ways that responsible 911 citizenship is resisted is through defensive violence, which often serves as a critique of 911 technologies and their rituals of regulated state intervention. When victims of home invasions "stand their ground"— that is, when they shoot or otherwise attack invaders rather than simply calling 911—the question of 911 as an effective mediator of citizen violence comes to the fore. For example, in 2013 Milwaukee County sheriff David Clarke sparked a national controversy when he urged citizens to arm themselves in anticipation of growing violence and crime. In a public service announcement targeted to his constituency, Clarke begins by telling his audience that he wants to talk about their safety: "It's no longer a spectator sport; I need you in the game, but are you ready? With officers laid-off and furloughed, simply calling 911 and waiting is *no longer* your best option. You can beg for mercy from a violent criminal, hide under the bed, or you can fight back; but are you prepared? Consider taking a certified safety course in handling a firearm so you can defend yourself until we get there. You have a *duty* to protect yourself and your family. We're partners now. Can I count on you?"[90] Clarke's rhetoric about partnership, duty, and preparation are standard neoliberal fare, and this part of his message failed to elicit any public anger. What infuriated Clarke's critics was that he urged citizens to be willing to transgress the communication/violence boundary in order to directly attack their fellow citizens. Not only did he encourage his constituents to take a firearms safety course, but he also made the provocative suggestion that calling 911—that *communication*—is often an inappropriate response, and that people should be prepared to commit defensive physical violence.

Clarke's statement set off a bitter debate over the policing responsibilities of good citizens. Expectedly, much of the reaction was intensely negative. Milwaukee's mayor, Tom Barrett, called the ad "irresponsible," while Jeri Bonavia, an activist with the Wisconsin Anti-Violence Effort, remarked: "I think he did a great disservice to the people of this community. . . . It's encouraging people to take the law into their own hands or to only rely on themselves and not rely on trained law enforcement officers."[91] Bonavia made parallels between Clarke's statement and the autonomous citizenship that prevailed in the vigilance era: "What [Clarke's] talking about is this amped up version of vigilantism. . . . I don't know what his motivations are for doing this. But I do know what he's calling for is dangerous and irresponsible and he should be out there saying this is a mistake."[92] Roy Felber, president of the Milwaukee Deputy Sheriffs' Association, invoked the sovereign exception in his criticism of Clarke: "That doesn't sound smart. . . . That's why society has police officers."[93] In a debate on the CNN evening program *Piers Morgan Tonight*, Mayor Barrett echoed these concerns, emphasizing that it was a citizen's duty to contact authorities rather than take matters into her own hands: "We respond to anything. . . . The 911 calls from homes in the city of Milwaukee are responded to by the Milwaukee Police Department."[94] This controversy illustrates how surveillance and communication, through the mediation of 911 technologies, serve as a pivot point for the assertion of responsible citizenship. The question of violence, of course, repeatedly frames these questions of civic responsibility. For renegade sheriffs like David Clarke, good citizenship means being prepared to take the law into one's own hands; for his critics, the key to civic duty lies in the telephone.

Conclusion

These struggles over the use and abuse of 911 illustrate the centrality of surveillance and communication as complementary sites of liberal governance. While the U.S. police apparatus has used 911 technologies to gradually democratize citizen participation in policing, police agencies have had to balance that extended access with increased surveillance and control. As this history shows, seeing/saying culture in America is about seeing and saying *the right things*. If a caller says the wrong thing—as with pranksters, Swatters, and others who violate the established protocols of citizen-police communications—then s/he will face severe penalties at the hands of the police and the justice system. Through restricted access, surveillance, technical and conversational protocols, and legal regulations, police have used 911 technologies as a means of surveilling and governing the social practices of witnesses, informants, and the public at large. This mass "democratization" of citizen-police communications, therefore, is more complicated and politically ambivalent than it seems at first glance.

Ultimately, the technologies and rituals through which we communicate with agents of the state help determine our relations with our protectors, leaders, and public servants. With the explosive growth of 911 technologies, the police have gradually found their way into the very depths of our local solidarity. As I will discuss in greater depth in the next chapter, our legal and cultural norms are heavily biased toward cultivating civic action that is highly restricted to disciplined acts of seeing and saying. Recent 911 outreach efforts emphasize the citizen's embodied epistemological utility: programs like Los Angeles's iWatch LA program, for example, openly ask citizens to lend their senses to the policing apparatus. As iWatch LA's outreach urges, "Trust Your Instincts: We rely on our senses every day of our lives. If a behavior or activity makes you feel uncomfortable, report it!. . . . If it doesn't look right, report it. . . . If it doesn't smell right, report it. . . . If it doesn't *sound* right, report it."[95] With the iWatch LA program and its companion efforts across the country—including iWatch Dallas, Eyes and Ears Kentucky, Colorado's Recognizing Terrorism program, New York's Operation Safeguard, and Pennsylvania's Terrorism Awareness and Prevention Training program[96]—citizens' eyes and ears are captured and put to use as mechanisms of lateral surveillance. Their mouths, as well, are transformed into instruments for reporting crimes and suspicious activities. And now, with the advent of ubiquitous computing, their dialing hands have become excellent tools for capturing and transmitting data—such as photographs of criminals and text messages with tips—to local police agencies. In many of the activities that bring the police into contact with the public, the citizen-subject is reduced to its barest biotechnical utility.

Reflecting on these political deployments of the body, Foucault recognized that human subjects "are not only [power's] inert or consenting target; they are always also the elements of its articulation. . . . The individual is an effect of power, and at the same time, or precisely to the extent to which it is that effect, is the element of its articulation. The individual which power has constituted is at the same time its vehicle."[97] Today, these rituals of seeing and saying provide an important point of our social and political articulation. This technologization of the citizen gives rise to a situation that Torin Monahan has eloquently described: "By reducing people to instrumental objects, which are seen either as pawns to be manipulated or as receptacles of information that must be extracted, humanity is excised from the object *and* the subject. . . . Paradoxically, such practices are done in the name of preserving their opposite: civil society, human rights, political accountability, and democratic processes."[98] Transforming the citizen into an instrument of liberal political experiments is not only disempowering to those who are promised freedom through responsibilization; it also threatens the bedrock of social and political values to which that responsibilization appeals. This brand of civic responsibility, needless to say, is not affirmative of community or an emancipatory politics; rather, with the simultaneous rise of mobile technologies and neoliberal campaigns to empower citizens through lateral surveillance and snitching, we can see the outline of a pernicious form of communicative citizenship. Communication, paired with surveillance and stripped to its barest informational content, falls far short of its political promise. It appears, instead, as a means by which citizens fight *against* rather than *for* one another.

3

Neighborhood Watching

Regulating the Citizens' Patrol

A little before 7:00 p.m. on February 26, 2012, a seventeen-year-old high school student was returning to his father's Sanford, Florida, home after a trek to a nearby convenience store. The young man, Trayvon Martin, was visiting his father in a gated community called the Retreat at Twin Lakes. After buying some candy and calling his girlfriend, Martin was spotted by Neighborhood Watch volunteer George Zimmerman, who called the authorities to report a young male that was "up to no good."[1] Zimmerman followed Martin while driving his truck around the neighborhood, informing the police operator of Martin's whereabouts and his "suspicious" behavior. When the operator told Zimmerman that she was dispatching an officer to the scene, she advised him to stop following the suspicious boy in a black hoodie. Zimmerman, however, continued to follow Martin throughout the community, telling the dispatcher that "these assholes always get away."[2] In fact, Martin did eventually evade Zimmerman, who complained to the police operator that he no longer knew Martin's whereabouts. A few seconds later, at 7:13, Zimmerman ended his call with the police. Yet when the responding police officer finally pulled into the community at 7:17, he found Zimmerman bloodied and bruised, while Martin was lying face down on the ground, motionless, with a single gunshot wound to the chest. Martin was pronounced dead on the scene at 7:30.

When the Trayvon Martin tragedy burst into the national imagination, it gave rise to a number of provocative cultural conversations about race, crime, policing, and vigilantism. One central element of this public discourse was the insight it provided into the relationship between surveillance/communication, violence, and civic responsibility. As Michael Thompson, a journalist and former Neighborhood Watch volunteer, observed: "Whether he is found innocent or guilty in his upcoming trial,

George Zimmerman gave Neighborhood Watch a bad name simply by carrying a weapon. To tote a gun violates the basic tenets of Neighborhood Watch."[3] Reflecting on his own experience as a young Watchman in the 1970s, Thompson writes that, contra the actions of Zimmerman, the local police "taught us how to watch one another's homes and what to do, and what to look for as a potential witness in court, when observing a crime or suspicious behavior."[4] Thompson's observations reflect the moral and political tone of much public discourse that followed in the wake of the Trayvon tragedy. According to this conventional wisdom, Watch volunteers should basically act as sensing/signaling devices for the police: as the National Crime Prevention Council puts it, "This strategy attempts to provide local law enforcement with additional eyes and ears to watch out for all types of criminal activity and promote neighborhood security."[5] Watch volunteers are educated in the visual and aural semiotics of crime, so they can use their "eyes and ears" to decipher what behaviors are suspicious. Once they detect this suspiciousness in their peers' conduct, they are to contact authorities and prepare themselves to record and pass along whatever information would be most useful in a criminal case. Zimmerman, therefore, should have remained a *speaking* subject: after he called 911 and offered a description of the hoodie-wearing teenager, he should have let the authorities handle the situation. The national office of Neighborhood Watch, too, expressed this ideal of the seeing/ saying subject in its official condemnation of Zimmerman's actions: "The Neighborhood Watch Program fosters collaboration and cooperation with the community and local law enforcement by encouraging citizens to be aware of what is going on in their communities and contact law enforcement if they suspect something—*not* take the law in their own hands. . . . The alleged participant ignored everything the Neighborhood Watch Program stands for."[6] What Neighborhood Watch stands for, in other words, is the cultivation of a very specific, nonviolent modality of the citizen-subject—a subject that patrols her or his neighborhood for potential criminality and then reports any suspicions to authorities.

This chapter examines how Neighborhood Watch and other citizens' patrols have been culturally and legally regulated, especially since their rapid rise during America's "war on crime." The essential crux of this regulation has involved channeling citizen vigilance into acceptable forms of seeing/saying citizenship. Since the emergence of Neighborhood Watch and similar state-sponsored programs in the 1960s and 1970s, citizen patrols have been assigned very limited tasks that revolve around communication and lateral surveillance—a stark contrast, no doubt, from the days of watch-and-ward citizen patrols and vigilante justice that characterized most American policing from colonial times to the end of the nineteenth century. This shift is perhaps best characterized as the process by which "Wanted: Dead or Alive" was gradually transformed into "Armed and Dangerous: Do Not Approach—Contact Authorities Immediately." As sovereign governance spread unevenly throughout the U.S. territories, the state gradually asserted its monopoly over legitimate violence. While the state still needed citizens to remain active in the police apparatus—to function as concerned community members, witnesses, and snitches—a range of public and private institutions emerged to properly cultivate these citizens in standards of seeing/saying conduct that would not violate the state's privilege of violence. In a word, these institutions set out to turn vigilant citizens into *communicative* citizens. The tools of this transformation have been primarily cultural, taking the form of neighborhood meetings, speeches, fliers, pamphlets, editorials, television specials, and supervision and mentoring from police officers. Yet when its exclusive right to violence has been challenged, the state has resorted to more extreme measures: radical citizens' patrols that threaten the state's defining monopoly have often faced threats, arrest, and violent reprisals. Thus Neighborhood Watch, as an institution that mediates citizens' relationships with the state and their peers, is an important means by which responsible citizenship is cultivated and the state's monopoly on violence is reinforced.

While several police historians and activists have provided their own histories of American citizen patrols,[7] the main task of this chapter is to map out the key cultural and legal processes by which authorities have attempted to transform citizen patrols from a threat to the state to a tool *for* the state. As such, the chapter will elaborate on a theme found throughout the book: while instructing citizens to see and say serves an intelligence-gathering function, it also serves as a practical reinscription of the sovereign's privilege of violence. Therefore, while in Chapter One I examined how police agencies have used crowdsourcing technologies to disseminate responsibilities to the broader public, this chapter will focus specifically on how the state and allied institutions have tried to domesticate citizen patrols like Neighborhood Watch into nonviolent, seeing/ saying servants of the public good. The duties of these citizen patrols, however, have provided a site of contestation at which the police, protestors, cultural authorities, and the volunteers themselves struggle over the appropriate boundaries of responsible citizenship. The questions driving these struggles include: should citizens ever physically engage suspects, or should they merely see something and say something? When, if ever, is a citizen's arrest permissible? How should police accountability patrols, such as Cop Block and the Huey P. Newton Gun Club, engage and observe the police? As we will see, this contested ground becomes even shakier when resistance groups are added to the mix, as they use the patrol model to fight—rather than enhance—police power.

Citizen Patrols and Autonomous Citizenship

The citizens' patrol has been an essential part of U.S. policing and surveillance history. Indeed, as I discussed in chapter one, we can see this process as far back as the colonial town watch system prominent in seventeenth- and eighteenth-century North America. Participation in town watches was compulsory for adult males: in colonial America, "every colonist was a police man."[8] From New England to Georgia, these community-based customs of policing were typically effective at crime control because of the small size, homogeneity, and restricted population flow of most colonial communities.[9] Larger cities eventually divided themselves into wards, each under the jurisdiction of a constable. For example, in 1790 Philadelphia was divided into ten constabulary districts in order to accommodate its relatively large population of twenty-eight thousand.[10] In colonial America, the state's specialized law enforcement institutions slowly supplanted the local justice systems that required extensive participation from community members. Salaried constables and judges steadily spread throughout the American territories in the eighteenth and nineteenth centuries, and police officers became prominent in eastern urban areas in the middle of the nineteenth century: Philadelphia founded its police force in 1833, followed by Boston in 1838 and New York in 1844.

The emergence of the police officer proved to be a crucial moment in American political history. Not only did it signal the rise of a formal sovereign justice system, it also gave birth to a dissociative rupture between different classes of the American population. On the one hand were regular citizens, who were bound by unique restrictions and terms of conduct; and on the other hand were police officers, who were subject to a different set of responsibilities and who enjoyed special privileges vis-à-vis their fellow citizens—a set of privileges that constitute what Kristian Williams calls "blue power."[11] The defining privilege that this blue power entailed, of course, was a monopoly over legitimate violence. The size and independence of the American frontier, however, led to a layered and uneven enforcement of this monopoly. As Michael J. Pfeifer observes, "the United States' transition to a capitalist economy was not accompanied by the emergence of a strong, centralized national state that claimed and enforced an exclusive monopoly over violence and the administration of criminal justice to secure the rule of law."[12] Lacking a well-developed system of courts, jails, and sheriffs, British colonial authorities struggled to navigate the tensions between delivering justice and preventing citizens from taking the law into their own hands. The Crown's solution was to promise justice to those citizens who could capture, detain, and transport subjects to the nearest court for a hearing. Yet in colonies like South Carolina, where there was only one court of law—in coastal Charleston—citizens' patrols like the South Carolina Back Country Regulators often chose to pursue justice without recourse to the formal rituals and processes of sovereign law.[13]

The slow and demanding nature of this peculiarly American justice system fueled amateur policing cultures across the U.S. territories. Typically, we associate these citizen patrols with "vigilantism"—that is, those subjects, operating under autonomous norms of citizenship, who reject the state's exclusive right to judge and punish suspects. In the century preceding the Civil War, several hundred vigilance movements would take root, most of them in the South or on the western frontier.[14] From the Back Country Regulators in the revolutionary period, to the mining town vigilantes that flourished in the "Wild West" a century later, and to the popular sovereignty movements of the antebellum South, these groups revolted against the sovereign's signature monopoly. Empowered by the "dead or alive" justice culture of the frontier, vigilance movements like the Fierce Missouri Bald Knobbers, the Tin Hat Brigade of Texas, the Montana Stranglers, the Dodge City Vigilantes, and the

San Francisco Vigilance Committees dispensed justice without regard for the state's legal processes,[15] using hasty violence as a critique of the sovereign's monopoly over the capture, judgment, incarceration, and punishment of suspects.[16]

In the early years of the twentieth century, as this ad hoc, Wild West justice threatened to spread to more and more urban areas back east, public opinion turned sharply against the vigilantes.[17] Federal and state governments eventually made a concerted effort to crack down on vigilance movements, attempting to transform these *autonomous* citizens into *responsible* citizens—that is, attempting to ensure that citizens' policing activities respected the procedures and privileges of sovereign power. Between 1900 and 1920, states like Ohio, South Carolina, Indiana, and Alabama attempted to suppress autonomous justice by prosecuting sheriffs who allowed vigilantes to break into their prisons and carry away inmates for summary justice. This political shift even drew the attention of Supreme Court justices, one of whom, David J. Brewer, suggested abolishing the right of appeal in order to eliminate one of the primary rationales for vigilante justice: the slowness of the justice system.[18] The state's answer to vigilantism, therefore, was (1) to enforce the established *processes* of sovereign law, such as suspect confinement, hearings, and jury trials, and (2) to reassert the sovereign's exclusive privilege of violence by developing and supporting alternative forms and programs of citizen-police cooperation. Thus in order to ensure the maintenance of sovereign political and juridical norms, autonomous citizenship had to be delegitimized and suppressed; it had to be tamed into appropriate expressions of responsible citizenship, particularly as citizens' social and political engagements were bounded by the sovereign's monopoly over legitimate violence. The so-called "vigilant era" of American citizen policing, therefore, came to a gradual end as the vigilant South and the Wild West—characterized by their wanton "dead or alive" justice—were tamed, and their participating subjects were instructed in the seeing/saying rituals of responsible citizenship.

The Turn to Responsible Citizenship

As state and local governments strove to thwart vigilante justice, they did not eliminate citizen participation in law enforcement. As this book has taken pains to show, throughout the twentieth century official police institutions remained highly reliant on citizens to watch their peers, report crimes, track suspects, provide tips, give testimony, file reports, and carry out other seeing/saying responsibilities. The police and their allies, therefore, were faced with a dilemma of governance: on the one hand, the liberal police force demands the active assistance of everyday citizens. On the other hand, the police must prevent these responsibilized citizens from violating the state's monopoly on violence. Therefore, as we see with organizations like Neighborhood Watch, regulating the conduct of citizen patrols becomes a matter of cultivating the seeing/ saying habits of the public while preventing their behavior from escalating into vigilantism and other acts of direct physical engagement. In fact, as police historian Martin Greenberg has argued, police authorities have designed and nurtured contemporary citizen patrols in such a way that they have become "antithetical" to the vigilance movements of years past: "The advent of extralegal vigilante groups in many ways represents the antithesis of the role of modern-day volunteer police."[19] The violence and autonomy of vigilance movements provide an illustrative contrast to the kind of responsible, seeing/saying citizenship the state strove to cultivate with official organizations like Neighborhood Watch.

After World War Two, and especially as the 1950s gave way to the turbulence of the 1960s, urban police departments across the country carried out new experiments in citizen responsibilization.[20] While this included the heavy recruitment of auxiliary volunteer police officers (according to a federal report, "auxiliaries put more sets of eyes and ears onto the street to detect crimes and summon the police"),[21] it also included the rise of federally funded citizen patrols like Neighborhood Watch. The same federal commission that spawned the national 911 Emergency system—President Johnson's Commission on Law Enforcement and Administration of Justice—energized the state's efforts to recruit, support, and regulate citizen patrols. As the Johnson and Nixon administrations began waging America's never-ending war on crime, citizen patrols became an essential element of community policing and related liberal social schemes. At a time when urban areas like New York City and Detroit were laying off hundreds of police officers, the state threw considerable support behind citizen patrols and related lateral surveillance programs.[22]

Largely owing to what Richard Maxwell Brown calls the "destabilizing context of postindustrial society"[23]—which was fueled by the confluence of ghettoized urbanization, the collapse of America's industrial economy, and the rise of neoliberal economic austerity[24]—violent crime rose dramatically in the mid-1960s, especially among young people.[25] While the American homicide rate had remained at about five or fewer per hundred thousand during the 1950s and early 1960s, in 1966 that rate rapidly increased: by 1974, homicides per capita had nearly doubled, and they peaked at more than ten per hundred thousand in 1980. Property and drug crimes, too, rose drastically throughout this period.[26] Responding to this rise in crime, local and federal police agencies began experimenting with new citizen responsibilization schemes. In 1968, President Nixon's Executive Order 11412, "Establishing a National Commission on the Causes and Prevention of Violence," empowered a federal task force to study the "causes and prevention of violence." In a defining moment of early neoliberal policing strategy, the report found that citizen responsibilization should take center stage in federal crime control efforts: "commitment and involvement are a solution—far better, more extensive and beneficial to society than arming oneself and hiding behind locked doors waiting for *them* (the government, the police, the courts, the elected representatives) to do it all."[27] In addition to encouraging increased citizen participation in crime control, the report also identified two dangers of this responsibilization: "From our national experience, two major dangers apply to citizen participation in law enforcement: first, vigilantism—volunteers exercising full police powers with no police discipline and few legal constraints—and second, the anti-police patrol—a community organization created independently of and in opposition to the police and serving as a roving check on its behavior. . . . Because of these dangers, therefore, individuals and groups should participate in the fight against crime in conjunction with officially sanctioned programs."[28] These two dangers—vigilantism and anti-police citizen patrols—provided the state with two distinct obstacles of governance. When promoting active citizen involvement with the police apparatus, how can violence, vigilantism, and related expressions of autonomous citizenship be kept in check? And when encouraging citizens to take organized action against local threats, how can those citizens be prevented from mobilizing against the threat of the state (in particular, against police brutality)?

Against the backdrop of these constant "dangers," during the 1960s and 1970s an interesting assortment of citizen-policing groups emerged throughout urban America. In working-class communities, and particularly in urban communities of color, many citizens had a rancorous relationship with the police. The citizen patrols that emerged in these areas, therefore, often lacked the support and oversight of local police departments. As I will discuss in a moment, this mutual distrust helped give rise to autonomous citizens' patrols that posed the two "threats" identified by the Nixon administration: by carrying guns or adopting militant facades, they threatened the state's monopoly on violence; and by turning their sights on police abuses, they frequently operated in a state of mutual hostility with the police. However, in most middle-class areas—where citizens' relationships with the police were typically less tense—the police and local citizens had better success working together to ensure a clear division of policing labor. While the sovereign police would retain their monopoly on violence and physical engagement, citizen patrols would be empowered to function as the "eyes and ears" of the authorities. This rhetorical theme, in fact, was consistent among many early citizen patrols in the United States: take, for instance, the California Neighborhood Safety Team in Los Angeles (whose stated purpose was to "observe and report"),[29] Newark's Triquonic Citizens Patrol (which insisted it functioned as the "eyes and ears of the Police Department"),[30] and the Azalea Hills Patrol in Norfolk, Virginia (which claimed to offer "an extra set of eyes for the Norfolk police").[31]

The case of the Chicago Organization of Radio Operators (COP) illustrates how this division of labor permeated the identity, behavior, and rhetoric of responsible citizen patrols. In the late 1960s, a group of citizen band radio operators collaborated with the Chicago Police Department to develop a network of local security organizations. In a familiar rhetoric of responsible citizenship, COP's membership director, Melvin Dixon, said that he decided to join COP because he knew the police "can't be everywhere all the time. . . . I get an inner satisfaction from doing my part in the community, and making the neighborhood safe for my wife. . . . This combination of social and service activities makes the patrol more fulfilling than I had ever expected."[32] To help carry out this responsible citizenship, Dixon and other COPs carried a variety of media technologies—a pencil, paper, a flashlight, and a CB radio—yet were prohibited from packing guns.[33] Not only did the COPs have direct police oversight from the Chicago PD, they were also careful to restrict membership only to those participants who used their eyes and ears rather than their fists and trigger fingers. Insisting that COP's role was to act as "the eyes and ears of the police," Dixon proudly declared that two members had been expelled because they exited their cars to "harass" people in the street."[34] In fact, Dixon remarked that "the cardinal rule" of COP was to never physically intervene in an incident: "I would never take the law into my own hands."[35] Agreeing with Dixon, COP's liaison officer at the Chicago Police Department boasted that COP volunteers had never "degenerated into vigilante activity," and that "no one wants a COP member to play policeman."[36] These themes reappeared in the discourse of civilian patrols across the country: the Azalea Hills Patrol in Norfolk, for example, was governed by a mission of nonconfrontational seeing and saying that is highly reminiscent of COP. Charley Tweed, an early member of the Hills Patrol in the 1960s and 1970s, emphasized that his group took great pains to eliminate violence and vigilantism from their ranks. According to Tweed, "You can't minimize the fact that people like to play cops and robbers. . . . We had to prove that we were only doing what an ordinary citizen would do. We were not vigilantes. We were only the eyes and ears of the police."[37] Tweed went on to boast that the Hills Patrol never carried clubs or guns—perhaps the two classic symbols of police violence.

During this process of widespread public responsibilization, "the neighborhood" became an idealized site of citizen discipline as public and private institutions collaborated to produce territorial arrangements that would promote responsible practices of seeing/saying citizenship. One of these schemes, now known as the Hartford Experiment, was launched under a grant funded by the DOJ's National Institute of Law Enforcement and Criminal Justice (NILECJ). In 1973, a group of NILECJ researchers affiliated with local nonprofits, Harvard University, and the Massachusetts Institute of Technology examined how the geographic layout of urban neighborhoods could be adjusted to facilitate lateral surveillance and informal social control. According to the researchers, the way in which many neighborhoods were geographically organized prevented the police and citizens from carrying out surveillance, primarily because (1) citizens were not encouraged to use their neighborhoods' outdoor resources, so they stayed indoors and out of sight, and (2) the organization of traffic patterns encouraged transient flow in and out of neighborhoods. According to the report's hypothesis, "Neighborhoods in which residents are out of doors, where surveillance is easy and where non-residents without identifiable purpose are likely to attract attention, are less attractive to offenders."[38] Thus by getting residents to actively roam about their neighborhoods, the Hartford Experiment tried to rearrange urban space in such a way that would "permit more surveillance" on residents and strangers.[39] To encourage widespread lateral surveillance among the community, the Experiment introduced perimeter street cul-de-sacs and narrowed intersections, thus preventing access to the neighborhood from its east, west, and south boundaries. These measures were intended to better define the neighborhood's interior from its exterior, as well as reduce transient pedestrian and automobile traffic.[40] The report's analysis of criminal geography observed that offenders operate in a complex urban atmosphere that includes police officers, citizen bystanders, and a physical environment. By rearranging the relationships between these three primary variables, urban planners could encourage lateral surveillance and community responsibility in a most liberal and noncoercive fashion. According to the report, "Offenders are deterred by citizens who use the spaces in their neighborhoods, thereby exercising surveillance, and who exercise control over who uses the neighborhood, thereby making extended waiting for an opportunity less comfortable. . . . To the extent that physical surveillance is easy, the citizens' ability to exercise surveillance is improved. To the extent that the environment encourages residents to use their neighborhood, their opportunities for surveillance are increased. . . . Increased use by residents was seen as a key step to increased resident surveillance and control."[41] By rearranging the public space of urban life, the police and their institutional allies sought to produce the geographical conditions in which local residents and citizens' patrols were most likely to carry out practices of seeing/saying citizenship.

Neighborhood Watching (and Speaking)

The "job" of a citizen in a Neighborhood Watch area is to be suspicious, alert, and to report any suspicious activity to the police department. It is the responsibility of the police to apprehend the criminals. Yours is to report crime.
—Neighborhood Watch Captain's Guide[42]

This focus on "the neighborhood," of course, was most influential in the creation of Neighborhood Watch, which the National Sheriff's Association founded in 1972 as the National Neighborhood Watch Program. Kick-started with support from the Department of Justice, the U.S. Jaycees, the Chamber of Commerce, and the Sons of the American Revolution, Neighborhood Watch began with the broad support of the federal government in its call for "cooperation between police, sheriffs, and the citizens of America to reduce crime."[43] Founded on the basic belief that "efforts to encourage citizen surveillance and reporting could have potentially significant impact on crime,"[44] Neighborhood Watch was highly successful at attracting federal funding and local participation, and by June 1976 it had spread to more than sixteen hundred local communities throughout the United States.[45]

The organization's founding documents give us valuable insight into the rationalities and strategies that informed its development. The National Sheriffs' Association, for example, asserted that the "principal objective" of Neighborhood Watch "is to develop within local law enforcement agencies an ongoing program of burglary prevention based on creating and sustaining a citizen education, property security, and cooperative action effort."[46] From the beginning, therefore, law enforcement agencies designed Neighborhood Watch as a program that would enjoy the constant monitoring and guidance of the police. These local police officials were instructed to "train" citizens in Neighborhood Watch's four "secondary objectives": (1) "Increase citizen awareness of burglary through a continuing information program"; (2) "Train citizens in the means to improve the security of their property and assist them in making their residence more secure"; (3) "Develop a neighborhood action program where neighbors help watch each others [sic] property and report suspicious persons and activities to law enforcement agencies"; and (4) "Encourage all citizens to cooperate with law enforcement agencies in reporting crime."[47] While the first two secondary objectives deal with informing and training citizens, the second two directly identify surveillance and communication as essential duties of responsible citizenship.

These outreach methods were highly effective in cultivating seeing/saying citizenship: during Neighborhood Watch's first five years of existence, over eighty percent of participating police agencies reported increased calls from citizens.[48] Cops also showed some enthusiasm for the program. In a 1977 survey of participating police departments, most officers reported having a positive view of it. Many of the responses lauded the program's success in promoting citizen surveillance: one cop, for example, related: "They [citizens] have police monitors and they go to the window and start watching—we got three stolen cars this way."[49] Another remarked: "It's good—the people are nosy and active."[50] The chiefs of police, however, were a bit more reticent about the program: summarizing their opinions, the survey reported: "Only the police can (and must) dominate and control a Neighborhood Watch Program. . . . Police must emphasize to citizens that their role is to *watch and report*, not take action" (emphasis in original).[51] This sharp division of labor, in fact, was emphasized at the very outset of Neighborhood Watch: cops must "dominate" local citizens' participation, which includes ensuring that citizens know their place (to "watch and report, not take action"). Early Neighborhood Watch even used classic eyes/ears rhetoric to preempt the emergence of citizen violence and vigilantism: as an implementation guide for New York State Neighborhood Watch emphasized, "Check tendencies toward vigilante action. Stress constantly that group members should always call police in suspicious circumstances, and must not take action themselves."[52] The official implementation guides used to train Watch liaisons, therefore, taught cops to curb vigilantism by promoting lateral surveillance and communicative action.

Neighborhood Watch's success at enforcing this clear division of labor has made it highly popular among police officials, helping make it the best-funded and most influential citizen-surveillance patrol in the United States. Their success, of course, continues to the present day. According to the U.S. State Department, Neighborhood Watch is practiced in every state of the U.S. And while more than twenty thousand Neighborhood Watch programs are listed in the nation's official registry, it is estimated that there are more than fifty thousand others that operate on an unofficial basis.[53] Every volunteer who works with these local organizations undergoes a training regimen in which s/he is instructed in the appropriate practices of responsible seeing/saying citizenship. Official Watch representatives, who are typically police employees, visit local gatherings in order to train volunteers in the arts of responsible Watch citizenship. One of these representatives, Wendy Dorival—who served as George Zimmerman's liaison to the Sanford Police Department—describes the familiar tone of her presentation: "I go through what the rules and responsibilities are,"[54] instructing volunteers that they are to act as "the eyes and ears" of the police force, "not the vigilante."[55] Watch volunteers, Dorival emphasizes, "are not supposed to confront anyone. . . . [The police] get paid to get into harm's way. You don't do that. You just call them from the safety of your home or your vehicle."[56] A Watch manual that Dorival distributes to volunteers also hammers home the point: Watch members should "not attempt to apprehend a person committing a crime or to investigate a suspicious activity."[57] Their responsibilities stop, therefore, at simple acts of seeing and saying—they stop where the state's exclusive privilege of violent engagement begins. Watch volunteers are repeatedly reminded that "they do not possess police power," and that the consequences of not following strict legal guidelines are severe: "Each member is liable as an individual for civil and criminal charges should he exceed his authority."[58] Watch volunteers, therefore, are instructed in the legal constraints that responsible citizenship places upon their civic duty, and the state's special privilege of violence is the animating logic behind these constraints.

Seeing Suspicious Activities

This training also teaches volunteers how to interpret and respond to "suspicious" phenomena, attempting to galvanize a renovated sense of community by forging a very specific set of responsibilities between neighbors. In its early days, police agencies promoted Neighborhood Watch by evoking nostalgia for an idyllic, crime-free past complete with unlocked doors and stay-at-home moms. In a federally funded study conducted by the RAND Corporation in 1976, researchers claimed that

Neighborhood Watch had emerged in response to the "reduced sense of public safety during the 1960s and early 1970s."[59] Illustrating how police officials tapped into this reduced sense of public safety, a 1981 Watch brochure released by the Virginia Division of Justice and Crime Prevention waxed dreamily on a crime-free era long gone: "In any discussion about crime, a frequently expressed desire is to have neighborhoods return to the way they were in the good old days when one could leave the home unoccupied and not have to worry about locking doors."[60] In the old days, the brochure claims, "neighborhood watching" occurred naturally because homes were always occupied (typically by women working in the home). In the chaotic and volatile word of today, however, citizens have to learn to be "nosy": "The best way to describe Neighborhood Watch is neighbors being 'nosy' about their neighbors. The prying eyes of neighbors may at times seem a nuisance but those prying eyes are enhancing neighborhood safety and security."[61] In addition to distributing local Neighborhood Watch stickers that said, "Use your eyes and your ears. Be nosy,"[62] Virginia's Watch organization reminded citizens of the fundamental duties of the citizen officer: "Trust your eyes, your ears, and your common sense."[63]

A 1984 Department of Justice report emphasized the importance of reorienting citizens' sociality toward these rituals of suspicion: "If citizens are to recognize crimes while the crimes are being committed, citizens need to know what a crime looks like and where it is likely to occur: to provide such knowledge is the goal of programs like Neighborhood Watch. When Neighborhood Watch works, it is because citizens share information about each other's habits and activities. A man who sees a woman rummaging in a neighbor's house may think little of it; but, if he knows that his neighbor is on vacation he may recognize that a burglary is in progress and call the police."[64] Recycling a theme that has long played a central role in Watch propaganda, a recent Neighborhood Watch pamphlet laments the atomized urban sociality that gave rise to the organization: "Neighbors stopped being concerned about their neighbor's property and began keeping more to themselves. The unity and cohesion of the traditional neighborhood gradually deteriorated. Neighbors were not looking out for each other. . . . It was also noted that communities able to obtain the assistance of their citizens in observing, recognizing, and reporting suspicious or criminal activities were much better able to keep the burglary rate down."[65] "Community," according to this pamphlet and to the Neighborhood Watch sensibility more generally, is fulfilled through assorted rituals of "observing, recognizing, and reporting."

Through in-person training sessions and official outreach materials, Watch volunteers and recruits are taught: "One of the most important aspects of Neighborhood Watch is getting to know your neighbors."[66] Indeed, neighborhood sociality is reconstructed as a primarily investigative project, as neighbors, their habits, and their belongings are reduced to data that must be mastered in order to protect the community. In other words, Neighborhood Watch makes the conditions of "community" those very rituals of suspicion that do much to undermine any promising possibility for being-with-others. Neighbors are instead reimagined as information that can be remembered, recorded, compared, and profiled—information that becomes valuable only to the extent that it informs surveillance strategy or facilitates the determination of suspicious and unsuspicious activities. We find this sentiment promoted in a 2010 Watch activist instruction manual:

> [I]t is important that you share information about the composition of your households and activities. By doing so you make it easier for your block members to recognize and respond to any suspicious activities in your area. To "profile" your block, share with each other the following information: Names of household members, address, phone numbers (include work numbers), makes, models, colors, license numbers of family cars, pets, medical problems. . . . Remember, the more information you share with each other, the better protected you will be. The more you know about the activities on your block, the better your chances of preventing a crime in your neighborhood.[67]

The sort of sociality prescribed in this manual is purely investigatory: neighbors should get to "know" their neighbors to the extent that that knowledge helps them construct a binary epistemology of suspicious/unsuspicious phenomena. Yet recruits, however, are warned that the semiotics of suspicion is a tricky business: "Burglars may case an area posing as: joggers, someone looking for an address or a friend, etc."[68] Barking dogs, too, may signify an unacceptable state of insecurity. While some of the listed activities might reasonably connote criminal activity—such as "Someone peering into cars or windows"—most others do not. For example, the pamphlet lists as suspicious the tautological "multiple persons who appear to be working in unison and exhibiting suspicious behavior," as well as warning of "persons arriving or leaving from homes or businesses at unusual hours."[69]

Yet this lateral surveillance and investigative labor constitute only one half of the watch volunteer's duty: the other half requires communicating one's observations to authorities. The pamphlet asserts, for example: "one of the keys to a successful Neighborhood Watch program is recognizing the importance of using good observation skills to keep your neighborhood safe. Practice looking at pictures of people to know how to describe them."[70] Surveillance and disciplined communicative practice, in fact, go hand in hand for the Watch participant—not only should volunteers hone their "observation skills," they should also practice rendering these observations into precise, easily decipherable language. And above all, of course, recruits are explicitly warned against transgressing the sovereign's violent privilege: "Community members only serve as the extra 'eyes and ears' of law enforcement. They should report their observations of suspicious activities to law enforcement; however, citizens should never try to take action on those observations. Trained law enforcement should be the only ones ever to take action based on observations of suspicious activities."[71] Denied the implied violence of "action," recruits learn that their utility has been reduced to the purely biotechnical: they are merely "the eyes and ears" of law enforcement, allowed simply to "report" their observations: "Dial 9–1–1 and call the police department of sheriff's office, *Tell the call taker what happened and the exact location, *Provide a detailed description of individuals or vehicles, *Remain on the phone and stay calm, *Be prepared to answer follow-up questions."[72] Theirs is a communicative citizenship, to be sure, but it is a citizenship stripped down to its barest mechanical engagement, a fact perhaps best attested by the infantile slogan of one of the nation's largest Neighborhood Watch two-way radio companies: "We talk, we act!"[73]

Neighborhood Watching after Trayvon

Despite this training in seeing/saying citizenship, Neighborhood Watch captain George Zimmerman failed to take the message to heart. After

Figure 3.1. Neighborhood Watch material distributed by George Zimmerman. *Trayvon Martin Killing: Neighborhood Watch 2* (n.d.): 4; available at http://documents.latimes. com/trayvon-martin-and-george-zimmerman.

Zimmerman shot Trayvon, Neighborhood Watch's local and national officials frantically adopted more intensive procedures and programs to guide and mediate their volunteers' actions. These efforts were per-haps most contested and controversial in the Sanford area in which Trayvon was shot. After he was killed—and after Sanford police chief Bill Lee was fired from his job—local police officials moved quickly to place local Neighborhood Watch crews under the direct supervision of police officers rather than civilian liaisons.[74] And to emphasize the strictly communicative-surveillant responsibilities of Watch volunteers, in November 2013, several months after Zimmerman was acquitted for Trayvon's murder, new Sanford police chief Cecil Smith moved to ban volunteers from carrying concealed weapons.[75] Speaking on Smith's behalf, a Sanford PD spokeswoman argued that the conceal-carry ban would restore the original seeing/saying mission to Sanford's "dysfunctional" Neighborhood Watch program: "Neighborhood watch was always intended to be a program where you observe what is going on and report it to police. In light of everything that has gone on, that's what we're really going to go back and push. That's what this program is and that's all it is."[76] In light of Trayvon's death at the hands of an armed Watch volunteer, the Sanford PD attempted to enforce this seeing/saying responsibility by removing the temptation for volunteers to physically engage suspects. Without guns, Chief Smith reckoned, volunteers wouldn't be emboldened to cross the threshold from "observing" and "reporting" into physical altercations. For Chief Smith, then, establishing the volunteers' responsibilities firmly within the communicative/surveillant required taking firearms out of their hands. Pleading with volunteers of Neighborhood Watch and similar groups to reject violence, Smith reminded them of their fundamental responsibilities: "If you see something, hear something, say something, call us and allow us to do the job we are being paid for. . . . Our goal is to teach [volunteers] to be great observers and fantastic witnesses. . . . It's about communications. It's not about firearms."[77] Smith went so far as to compare Watch volunteers' responsibilities to that of *Bewitched* character Gladys Kravitz, whose name has become synonymous with snooping/snitching neighborly conduct. "Your responsibility is to be Gladys Kravitz," Chief Smith informed the public. "She worked it, and she worked it without a firearm."[78] For Smith, the key to reinstantiating volunteers' communicative citizenship was to remove guns from the Neighborhood Watch equation, thus narrowing citizens' range of possible action.

Yet this attempt to regulate Watch volunteers ignited a controversy about the rights and privileges of responsible citizenship. As soon as Chief Smith announced his intent to implement the conceal-carry ban, local citizens responded with outrage. Sean Caranna, executive director of a gun rights organization called Florida Carry, argued that Watch volunteers needed to carry guns because their anti-crime activism made them popular targets of violence and revenge attacks. According to Caranna, "What you are doing is asking people to be out in their community, be visible and take note of what's going on. . . . They can be more of a target for criminal aggression. We certainly don't want the only person to be armed in a confrontation to be a criminal."[79] Taking a more legalistic approach, Carrie Lightfoot, founder of an organization called The Well Armed Woman, remarked: "If they're licensed to carry, they're licensed to carry, and that should not be restricted."[80] As this chorus of dissent rose in volume and pitch, the old wounds from Trayvon's death reopened, and Chief Smith's press conference threw Sanford back into the national spotlight. The press conference at which Smith planned to ban guns received international attention, drawing representatives from *Al Jazeera*, an array of network television affiliates, National Public Radio, the *Huffington Post*, and other outlets. Yet many onlookers were disappointed to find that, under considerable pressure, Chief Smith decided at the last minute to scrap his plan to disarm Watch volunteers. In a resigned tone, he addressed the press, painting a romanticized portrait of Neighborhood Watch: "Neighborhood Watch is a very simple organization. It's about neighbors helping neighbors, talking to neighbors about ways to make their neighborhood safe. That's it."[81] After begrudgingly admitting that Watch volunteers have the constitutional right to carry a gun, he pleaded with them: "Do not intercede or pursue." After all, he averred, volunteers were simply supposed to serve as "communicative vessels."[82]

The Threat of the Citizens' Patrol

As a state-sanctioned institution, Neighborhood Watch and its police liaisons have taken care to train citizens in the rituals of nonviolent citizenship. While these tactics do not always succeed—as George Zimmerman's case so starkly illustrates—Watch officials take care to use training seminars, fliers, and other modes of oversight and outreach to govern volunteers' activities toward responsible outlets of surveillance and communication. Yet, as many scholars have pointed out, Neighborhood Watch has tended to take hold in suburban and middle-class communities where serious violent crime is rarely a threat.[83] In urban working-class and poor communities, however, the decline in police resources during the 1970s struck a disproportionate blow—not to mention the fact, of course, that these underserved neighborhoods struggled to draw and sustain citizens' participation. So while the bourgeois strictures of "observe and report" governed the conduct of citizens who volunteered with Neighborhood Watch and other federally sanctioned programs, many urban citizen patrols developed their own rules of engagement (and, in doing so, often attracted the hostility of the state). Some of these groups included Boston's Urban Citizens Patrol, the Fifty-Fourth Ward Patrol and the Maccabees in Brooklyn, Kansas City's Ad Hoc Group Against Crime, the Boonton Crime Patrol in St. Louis, and the Mayberry Glen Security Patrol of Washington, D.C. While these groups had occasional interactions with the police, they lacked the disciplinary oversight and training enjoyed by Neighborhood Watch and other officially sanctioned patrols. This independence often gave rise to patrol strategies and aggressive public postures that openly called into question the state's monopoly on violent engagement.

Some African American organizations, in particular, took a more militant stance toward community policing. For example, the Deacons for Defense and Justice deployed armed patrol cars around Louisiana to protect civil rights activists from Klansmen and the police. Other radical African American groups, such as the Community Alert Patrol in Los Angeles, emerged in the wake of the Watts riots in order to protect protestors and carry out surveillance on the police.[84] In fact, the 1960s saw many lateral surveillance patrols turn against one another: groups such as Newark's Triquonic Citizens Patrol and North Ward First Aid Squad, and Detroit's Citizens Organized Radio Patrol Service were organized to "fight rioting"—which, in the context of the civil rights movement, often meant carrying out surveillance and/or violence against African Americans and their allies. In an attempt to protect African American communities from these opposing citizen patrols—and others, including the Ku Klux Klan—a Louisiana group known as the Alliance for Safety (AFS) carried guns and other weapons as a means of community protection. Organized by activist Isaiah Tripp, the AFS had a weapons policy that mirrored its militant stance against state power. In 1965, Tripp took over the Voting Rights Committee, which had been organized by the Congress of Racial Equality (CORE), and changed its name to the Alliance for Safety. Declaring that Louisiana officials were failing to enforce the 1964 Civil Rights Act, Tripp promised that the AFS would form armed patrols to protect African Americans as they sought to vote and protest amid the coordinated interference of state officials, the Klan, and other racist Louisianans.[85] According to Tripp, "The local police and the

U.S. Department of Justice knew what we were doing and knew that we were armed . . . but it had to be done. I always said though, that when citizens of this town began to work with their black residents, then we would hang up our guns."[86] The police and the local Louisiana political machine, however, had little interest in working with Tripp and other African Americans. In fact, powerful factions of the local government and the business community went to work against the AFS, crushing Tripp's cab business when he refused to back down. His creditors demanded immediate payment, and he lost much of his fleet. After he refused bribes to fold up the AFS and return to responsible seeing/saying citizenship, the insurance policy for Tripp's cabs was cancelled, and vandals poured acid on his personal Cadillac and slashed its tires. And because one of AFS's main missions was to "protect black citizens from police harassment,"[87] Tripp and his patrols encountered their own fair share of police harassment and violence. Yet for Tripp, armed resistance patrols helped keep the state in check until it was able to deliver on its promises of peace, justice, and civil rights. The police and responsible citizens, however, were threatened by the radicality of the AFS, and they exerted many forms of cultural, legal, and physical pressure in order to force the group's members onto the path of responsible seeing/saying citizenship.

Another interesting example is provided by the Guardian Angels, an organization founded in 1979 by a charismatic young New Yorker named Curtis Sliwa. As with the Alliance for Safety, the Angels clung to expressions of autonomous citizenship, making them popular targets of the state. Rather than taking a purely surveillance-based approach, in the 1970s Sliwa and his comrades began attacking and detaining criminals on New York subways. With their uniforms and berets—not to mention their required training in martial arts—the Angels struck a militant posture that smacked of autonomous citizenship. The Angels' volunteers, who largely comprised young African Americans and Chicanos, flipped society's prevailing surveillance roles: rather than being policed and scrutinized by the state, these young citizens were adopting the role of police officers. Yet most of all, what set the Guardian Angels apart was their resistance to seeing/saying dogma: they are perhaps best known for carrying out dramatic citizens' arrests. As constitutional rights advocates Michael Cicchini and Amy Kushner have pointed out, "A citizen's arrest is likely law enforcement's last choice for apprehending a criminal suspect."[88] Yet in its first six years of existence, the Angels claimed to have made five hundred citizen's arrests,[89] quickly putting them on a collision course with the state.[90]

Before the official launch of the Angels, when Sliwa was gaining local notoriety by threatening to organize a militant citizens' patrol, he began to encounter the hostility of the press and the police. Emphasizing his determination, Sliwa remarked: "it's being reported that if I am going to try this new idea, the police are going to do everything within their power to stop us."[91] It turns out that his fears were warranted. Just before the official launch of the Angels, Sliwa attacked two assailants who had used a broken bottle to threaten and rob an elderly man. Sliwa rushed the two assailants, knocking their bottle away and detaining them in the back of a train car. He then refused to let the conductor pull the train out of the station: because Sliwa did not have access to a phone, he simply pulled the emergency brake and waited for the cops to show up. "They hate that," he later recalled.[92] As the cops arrived on the scene, they were flabbergasted. When Sliwa informed them he had made a citizen's arrest, they replied: "Citizen's arrest? . . . This ain't the movies. You can't do that. There ain't no such thing."[93] He was then detained by the NYPD and escorted to a local precinct station, where he was interrogated and threatened with arrest. Although the police were eventually compelled to release him, the case proved so controversial that, despite his testimony, the city was unable to convict the two thieves of any crime. According to Sliwa, the justice system was trying to teach him a lesson about threatening the state's monopoly on violent engagement: "They were trying to prove a point: hey, wise guy, you're going to be a wise guy, you're going to say it's a citizen's arrest, well now you see what's going to happen."[94]

This animosity toward the Angels was widespread among public officials. New York City mayor Ed Koch, for example, condemned the Angels as vigilantes and "paramilitaries." According to Koch, the Angels should adopt seeing/saying citizenship or leave the policing labor to the state: "I suggest they join the police force if they want to continue their efforts to increase public safety."[95] A member of Koch's staff remarked that the city would increase its efforts to domesticate the Angels, promising citizens: "At the moment . . . we are trying to balance the Angels' potential for good with the risk of disaster."[96] In return, Sliwa prom-ised to amplify his antagonism vis-à-vis the state: "I know that Koch is totally uncomfortable with the idea of a black or a Hispanic. . . . I was going to confront him with four hundred and fifty of them, but not with everybody screaming in some auditorium where he could walk out. I was going to make Koch go to sleep at night with four hundred and fifty blacks and Hispanics right under his bedroom window."[97] To be sure, the NYPD had never had to worry about Neighborhood Watch volunteers staging mass protests outside Gracie Mansion. But with Cur-tis Sliwa's rebellious band of young men of color, the state encountered an autonomous citizens' movement that proved difficult to control.

Unsurprisingly, local cops complained that the Angels, unlike Neigh-borhood Watch and other responsible citizen organizations, would not subject themselves to the oversight and command of the police. While the Angels proved to be popular among New York citizens, the majority of police officers—and the vast majority of public officials—disapproved of the Angels' activities.[98] Frustrated by the Angels' success with citizens' arrests—and perhaps intimidated and incensed by their activists' regi-men of martial arts training and their dedication to aggressive citizen responsibility—a local transit cop remarked: "I wish they would report directly to us. . . . But they have this idea that they shouldn't work too closely with the cops."[99] According to a federally funded study of the group, a national survey of law enforcement officers found that seventy percent of officers who had encountered the Angels accused them of carrying out "inappropriate" interventions.[100] Increasingly frustrated with the Angels' autonomous interventions, a contingent of New York City cops set out to teach Sliwa a lesson in the bounds of responsible citizenship. After making more than twenty citizens' arrests on the New York subways between 1977 and 1978, Sliwa had a direct run-in with a cop who happily demonstrated the state's monopoly over violence. In Sliwa's words, after the police officer arrived on the scene to answer his call, "Cop lets the guy go. He takes his gun, right, he points it at me, he says, 'This is the third time I've run into you doing this shit. You trying to play cop?' He's pointing the gun at me, and playing macho man, and, 'If I catch you out here again . . .'"[101] Pointing his gun in Sliwa's face, the officer demonstrated the essential political boundary that separates citi-zens from the state.

While Sliwa claims to have softened the Angels' strategy following this incident, he and the Angels continued to emphasize their uneasy relationship with the police. According to Sliwa, the Angels could never completely make peace with the cops: "The police just don't understand. . . . We're not trying to be cops. This is a movement. . . . We are independent. Many of our members are from neighborhoods where the police are stigmatized. We can't be part of the police."[102] This ambivalence has occasionally boiled over into violence. For example, on February 13, 1981, a crew of Angels got into a fight with local cops, landing eleven of them in jail.[103] The following year, a twenty-six-year-old Guardian Angel, Frank Melvin, was shot by a Newark, New Jersey, cop as the two were responding to the same burglary. While the policeman was never indicted for the man's death, Sliwa and his allies hinted that the officer's behavior was rooted in the local police's frustration with the Angels for crossing from seeing/saying citizenship into violent practices of suspect engagement and apprehension.

Discussing the growing hostility between the police and the Angels, a *New York Times* editorial that appeared after the shooting observed that the Angels were offering public services that the police could not or would not provide. According to the editorial, "The [Frank Melvin] shooting is tragic enough. The controversy it is generating exemplifies a deeper problem: the difficulty that groups like the Angels have in getting along with the police. In Newark as elsewhere, awareness has grown that the police are unable to prevent much of the crime that engulfs a community. That creates fertile ground for voluntary crime fighters, but it also poisons the atmosphere for their relations with authorities. . . . The police inevitably feel antagonistic toward groups that appear to symbolize official failure to stop crime."[104] Other local citizens expressed this sentiment, including Bronx district attorney Mario Merola, who lauded the Angels for their determination to fill the social service gaps left by the police: "To call them vigilantes is nonsense. . . . The municipal and state governments have not met their obligation to provide the kind of security that's needed on the subway. How do we say to any citizens who want to do some good that they should not be involved?"[105] The Angels, in fact, had grown quite popular with many prominent New York residents who were frustrated with the NYPD's failure to reduce crime. Taking the Angels' side, legendary New York journalist Jimmy

Breslin argued that the police were "terrified" of the Angels' success: "Of course, government fought him [Sliwa]. . . . We suffer the worst crime in the history of the city, and those who cannot protect us were busy trying to prevent anybody else from trying."[106] For Breslin, the Angels were simply a populistic expression of citizens' outrage at a corrupt and ineffective police force: "The only way the city can get anything done is for the people to do it themselves. You can't work through the political process. That failed us. We just have to do the work ourselves."[107] Abandoned by the state during the height of New York City's crime crisis of the 1970s and 1980s, many citizens agreed that they would simply "have to do the work themselves"—they were happy, therefore, to have citizens like Sliwa shoulder the workload.

Over the years, however, the NYPD has not been the Angels' only foe: Sliwa has repeatedly been attacked by gang members and other criminals, and in 1992 he was shot and kidnapped after he tried to enter a stolen taxi. In 2000, a fellow Angel was shot by a gang member while he patrolled his neighborhood.[108] Facing this sustained hostility from the police and volatile elements of the population, the Angels have often promised to abandon citizens' arrests and adopt a more responsible form of seeing/saying citizenship. Following a physical altercation with a New York cop, Sliwa remarked: "I realized that I had to create a mechanism where we didn't have to grab people necessarily, where we would deter by just being there."[109] Despite these reassurances that he would dedicate the Angels to seeing, saying, and being seen, the Angels continue to carry out citizens' arrests—and, as a result, they continue to encounter the violence of the state and of their fellow citizens. According to Sliwa, six Angels have been killed "in the line of duty" since the organization's founding.[110] And while the Angels now have more than five thousand members in more than eighty cities worldwide, their frequent outbursts of autonomous citizenship have prevented them from developing the public inroads enjoyed by tamer programs such as Neighborhood Watch.

Citizens' Patrols against Police Brutality

Given the resistance that the Angels and other relatively autonomous patrols have faced, it is hardly surprising that the state typically frowns upon citizens organizing to guard their communities from police violence. According to the FBI Uniform Crime Reports, police shootings reached a twenty-year high in 2013, as American cops allegedly killed 1,688 people between the years of 2010 and 2013.[111] These astonishing figures, however, are almost certainly understated: because the FBI's statistics rely on police departments to self-report fatal shootings, critics argue that the real numbers are significantly higher. To construct a more objective account of annual American police shootings, in 2015 the *Washington Post* carried out an independent national investigation into fatal police shootings. According to the *Post*'s findings, American cops fatally shot 990 people in that year alone.[112]

Following the death of Michael Brown, an unarmed African American teenager shot six times by a Ferguson, Missouri, cop in August 2014, many communities began to take more seriously community programs designed to protect citizens against police brutality. While some of these programs have entailed police education and community review boards, other citizens have taken an open stand against the state's monopoly on violence. One such group, the Huey P. Newton Gun Club, follows its predecessor, the Black Panther Party, by organizing armed citizen patrols in poor and working-class African American neighborhoods. Outfitted with an assault rifle hung over his shoulder, one of the group's leaders, Erik Khafre, told a Dallas news reporter in the days following Brown's death: "We felt it was up to us to patrol our communities—especially since a number of police acts of terrorism have occurred in Dallas. . . . Police are running rampant in the community, and they say police are to protect and serve, but basically they are gunning down our people."[113] According to a Gun Club press release, the group began to organize citizens' patrols in response to the shockingly high levels of police violence among the Dallas Police Department. The press release noted, for example, that in the preceding twelve years Dallas police officers had killed over seventy unarmed citizens. Not a single one of these deaths resulted in the indictment of a police officer; according to the release, only one Dallas cop had been indicted in the death of an unarmed citizen during the past four decades. In the wake of Michael Brown's shooting death, therefore, "The people, who are gunned down and murdered by violent and militarized police forces, have formed the Huey P. Newton Gun Club for the specific purpose of self defense and community policing. In response, Black and Brown residents of the City of Dallas *will conduct the first of an ongoing and necessary armed self defense patrols through our communities in the coming week.*"[114] As one Gun Club organizer put it, "We know our puny weapons won't be able to match Dallas police one for one . . . but what they fear is *seeing* us with weapons."[115] While armed cops are accustomed to patrolling neighborhoods in search of crime, they are less accustomed to openly armed citizens watching them as they sit in their patrol cars or walk their beats. The Gun Club's emphasis on self-defense, therefore, serves as an open indictment of the traditional rationale behind a strong centralized police force. The police are typically justified on the grounds that they protect decent citizens from dangerous citizens. But when the police in a single American city kill over seventy unarmed citizens in just twelve years, who is supposed to safeguard citizens from the brutality of their supposed protectors? The members of the Huey P. Newton Gun Club have an answer: in conjunction with their regular Saturday self-defense and training classes, Gun Club members march down the streets of South Dallas, chanting in unison, "No more pigs in our community!"[116]

While the Gun Club is unlikely to dislodge cops from South Dallas, they are not the only citizens' patrol trying to stamp out police brutality. One of the most interesting of these groups, Cop Block, sends its members to monitor police beats, highway checkpoints, and protest sites. While the group also has an innovative social media presence that publicizes police abuses, Cop Block's patrols have proven most controversial among police agencies and public officials. Like the Huey P. Newton Gun Club, Cop Block members routinely carry weapons on their patrols. Using radio scanners to track police activity, local Cop Block activists dispatch immediately to areas where citizens will have contact with the police: the sites of 911 calls and traffic stops are some of Cop Blockers' favorite targets. And while the Huey P. Newton Gun Club coordinates disciplined marches in paramilitary gear, some Cop Block activists prefer to show up with pig ears attached to their heads and to scream obscenities at cops. Openly provoking the police, Cop Blockers like Jacob Cordova have taken it upon themselves to anger cops—even to the point of trying to perform citizens' arrests on police officers who violate the law.

The actions of Cop Block activists, who make as many as twenty stops per night, have drawn the ire of the police. Cop Blockers are frequently arrested for interfering with cops; Cordova and his comrades are quick to take a misdemeanor charge in order to film the police arresting, harassing, and sometimes assaulting them. Yet as Cop Block and allied groups have become a growing presence in cities across the U.S., police agencies are attempting to develop more diplomatic methods for defusing the threat of armed citizen watch groups. While cops in open-carry jurisdictions cannot legally prevent Cop Blockers from packing heat, they often plead with activists to leave their guns at home. When the Arlington, Texas, police department sent certified letters to local Cop Block headquarters inviting them to a meeting with police officials, Cop Block ignored them. While the Arlington Police Department and its allies are hoping that activists will agree to leave their guns at home, Cop Blockers, like their counterparts in the Huey P. Newton Gun Club, assert that their revolt centers upon depriving the state of its monopoly on potential violence. In the words of Tov Henderson, a Cop Block ally and organizer for the Open Carry Texas organization, "Firearms make us equal to those who aggress us."[117]

For the Huey P. Newton Gun Club, Cop Block, and similar organizations around the U.S., disrupting the asymmetry of the state's capacity for violence and surveillance puts citizens on an equal footing with the police. Just as patrolling their neighborhoods protects their communities from police brutality, it also broadly illustrates that citizens—some with military fatigues, others with pig ears—can at anytime challenge the state's monopolies on violence and armed surveillance. In the end, these provocative activist tactics may prove to extract important concessions from the police. As I discussed in Chapter One, cop watching is frequently suppressed by legal and technological means—yet in some jurisdictions, gutsy, armed cop watchers have shifted police attention away from preventing anti-cop surveillance and onto preventing cop watchers from carrying guns. Arlington Police Lieutenant Christopher Cook, who has encountered the cop watching styles of both the Huey P. Newton Gun Club and Cop Block, leaves an open door to these groups' police antagonism: "We don't mind them cop-watching. Just leave your guns in the car. Leave your guns at home."[118] By shifting the discourse in this way—so that at least some cops publicly assert that they don't "mind" cop watching—gun-toting cop watchers have the potential to give rise to a new logic of acceptable citizen-to-police surveillance. Pushing the limits of acceptable citizen action vis-à-vis the police, therefore, has encouraged some cops to cede important ground in the political struggle against police brutality.

Conclusion

America has a long tradition of citizens' patrols—one that goes back, indeed, to the colonial period that preceded the nation's founding. Due to their ambivalent relationship to the state, these patrols have come in all political shapes and sizes: some have fought capitalist exploitation, while others have protected capital; some have been anti-racist, while others have fought under the banner of white supremacy; some have guarded against the violence of the state, while others have provided simply another articulation of state violence. In his discussion of the South Carolina Back Country Regulators, a vigilance movement that gained prominence in the 1760s, Howard Zinn argues that we have inherited a distorted view of these groups. According to Zinn, early vigilance movements and other citizens' patrols were mainly comprised of the "rebellious poor" and acquired their stained reputation by revolting against capital and a corrupt state.[119] So while we don't want to develop a romantic view of America's tradition of citizens' patrols, we should recognize their diversity, and, with that, the broad range of their motivations, political goals, and tactics.

During the twentieth and twenty-first centuries, and especially since the 1970s, the police and their allies have proven quite adept at capturing these patrols and putting them to work for the state. For many communities, the political stakes of this transformation have been particularly high. Despite high-sounding neoliberal rhetoric about citizen participation and community policing, fostering "community" through rituals of surveillance and suspicion can simply lead to more alienation, vulnerability, and even violence. Although the democratization of some policing roles has been a positive development for *some* middle-class and privileged communities, the ongoing recession of the police from whole sectors of urban life—and their increasing reliance on community-based surveillance and enforcement initiatives—has proven generally disastrous.[120] Moreover, despite the state's best efforts to train nonviolent, seeing/saying patrols, this widespread responsibilization results in the occasional eruption of violence.

In the earlier days of Neighborhood Watch, criminologist Harold Pepinsky noticed these antisocial tensions simmering under the lid of Neighborhood Watch's carefully crafted façade of care and community: "While neighborhood residents may build some measurement of cooperation in the process of turning people in to the police, the inherent violence of the collective effort builds more violent tension—more of a sense of isolation and vulnerability."[121] As a result, Pepinsky argues, Watch volunteers "can be expected to find themselves more isolated from other community members in the process."[122] By asking these citizens to carry out the traditional tasks of the police, Neighborhood Watch and other responsibilization efforts encourage citizens to flirt with the rupture of violent privilege that separates citizens from cops. Amateur citizen-officers like George Zimmerman have become far too comfortable exercising the exceptional violence typically reserved for the state. As these men and women play out the drama of state-sanctioned patrol, amateur investigation, and law enforcement, they identify with the activities and mentality of sworn police officers.

As Mark Andrejevic has warned, this identification between citizens and the police can have important social consequences: "Thanks to the promise of interactive participation in the policing process, the authorities can exploit the free labor of selected members of the community. The wager, of course, is that entrusting members of the populace with access to surveillance technology will encourage them to internalize the norms of state surveillance and policing: they will identify the problem the same way the police do, thanks, at least in part, to having been accorded the role of an agent of the state. . . . [This is] a strategy that enlists the appeal of participation as a shared responsibility."[123] As we have seen throughout this book, this process of identification with the raw activity of policing disproportionately leads to individuals reporting their neighbors, coworkers, and even family members for petty infractions. In this regime of responsibilization, citizen action is centered on and filtered through civic obligations, such that one's duty to one's community is overshadowed by—and often redefined as—duty to the state. It is hardly shocking, therefore, that Watch volunteers will sometimes slip from seeing and saying into the exception of violence that is legally reserved for the police officials who serve as their role models.[124] There is considerable wisdom in what Natalie Jackson, the attorney representing Trayvon Martin's family, said about the relationship between the police and wannabe cops like Zimmerman: according to Jackson, "What made [Zimmerman] shoot was that he was one of them; he felt he was a cop."[125] Indeed, as Zimmerman was the captain of the Retreat's Neighborhood Watch patrol, perhaps we shouldn't be surprised when he acted out the defining privilege of the police officers with whom he so intimately identified.

4

Recognize, Resist, Report

D.A.R.E. America and the Kid Police

In April 1990, a guidance counselor at a Searsport, Maine, elementary school summoned a fifth-grader to her office. The counselor asked the eleven-year-old, Crystal Grendell, whether her parents used drugs. After the counselor reassured her that "nothing would happen," Crystal eventually admitted that her parents smoked pot on occasion. At school a few days later, Crystal was greeted by three D.A.R.E. police officers who interrogated her about her parents' drug use. The officers threatened Crystal, saying that her parents would be arrested if she didn't tell them everything she knew about her mother and father's recreational drug habits. The officers then warned her against telling her parents about their encounter, claiming that "often parents beat their children after the children talk to police."[1] Scared, the eleven-year-old agreed to carry out a spy mission on her parents. The D.A.R.E. officers instructed Crystal to count her parents' marijuana plants and provide details about their schedules and the layout of their home. When Crystal reported back to the cops, they informed her that her house would be raided and that she would not be able to stay there that night—again, because "in most cases like this, children are beaten by their parents."[2] After the police raided the house, finding a number of marijuana plants, Crystal's parents were arrested and her mother was fired from her jobs as a teacher's assistant and a bus driver. The D.A.R.E. officers had failed to make arrangements for where Crystal and her younger sister would stay while their parents were in police custody, and when the police couldn't find any nearby family members they had to take the girls to the house of a distant relative. Feeling that the police and school officials had manipulated her, Crystal—who was once outgoing and gregarious—became socially withdrawn and suffered from psychological distress. Reflecting on how the incident had turned her life upside down, Crystal later told the *Wall Street Journal*: "I would never tell again. . . . Never. Never."[3]

When a federal judge awarded Crystal a civil judgment against the D.A.R.E. officers, he issued a strong condemnation of how they had turned the fifth-grader into an informant against her own family: "This type of coercive extraction of indicting information from an eleven-year-old girl about her parents is reprehensible behavior unworthy of constitutional protection."[4] This reprehensible behavior, unfortunately, is all too characteristic of a program that has long been criticized for its tendency to use children to gather information about their families and communities. The only thing unique about this story is that the D.A.R.E. officers coerced the young girl in an especially callous way; indeed, most D.A.R.E. programs involve coloring books, stuffed animals, and special certificates rather than bullying and threats. Whether they use coercion or gentle persuasion, however, D.A.R.E. and similar youth programs have much to teach us about American spy/snitch culture. Indeed, while we tend to think about the neoliberal subject as a responsible adult, the D.A.R.E. phenomenon illustrates how programs of enterprising civic duty cultivate responsible child-subjects throughout their schooling years.

D.A.R.E. and similar youth/police collaboration efforts kill two birds with one stone: from the perspective of the police, the youth who participate in these programs are taught to identify with cops, thus readjusting their social values in accordance with the law-and-order objectives of police agencies. In addition, these programs teach children to scrutinize and regulate their parents' and peers' conduct. Youth/police collaboration, therefore, is often promoted as a solution to the youth problem.[5] As Dick Hebdige notes, in the twentieth century—and especially since World War Two—we have repeatedly seen the emergence of marginalizing discourses that fret over the ungovernable and "illegible" nature of youth cultures.[6] While authorities seek to break through this "illegibility" in diverse ways—including disciplinary surveillance, arrests and incarceration, and other harsh measures associated with law-and-order policing—one of the more liberal ways to address this problem is to recruit local actors who can provide the inside scoop on youth misbehavior. While these local actors might include parents, pastors, and community leaders, they also include youth themselves. Through youth/police collaboration efforts such as Junior Police programs and D.A.R.E. America (originally Drug Abuse Resistance Education, or simply D.A.R.E.), cops teach kids to keep an eye on their peers and to report any misdeeds to the authorities. In lieu of tackling structural social problems that alienate and disfranchise teens,[7] the police and allied institutions have developed cultural technologies that train kids to keep an eye on their peers and parents.

While a number of scholars have looked at how Head Start programs, the Boy and Girl Scouts, and local recreational initiatives have influenced the behavior of teens, less attention has been paid to how the police have used youth/police collaboration programs to form and regulate young citizens.[8] This chapter will give a broad historical analysis of how American youth have been policed through programs that, in essence, encourage kids to act like cops. An essential element of this has been the cultivation of civically engaged seeing/saying habits. The most basic goal of D.A.R.E. America, for example, is to teach kids to say the right thing: to *just say no*. In fact, the D.A.R.E. project is often characterized as a plan to teach children "The Three R's": *recognize, resist, report.* "Recognize," of course, encourages a lateral surveillance sensibility, prompting kids to be vigilant against suspicious activity in their midst. "Resist," on the other hand, is tied to a carefully cultivated form of speaking subjectivity: to just say no. And "report" provides a complementary communication imperative: once kids have seen unapproved behavior and, if asked to join in, have just said no, they are then compelled to inform the police about what they've seen. This is D.A.R.E.'s basic formula: to cultivate specific practices of seeing and saying that help authorities monitor, police, and engage a relatively hard-to-reach sector of the citizenry.

In this chapter I will illustrate how a series of social crises (idle working-class teens, wartime lack of parenting, and the drug war) have been addressed by youth/police collaboration. With the Children's Aid Society, the Boy Police, the Juvenile Coppettes, the Youth and Police Initiative, D.A.R.E. America, and similar youth/police programs, the police apparatus has infiltrated youths' social networks, effectively disrupting their traditional allegiances to friends, community, and family. While working-class kids in the early twentieth century were assailed by innumerable private and public welfare programs aimed at monitoring and governing their behavior, many of the youth engagement programs which were state-sponsored—particularly those organized by police agencies—strove to civilize youth by having them serve the state. Although these youth/police programs were only one element of a much larger apparatus of youth governance, they were unique in their emphasis on cultivating habits of seeing, saying, and patriotic duty. Yet important cultural forces have organized resistance to the spy/snitch culture promoted by the police and their allies—kids today are barraged by a police apparatus that urges them to "keep talking," while cultural figures and local codes of silence warn them that "snitches get stitches." This chapter provides a historical perspective on the complexities and pitfalls of "D.A.R.E. America," a society in which the police, activists, and cultural authorities fight over the seeing/speaking subjectivity of American youth.

Youngsters of the Dangerous Classes

It was not long ago that practically all the gamins of the poorer sections of American cities were regarded by the authorities as incipient criminals. Now the authorities seem bent on making all of them into police officials. Instead of the enemies of order, the youngsters are learning to be its guardians.
—New York City journalist, 1915[9]

It's no secret that America has long reserved a special anxiety for its youth, particularly youth of color and boys of the working class. The "boy problem," as Julia Grant calls it,[10] has given rise to countless moral panics about immorality, crime, and revolution from below. Such a problem has demanded the effort of a layered and multidirectional apparatus of conduct regulation. While in the nineteenth century public schools detained youth in a constantly monitored atmosphere, private institutions such as the Children's Aid Society began to vie for these kids' time outside of class. By providing working-class kids with the close mentorship of positive role models, these institutions worked hard to transform youth into productive and moral citizens.

For Charles Loring Brace, who founded the Children's Aid Society in New York in 1853, these efforts at promoting child welfare could be best described as "moral disinfectants."[11] For Brace, poverty and crime were largely the result of a swelling underclass of undisciplined youth. To cure the cyclical social maladies of the "dangerous classes," therefore, activists would have to intervene in the everyday lives of youth in order to make them a credit to society: "The objects of those engaged in laboring for this class are to raise them above temptation, to make them of more value to themselves, and to Society, and, if possible, to elevate them to the highest range of life."[12] For Brace, this meant disrupting the socially reproductive logics of working-class family life:

> fathers die, and leave their children unprovided for; parents drink, and abuse their little ones, and they float away on the currents of the street; step-mothers or step-fathers drive out, by neglect and ill-treatment, their sons from home. Thousands are the children of poor foreigners, who have permitted them to grow up without school, education, or religion. All the neglect and bad education and evil example of a poor class tend to form others, who, as they mature, swell the ranks of ruffians and criminals. So, at length, a great multitude of ignorant, untrained, passionate, irreligious boys and young men are formed, who become the "dangerous class" of our city.[13]

For Brace, the kindred evils of alcohol use, neglectful parenting, irreligiousness, and poor education naturally gave rise to juvenile delinquency among the working class. Eventually it became clear to Brace that "what New York most of all needed was some grand, comprehensive effort to check the growth of the 'dangerous classes.'"[14] This grand, comprehensive effort included "Boys' Meetings," where youth were lectured about criminality and delinquency,[15] and eventually grew to include industrial education and reading rooms where working-class kids could be chaperoned and supervised.[16]

While the comprehensive efforts aimed at governing working-class youth are a bit beyond the scope of this book,[17] these early programs give important insight into how diverse organs of American culture have approached the task of youth correction. While private institutions like the Children's Aid Society focused on things like cultural education, personal responsibility, and labor training, these programs often took on a unique inflection when they were guided by the state apparatus. Under the direction of public institutions, these activities naturally emphasized various forms of civic participation. We shouldn't be surprised, therefore, that in the hands of the police these activities were geared toward developing the habits and skills most valued by the police (in particular, communal vigilance, lateral surveillance, and crime reporting).

The Boy Police

At the turn of the twentieth century, a number of "Boy Police" patrols sprouted throughout the United States.[18] As crime rose in many of the nation's cities, burgeoning urban police departments sought to kill two birds with one stone: by recruiting a large number of young boys, the police could maximize their forces' urban presence while also enticing youth to choose the side of law and order. Having kids police their own communities, therefore, was often an attempt to lure youth away from petty crime and into the orbit of responsible citizenship. A good case in point is the Des Moines Boy Police, which was formed in 1900 when the State of Iowa passed new laws against shooting fireworks at Fourth of July celebrations. Because the Des Moines police force was unable to enforce this new law over the entire city, a number of anxious citizens came forward with enforcement ideas. When one of these citizens suggested forming a company of Boy Police, a local activist, Elizabeth Jones-Baird, took it upon herself to organize the patrol.

Emphasizing "the sacred necessity of keeping the laws of the State,"[19] Jones-Baird told her new recruits that if they ensured the other kids would keep the peace—and if they agreed to avoid early partying and shooting fireworks—then they would be appointed "special policemen." According to a contemporary supporter of the Des Moines Boy Police project, this "idea of authority captivated the boys at once. . . . With acumen which would have put to shame many a regular detective these little fellows went to work to track down every specimen of explosive which was being secreted for the big celebration. They told all their young friends that they would be obliged to obey the law, or else be arrested."[20] The primary role of the Boy Police, therefore, was to patrol their towns and "track down" any of their peers' youthful offenses (even as petty as swearing). By policing their peers' conduct, the boys would absorb invaluable lessons in masculine duty and civic responsibility: as one observer put it, the Boy Police would force youth to "absorb the lessons of integrity, uprightness, and obedience" that policing teaches, thus "promoting those qualities of manliness, self-reliance, and order."[21]

In nearby Council Bluffs, this holiday policing project was also adopted by Police Chief George Richmond. Starting in the early years of the twentieth century, from the first to the fifth of July twenty-five junior officers were recruited to keep tabs on their friends. According to an admiring journalist for the *Chicago Examiner*, Council Bluffs' Boy Police project was a potent way to instill vigilant modes of responsible youth citizenship: "The children are interested in law and order, consider themselves the guardians of property, and are early inoculated with the spirit that makes for good citizenship. . . . They go about the task with all the vim and vigor with which other young Americans commemorate the day."[22] While most Americans viewed Independence Day as an opportunity to celebrate, Council Bluffs' "diminutive bluecoats" spent the day patrolling the city and policing their peers. As the *Examiner*'s endorsement demonstrates, lateral surveillance was tied up with many Americans' visions of patriotic duty. It is hardly surprising, then, that these patrols were first gathered to protect the sanctity of Independence Day, as young citizens celebrated their nation's birth by surveilling their peers and ratting them out to local authorities.

This fervor for "boy police" was not confined to the sleepy fields of the Midwest. In New York City, Captain John Sweeney developed a Boy Police program designed to get budding young criminals off the streets. Sweeney, who presided over New York's Fifteenth Police Precinct, recruited boys between the ages of eleven and fifteen to patrol their own neighborhoods. The captain divided his precinct into twelve zones, each under the command of a single boy lieutenant. The boys on a street block constituted a "vigilance committee" that was responsible for enforcing the law on that block. As an observing journalist with the *Christian Endeavor World* remarked: "With rare insight into the weakness of boy nature, Captain Sweeney marks out a path for his young friends. . . . Instead of letting them strut about the whole precinct, flashing their badges, he decrees that no junior policeman has any authority except in his home zone, and that his special duty is right on his own block—under the eyes of his parents and neighbors! Far from grumbling at this restriction, each vigilance committee is striving to outshine the rest and secure for its members the coveted honorable mention for 'condition of the block."[23] Key to Sweeney's program, therefore, were a disciplined environment of supervision as well as a reward system that propelled a competitive spirit among the young officers.

While some critics objected that it was a mistake "to encourage the boys to undertake any such meddlesome and intolerable activity [because] their zeal would more than overbalance their possible good intentions,"[24] Sweeney moved forward with his plans to discipline delinquent youths through police collaboration. As the ranks of his Northeast District Boy Police program swelled to three hundred members in 1917, Sweeney announced that the program went a long way toward "keeping the boys out of trouble": "This problem is largely solved when the boyish love of adventure and mystery, which usually expresses itself in the exploits of criminal heroes of dime novels and the yellow press, is directed to the imitation of the deeds of the real heroes of American cities—the brave, honest, and unassuming members of the police force, in uniform and out."[25] By tapping into the untamed adventurousness of urban boys, Sweeney sought to channel that passion by having the boys imitate the "heroes" working in American police departments.

Yet this empowerment, of course, had important limitations: Sweeney stressed that the boys had to enforce the law without violence or physical engagement—their responsibilities were confined to various modes of seeing and saying. Their ultimate duties, he emphasized, were to file daily reports of criminal deeds and to "squeal" on anyone committing a crime: "The 'Kid Cops' avoid bullying and being bullied in enforcing the law. They carry no billies, and boast no 'strong arm squad.' If they can't gain their purpose by being 'polite' and 'helpful' in accordance with their motto, they report to the senior force. . . . 'Squealing' has become the virtue of 'loyalty to the force.'"[26] In lieu of billy clubs and a "strong arm squad," Sweeney's Boy Police were outfitted with the weapons of speech and surveillance—"squealing" became the ultimate expression of their civic duty.

When a boy decided to join the Boy Police, Sweeney gave him a long list of responsibilities to learn by heart. Before reporting for duty, each cadet was required to memorize a pledge ("To do my duty to God and my country, and to obey the law . . ."), a short motto, and a list of eleven basic duties—the essential parameters of Boy Police conduct:

1. Prevent swearing and vulgar language in the public street and public places.
2. Prevent the building of bonfires in the streets.
3. Prevent boys from breaking windows and street-lamps and from defacing buildings and sidewalks with chalk.
4. Prevent boys from smoking cigarettes and playing crap.
5. Prevent boys from engaging in dangerous or unlawful playing
6. Prevent persons placing encumbrances or obstructions on fire-escapes.
7. Prevent the mixing of ashes, garbage, and paper.
8. See that garbage cans are kept covered, and that ash and garbage cans are promptly removed from the sidewalk when emptied.
9. Request persons to keep the sidewalk and areaway in front of their buildings clean, and not to throw refuse into the street.
10. Make special effort to perform duties 6, 7, 8, and 9 at your own homes. See that your parents and relatives do not violate the laws and ordinances.
11. For the above purposes do not enter any building under any condition.[27]

Many of these duties revolved around carrying out surveillance on fellow youths—the Boy Police were charged with policing the language and conduct of their peers. Yet, as duty 10 makes clear, the boys were also required to keep an eye on their parents and families. The mission of the Boy Police, therefore, extended beyond carrying out surveillance and snitching on their peers. In fact, the boys' biannual progress reports would give special marks for "personal influence," which, in the words of Elizabeth Ellsworth Cook, a journalist with the *Christian Endeavor World*, measured a boy's success "in persuading grown-ups to obey the law."[28] The uniformed kids of the New York Boy Police, therefore, were given rewards for turning their vigilance toward the adults in their families and communities.

Junior Coppettes

Boys were not the only targets of the NYPD's youth responsibilization efforts. Alongside Sweeney's Boy Police, teenage "Coppettes" monitored the streets of New York City. To complement its Boy Police program, in 1915 New York City recruited five hundred teenage girls to try out for a new girls' patrol. After six months, fifty of these girls were selected for the program, and each selected Coppette was given a beat to monitor and patrol. The *New York Times* chronicled the activities of one of these girls, "Captain" Celia Goldberg, as she demonstrated the daily work of a "girl cop." Outfitted with a blue cap and a brass-buttoned blue coat, young Captain Goldberg roamed her beat, looking for illegal and unsafe activities. Responding to a question about whether her fellow citizens took her seriously when she tried to enforce the law, Goldberg remarked: "Surely they obey. . . . They see this uniform and they know it means the law."[29]

The responsibilities of Goldberg and other Coppettes, however, were somewhat different than those of the Boy Police. While the Boy Police often watched out for street crime and assaults, according to Goldberg the Coppettes had two main responsibilities: first, they kept a close watch over children and families, and only second did they police their neighborhoods for street crime. Goldberg reported, "Most of our work has to do with children and the home. . . . We have to see that our own mothers buy only pure, wholesome food, that our homes are clean, and that our own little brothers are well cared for. Then we are ready to take care of our other duties."[30] In fact, when describing her duties Captain Goldberg often emphasized her role in childcare: when walking their beats, "we take lost babies to their mothers. If we don't know the baby we take it to the girl-policeman on the next block, and she usually does."[31] Through this gendered division of labor, the NYPD used the Coppettes to extend their sensory resources into the homes of New York families. While the girls would sometimes join the boys to stamp out petty crime, the Coppettes were primarily tasked with regulating the health and morality of their parents, their siblings, and the children in their neighborhoods. These duties included preventing children from watching motion pictures without their parents, "getting after" merchants who sold tobacco to minors, ensuring that grocers sold clean and healthful food, and reporting underage girls who would attempt to enter dancehalls.[32]

The Coppettes thus illustrate how certain distributions of youth responsibility helped expand the police's sensory reach into the family and other social institutions. In its review of the *Times* article on Captain Goldberg and the other Coppettes, the *Literary Digest* posed: "the mind asks if this, or something like it, be not the ideal democracy, where every citizen is a policeman, assuming the responsibility not only for his own welfare and that of his family, but for the community at large, as well."[33] Of course, this idealistic rhetoric about democratic participation is nothing new: as this book has illustrated, police agencies and their supporters have routinely conflated democratic citizenship with the participatory policing of fellow citizens.

The Cowan Plan

From Berkeley, Spokane, and San Antonio to Washington, Boston, and Providence, the 1940s saw a tremendous upswing in programs that addressed juvenile delinquency through youth/police collaboration. Like Captain Sweeney's Boy Police and the Junior Coppettes, the young officers of the Junior Police and Citizen's Corps were tasked with patrolling their blocks, keeping neighborhoods clean, and safeguarding law and order.[34] Historically, these programs tended to gain momentum during times of social upheaval. During World War Two, for example, as millions of men left their families to fight overseas, "juvenile delinquency" became an object of special social concern. Public figures like FBI director J. Edgar Hoover and Senator Estes Kefauver were quick to blame parents, and women in particular, for these social maladies.[35] As women rushed to fill the jobs abandoned by men who had been drafted to fight the war, the specter of the idle child rankled many social welfare and law enforcement agencies.

As Malinda Lindquist has shown,[36] this discourse of "juvenile delinquency" was often fueled by social anxieties over race, class, and gender that laid responsibility for rising juvenile crime rates at the feet of single working mothers (and especially women of color). To address this delinquency, nonprofit groups like the YMCA and the Boy Scouts organized after-school programs, summer camps, and recreation initiatives aimed at governing the conduct of working-class and African American youth.[37] Local police departments, too, set their sights on these unparented "delinquents." In 1942, for example, an African American Washington, D.C., police officer named Oliver Cowan developed a "Junior Police Corps" aimed at steering young African Americans away from a life of crime. According to Elizabeth Jean Stanton, a social worker who worked with Cowan's Junior Police Corps in the 1940s, "The Negro Officer who initiated this club had hopes that through . . . encouragement, enlightenment, supervision, and a diversified activities program the Negro youth of Washington, D.C., would become worthy and better citizens of the community."[38]

By recruiting students to keep watch over their schools and communities, Cowan aimed to transform these future criminals into productive young citizens. With the support of D.C. public schools, he organized citizen-youths into hierarchical patrols modeled on the civic police force. In less than a year, he had enlisted more than seven hundred boy cadets and one hundred girl "auxiliaries."[39] By 1944, that number had increased to nearly twelve hundred boys and more than three hundred girls.[40] Cowan attributed his success to an interesting recruitment strategy that involved subverting the leadership of local youth gangs. He found that a great deal of youth crime in Washington was carried out by local gangs such as the Oil Burners, the Bulldozers, and the Bone Crushers. Rather than arresting the gangs and sending their members to juvenile homes or prison, Cowan floated the possibility of reorienting the gang's efforts toward more socially constructive activities: "They are kids, actually, with a lot of energy, and they merely need direction. That energy could be used constructively rather than destructively if somebody showed them how to do it."[41]

Cowan infiltrated these gangs by persuading their leaders to join the Junior Police Corps. In the spirit of a scheme put forward by legendary police official Eliot Ness,[42] he offered gangs various social and communal resources in exchange for them abandoning crime and collaborating with local authorities. According to Cowan, he would approach gang leaders and say, "I know you know all about breaking the law. I guess you fellows know best how to get others to respect and obey it."[43] Surprisingly, he had a great deal of success in convincing youth gangs to carry out lateral surveillance in their communities. Before long, the gangs developed an alternative urban youth culture based in fighting crime. Their organizational manual, which the former gang members produced on their own and distributed to new members, declared: "Congress made the laws, we enforce them. . . . We as junior citizens are determined to abolish juvenile delinquency in our neighborhood."[44]

Despite these successes, the Junior Police Corps and similar programs across the U.S. had unintended effects on local youth politics. On the

Figure 4.1. A cop cultivates relationships with elementary school students in a Washington, D.C., classroom. Police Foundation, *Experiments in Police Improvement*, 4.

one hand, integrating entire gangs into boy police programs prevented retaliation against newly recruited officers. By bringing whole gangs under the supervisory purview of the cops, boy police recruiters were able to reduce local crime while simultaneously forestalling retaliatory attacks from rebuffed gang leaders. But in many locales, animosity emerged between newly minted boy officers and the gangs that refused to join youth police programs. For example, in an attack that prefigured current anti-snitch campaigns, in 1951 several youths fired rifles at boy patrol officers while they were serving as crossing guards at an elementary school in Watseka, Illinois.[45] These attacks simply triggered more intensive efforts by police to target crime and violence among youth, especially through programs aimed at permeating the opaque and rebellious student bodies of American schools.

Just Say No

It isn't snitching or betrayal to tell an adult that a friend of
yours is using drugs and needs help. . . . It's an act of true
loyalty—of true friendship.
—Former Education Secretary William Bennett[46]

The Cowan Plan was simply one element of a much broader postwar
effort to regulate the conduct of America's "delinquent" youth. Fueled by
a rampant moral panic about out-of-control teens,[47] the 1960s and 1970s
gave rise to a broad range of strategies for using police collaboration to
channel kids toward the straight and narrow. As I discussed in Chapter
Three, just as the rising crime of the 1960s and 1970s gave rise to adult
citizens' patrols, it also gave rise to new kid patrols.[48] One of the most
successful of these groups, the Bay Youth Courtesy Patrol in Washington,
D.C., was organized by James Adler, a veteran social worker and probation
officer. Adler founded his patrol in 1968, after a local woman was mugged
by a violent youth gang. The victim turned out to be the mother of the
gang's leader, who decided to reform his organization into a responsible
citizens' youth patrol. According to Adler, the Courtesy Patrol adopted a
familiar aim: "the primary goal of the patrol is crime prevention through
surveillance of the neighborhood and diversion of potential delinquents
into constructive (crime prevention) activity."[49] Even though many of their
former friends and associates mocked them as a "snitcher patrol,"[50] the
Courtesy Patrol members took their seeing/saying citizenship seriously
and eventually developed an official relationship with the D.C. police.

While the Police Athletic League, the "White Hats" in Tampa,[51] and
other junior police programs used badges, uniforms, and official titles
to entice students to monitor their peers, nonprofit groups and police
agencies began experimenting with a new model of youth governance
that would turn everyday, sneaker-wearing kids into seeing/saying subjects. Searching for the best disciplinary space for carrying out these
experiments in citizenship training, the police and their allies turned to
public schools. As criminologist Denise Gottfredson has pointed out,
"Schools have great potential as a locus for crime prevention. They provide regular access to students throughout the developmental years, and
perhaps the only consistent access to large numbers of the most crime-

prone young children in the early school years; they are staffed with individuals paid to help youth develop as healthy, happy, productive citizens; and the community usually supports schools' efforts to socialize youth. Many of the precursors of delinquent behavior are school-related and therefore likely to be amenable to change through school-based intervention."[52] As scholars have long recognized,[53] schools are outfitted with countless mechanisms for surveillance and correction: classroom design, detention, student "tracking," examinations, and other disciplinary measures subject students to diverse pressures and programs of behavioral modification. To supplement the disciplinary surveillance that is so essential to the form and function of the modern school, police officials and allied institutions have introduced more flexible and modulating programs of surveillance. In fact, an essential characteristic of school programs like D.A.R.E. is their tendency to disrupt the asymmetry of traditional disciplinary relations. The surveillance monopolies typically held by teachers and parents, in particular, are challenged—while students have typically been monitored by their parents and teachers, they are now also faced with police-trained peers. This disruption hits its ironic zenith, perhaps, as police flip disciplinary surveillance structures on their heads by encouraging students to spy and snitch on their parents. Other differences, too, mark the spy-and-snitch programs promoted in today's schools: in lieu of the uniformed police collaborators of the Junior Police clubs, seeing/saying students circulate more or less transparently among their peers.

The most influential and far-reaching of these programs has been D.A.R.E., which attempts to turn kids into weapons in the War on Drugs. Founded in 1981 by Los Angeles police chief Daryl Gates, the D.A.R.E. program emerged as part of Nancy Reagan's "Say No to Drugs" campaign. The Reagan administration's drug war, of course, took a mostly "supply-side" approach to fighting drugs; however, it also involved attempts to inoculate future drug users by targeting them with an assortment of policies and programs. One of these early intervention programs, Project SMART (Self Management and Resistance Training), was developed by researchers at the University of Southern California. Aimed at students in the Los Angeles Unified School District (LAUSD), Project SMART was a collaborative effort between USC professors and administrators at local public schools—police simply did not fit into the plan. Chief Gates, though, had hopes of building a closer relation-ship between Los Angeles public schools and the LAPD. He approached Project SMART and offered to help by bringing uniformed officers into the schools. Alarmed by the idea of having armed and uniformed offi-cers act as mentors for students, the officials at Project SMART declined. Undeterred, Gates developed his own elementary school program that supplemented the SMART curriculum with police participation. Un-pleased with Gates's move, officials from Project SMART were quick to criticize how Gates and his associates assembled the D.A.R.E. program: according to a representative from SMART, "[D.A.R.E.] ripped off our materials," and "they took a version of the program that we had radically revamped because it wasn't working."[54] Yet D.A.R.E. quickly dwarfed Project SMART, gaining a national presence during the 1980s. Benefit-ing from massive drug-war grant initiatives, D.A.R.E. was able to spread to middle schools in 1986 and high schools in 1988.[55]

Active in seventy-five percent of American schools and in more than forty-three countries worldwide, and with annual expenditures exceed-ing one billion dollars, D.A.R.E. is today one of the most significant youth governance initiatives in the United States. While its central mission is still to "provide children with the information and skills they need to live drug and violence free lives," in recent years it has added new areas of focus: Internet security, bullying, school safety, and "community safety" now rank among D.A.R.E.'s core concerns.[56] To promote D.A.R.E.-approved conduct, uniformed police officers carry out a seventeen-session program that targets students from K-5 all the way to high school. In order to give these kids "the skills they need to avoid involvement in drugs, gangs, and violence," D.A.R.E. takes pains to cultivate an interac-tive environment that helps students identify with the police officers in their schools. In many communities, like that facing Chief Gates in the early 1980s, D.A.R.E. has singled out youth of color for special police attention. According to Michael J. Stoil and Gary Hill, D.A.R.E. "was de-signed to respond to the specific needs of African American and Mexican American neighborhoods" in Los Angeles, and "sought to reduce distrust of law enforcement officers in communities where the police often were viewed as an alien, racist presence."[57] At a time when many poor people of color saw police targeting their neighborhoods with a curious mix of militancy and cold disregard, D.A.R.E. gave police officers a chance to improve community relations with the marginalized youth of these neighborhoods. Indeed, early D.A.R.E. police officer Anthony Piergallini has been clear on this aspect of its mission: "A big plus to this in my eyes was that if you put an officer in an elementary school classroom talking to kids at their level, not talking down to them, if you communicate with them, now you are not the frightening men in the blue uniforms with badges who are going to put you away. . . . Now, you are human beings. You are friendly guys. A lot of people still don't understand the concept of how important this is."[58] D.A.R.E.'s mission, therefore, is more than simple "drug abuse resistance education"—as much as that, it seeks to build identification and empathy between youth and local police. Other D.A.R.E. figures, including DEA agent Robert Strange, have gone so far as to say that this identification outweighs the initiative's educational value: "Forget about the drug education. . . . We saw a relationship that could be built between the students and the police officers. There's no other vehicle for that that we're aware of."[59]

For D.A.R.E. officials, these "close and trusting" bonds of identification are essential because they make students more comfortable opening up about the forbidden habits of their friends and family members. In an assessment of its school outreach program, the Florida D.A.R.E. Officer's Association asserts, "Because of these highly credible D.A.R.E. officers in the schools, students develop a close and trusting relationship. This relationship results in students letting officers know if Johnny has a gun in his backpack or about other potentially violent situations that may occur on campus."[60] According to the identification-building logic of D.A.R.E.'s school programs, putting cops into classrooms encourages students to assist the police in their crime-fighting mission. This logic is perhaps best expressed in the "Three R's"—recognize, resist, report—promoted by many D.A.R.E. programs. While instruction in the "Three R's" helps students "recognize" drugs and drug paraphernalia, they are also taught to recognize "suspicious" behaviors among their peers, friends, and family members.

D.A.R.E.: Keep Safe, Keep Away, Keep Telling

And of course, like the other lateral surveillance programs discussed in this chapter, D.A.R.E. has taken great pains to cultivate an appropriate speaking subjectivity in its young targets. It is unique, however, in that it actively targets elementary students as young as five, in kindergarten and prekindergarten.[61] Through coloring books and games, D.A.R.E. promotes the same spy-and-snitch culture among kindergartners that, as we will see, it also encourages among older students. For instance, in the *Child Safety Coloring and Activity Book*, distributed by the Department of Justice in partnership with D.A.R.E., students are reminded—first and foremost—to "settle arguments with words, not fists or weapons."[62] And this classic liberal feature of seeing/saying discourse is not the book's only lesson: cartoon characters—including D.A.R.E.'s tough animated lion, Daren—instruct students how and when to snitch on their peers and parents. Indeed, the most frequently touted theme in the little book is "KEEP SAFE, KEEP AWAY, KEEP TELLING."[63] The book is filled with instructions on how to "keep telling"—kids are encouraged to "tell" if someone "bothers" them online, if they see someone being picked on at school, and, above all, if they see evidence of drugs, weapons, or gang activity. Thus by honing students' "communication, decision making, and refusal skills,"[64] D.A.R.E.'s outreach materials instruct students in appropriate forms of communicative citizenship. The coloring book even contains a completion certificate where students sign their names, promising to exercise this communicative subjectivity while keeping a close eye on the conduct of their family and friends: "I [student name] take the Safety Pledge and promise to always be safe and help my family and friends practice safety first."[65] While these coloring books are a relatively innocuous manifestation of D.A.R.E.'s outreach arsenal, they illustrate the strong pressure that even the youngest kids face to scrutinize the conduct of their friends and family members.

To trace D.A.R.E.'s vision of success, we can also look at the student-written testimonials it promotes in official publications. D.A.R.E. Alaska, for one, uses testimonials to demonstrate that students are absorbing the program's message. One young girl, Katrina, writes: "In D.A.R.E. I have learned that if someone walks up to me and tells me to do something that is bad or that I don't feel comfortable with, then I need to say something that has the Three R's and I need to make eye contact."[66] Other students, too, illustrated that they had mastered the "recognize, report, resist" procedure: Taylor writes, "D.A.R.E. has helped many people including myself make the right decisions. . . . I know that when I have

Figure 4.2. A D.A.R.E. coloring activity shows students
how to see something and say something. "Coloring Pages,"
South Carolina D.A.R.E. Training Center. www.rcsd.net/
dare.

a problem I need to tell an adult I trust. I would not have known that
before I started D.A.R.E. I would have tried to solve any problem I have
by myself and it would possibly get physical. Now I know that a fight
should never have to get physical. I have learned how harmful drugs
and alcohol is and I have learned how I can stop people from doing the
wrong thing without getting violent."[67] Taylor's testimony provides another illustration of how the perennial nonviolent imperative of lateral
surveillance programs persists in youth initiatives like D.A.R.E.: surveillance and reporting are contrasted with "getting physical," thus allowing
little citizens to be of use to the state while delegating physical interventions to the police and other figures of authority.

A young D.A.R.E. Alaska student, Stephanie, demonstrated one of
the most provocative lessons promoted by the group. She wrote that "the
thing that is most important to me during the D.A.R.E. class is not to

smoke not to do drugs or use drugs [*sic*]. . . . I will try to tell my mom to stop smoking or any body else that I know that smoke. I learned that if I smoke then I can get black lungs and you can't join any kind of sports and you can't run fast as you could."[68] While many of these students' essays suggest the confusing and dubious quality of D.A.R.E. education ("black lungs," for example), Stephanie pinpoints perhaps the most controversial element of the initiative's school program: that it encourages students to police and snitch on their families.

D.A.R.E. to Snitch

Although D.A.R.E. is reticent about this element of its program, its policies, outreach materials, and cultural track record demonstrate that it creates an ideal environment in which youth learn to scrutinize and snitch on their parents. This aspect of D.A.R.E. education, in fact, has been central to its mission since the 1980s. In 1988, a D.A.R.E. implementation manual released by the U.S. Department of Justice explains that D.A.R.E. officers, like social workers and many other school administrators, are required to pursue tips of a criminal nature, even if those tips are shared in confidence.[69] The manual even gives special instructions to officers who receive reports that parents are using "dope"[70]—that information, D.A.R.E. officers are informed, "cannot remain confidential."[71] When these mandatory reporting guidelines are combined with activities and outreach materials that promote *recognizing* and *reporting*, local police departments often find themselves pursuing the tips of a naïvely vigilant student.

Since at least the early 1990s, D.A.R.E. has been under fire for this element of its outreach. Publications like the *Washington Post*, *Village Voice*, and *New Republic* have criticized D.A.R.E. for its efforts to transform students into snitches. Despite the denials of administrators, many D.A.R.E. students, in fact, have used their recognize-and-report skills for just this purpose. In 1991, for example, a ten-year-old D.A.R.E. student in Colorado found a small stash of marijuana hidden in his parents' bookshelf. Instead of confronting his parents, the boy called 911, informing the dispatcher that he was a "D.A.R.E. kid" and that he had found drugs in his home. When the parents were arrested, the boy's local D.A.R.E. officer praised his actions. The next year, there were two separate cases in which Boston children who ratted on their parents showed their D.A.R.E. certificates to officers as they arrived to arrest their parents. According to Gary T. Marx, in the late 1980s school programs like D.A.R.E. led to Boston police authorities receiving twelve calls a day from kids turning in their parents for misdemeanor drug possession.[72] And many parents of D.A.R.E. kids—including, of course, those of Crystal Grendell, whose story introduced this chapter—have been arrested and fired from their jobs after their children ratted them out for simple drug possession.[73]

In their research on youth/police collaboration, Richard Ericson and Kevin Haggerty have found "a fine line between [police officers in schools] providing a reactive 'service' and proactively recruiting informants."[74] That is, while the police often claim that they do not actively recruit informants from the student body, there is a fine line between "proactive recruitment" and the kind of spy-and-snitch encouragement engaged in by programs like D.A.R.E. In many cases, the distinction between reactive support and active recruitment seems to disappear. In Georgia, for example, a nine-year-old D.A.R.E. kid called the cops when he found a small stash of speed hidden in his parents' bedroom. The cops showed up and arrested both of his parents, keeping his father in jail for three months. The distraught child said, "At school, they told us that if we ever see drugs, call 911 because people who use drugs need help. . . . I thought the police would come get the drugs and tell them that drugs are wrong. They never said they would arrest them. . . . But in court, I heard them tell the judge that I wanted my mom and dad arrested. That is a lie. I did not tell them that."[75] Indeed, naïve youth often recognize and report without understanding the potentially devastating consequences of their actions. We might also consider the tale of an elementary student in Matthews, North Carolina. In 2010, the fifth-grade boy sat with his peers during a D.A.R.E. lesson on the horrors of marijuana use. The boy was so affected by the lesson that he approached a D.A.R.E. officer, informing him that his parents sometimes smoked pot. To prove his point, the boy brought one of his parents' joints to school. When the local police arrested the boy's parents, social services removed the couple's two children from the home. Remarking on the case, a Matthews police officer seemed undisturbed by the fact that the children had been taken from their home over misdemeanor marijuana possession. With a hint of pride, the cop remarked: "Even if it's happening in their own home with their own parents, they understand that's a dangerous situation because of what we're teaching them. . . . That's what they're told to do, to make us aware."[76] While some cops might take pride in these successes, the cultivation of a spy-and-snitch ethic among youth has resulted in many kids unintentionally siding with the police against their friends and families, sometimes turning their lives upside down in the process.

The recognize/report mentality so characteristic of D.A.R.E., meanwhile, has seeped into other school programs. Combined with the entrepreneurial spirit of millennial neoliberalism, students are now learning that snitching pays—literally. Campus Crime Stoppers, the youth division of the national Crime Stoppers organization, offers cash rewards for students to snitch on their peers for drug offenses. Different rewards are meted out based upon the severity of the crime: while a student who reports marijuana possession might receive $200, a student who reports cocaine possession might be eligible to receive $500. For reporting certain drug offenses, in some jurisdictions students can be paid as much as $2,500. Some recent rewards divvied out by the Atlanta-area Campus Crime Stoppers include a seventy-five-dollar reward for snitching on a student who made a bong out of a Gatorade bottle; a $200 reward for turning in a classmate who possessed hydrocodone pills; and even a number of small rewards for students who ratted out their peers for skipping class.[77] To fuel this entrepreneurial spirit among students, the police in many jurisdictions have built a digital reporting apparatus: if a student is bashful about snitching over the phone, tips can be emailed, texted, or submitted on Crime Stoppers' mobile app, TipSubmit.[78] As we saw in Chapter Two, these digital reporting systems tend to energize the spy-and-snitch culture that is already prominent in schools.

Stop Snitching vs. Keep Talking

While some kids are happy to scrutinize and snitch on their peers, D.A.R.E. and other youth policing efforts have ignited a number of remarkable resistance practices. Some of these emerge in response to the relatively juvenile efforts of youth-oriented anti-drug programs. The "D.A.R.E." acronym and logo, of course, have become popular sites of satire. The iconic D.A.R.E bumper sticker, which features "D.A.R.E. TO KEEP KIDS OFF DRUGS" in large red letters, has been transformed into "D.A.R.E. TO KEEP COPS OFF DONUTS." Progressive organizations like Students for Sensible Drug Policy have designed their own apparel that raises awareness about the dangers of D.A.R.E.—one of their shirts, for example, calls on fellow students to "D.A.R.E. TO RESIST THE WAR ON DRUGS." And aside from these socially conscious critiques, many students simply reject the D.A.R.E. message out of hand. In a *Village Voice* article, Martha Rosenbaum, a former director at the Lindesmith Center, pointed out that D.A.R.E.'s freebie promotion culture makes it an easy object of teen critique. For Rosenbaum, the graduation certificates, tee shirts, pens, banners, coloring books, pennants, rulers, bumper stickers, and stuffed animals help make D.A.R.E. a corny cultural icon: "What happens is that the culture takes these messages and twists them around. . . . [W]hich is what happened with the 'This is your brain. This is your brain on drugs' commercials. And now there's a whole T-shirt line that's a spoof."[79] Many of D.A.R.E.'s middle and high school targets, in particular, are too culturally sophisticated to take the program seriously, and local police agencies are unlikely to get much help from them.[80]

Yet D.A.R.E. and allied youth spy-and-snitch program have also fueled more politically provocative critiques. The boy patrol officers who were shot in Watseka, Illinois, in 1951 are not the only youth/police collaborators to have elicited violence from local criminals and gangs. Abiding by what Elijah Anderson calls the "code of the street"[81]—a code of silence, solidarity, and police resistance that is prominent in many urban communities—a large number of teenagers actively resist the speaking/snitching subjectivity promoted by agencies like D.A.R.E. Articulations of this code of the street include the "Stop Snitching" movement, which has become popular in recent years due to the high cultural profile carried by some of its advocates. While the Stop Snitching movement is not exclusively a youth phenonenon, it has had an especially significant impact on youth culture. Hip-hop, in particular, has been a driving force behind the Stop Snitching movement, as artists like NWA, Busta Rhymes, Lil' Kim, Project Pat, and Cam'ron have taken public stances against police cooperation.[82] As Rachel Waldoff and Karen Weiss have observed, these elements of hip-hop culture endorse "a 'stop snitching' message aimed at black urban youth that implores listeners to refrain from police cooperation in *all* circumstances, whether simply reporting crime or becoming an official informant."[83] Hip-hop, which plays such an important role in defining many urban youth cultures, helps galvanize resistance to the diverse spy/snitch initiatives promoted by the police (including 911 and other crime reporting apparatuses).

The Stop Snitching movement entered the popular imagination in 2004, when basketball star Carmelo Anthony appeared in an amateur documentary called *Stop Snitchin'!* Anthony's controversial appearance gave the code of the street bourgeois credibility, and Stop Snitching rhetoric gained prominence among many American youth communities.[84] "Snitching" was tagged on metal stop signs, Stop Snitching shirts and bumper stickers became cult favorites, and other items of Stop Snitching outreach soon gained a cultural esteem among urban youth that D.A.R.E. could never obtain. And much of the Stop Snitching ethos, of course, centered on the violent implications of snitch resistance—many of the shirts and stickers were emblazoned with guns and knives, featuring slogans such as "Snitches Are a Dying Breed" and "Danger: Snitch at Your Own Risk." In fact, in recent years "snitches get stitches" has become a rallying cry among many youths and young adults, and kids who rat out their peers often find themselves faced with violent retaliation. Indeed, some scholars have argued that the Stop Snitching campaign has had a palpable effect on murder prosecutions, as a number of high-crime urban jurisdictions (such as Baltimore, Detroit, and Washington, D.C.) have suffered falling murder conviction rates since the emergence of the movement.[85]

In 2007, the National Center for Victims of Crime (NCVC) released a report on these anti-snitching pressures. Among students who had witnessed gang-related crime, one half never reported it to authorities. The primary reason they neglected to report crime, the report found, was that they feared being attacked for snitching. According to the authors, "Interviews made clear that being labeled a snitch carries a price, not just of potential violence, but of ostracism by neighbors and peers."[86] In many communities, this threat of violence is very real: in October 2009 a fifteen-year-old Florida boy, Michael Brewer, called the cops after a fellow student stole his father's bicycle. When the suspect was released from police custody, he and four of his friends confronted Brewer outside his parents' apartment complex. Yelling, "He's a snitch! He's a snitch!," the boys doused the fifteen-year-old with rubbing alcohol and set him on fire. Brewer suffered second- and third-degree burns on eighty percent of his body, and the ringleaders of the attack were charged with attempted murder.[87]

Alarmed by the cultural climate that fuels this kind of anti-snitch violence, the NCVC argues that more resources should be spent on convincing youth to communicate with police. Recommending media outreach campaigns that are aimed at "counter[ing] community 'norms' against snitching,"[88] the authors stumbled upon the same counter-strategy designed by the City of Baltimore during the heart of the Stop Snitching controversy. While kids were being urged through numerous cultural channels to cut off communication with cops, Baltimore kicked off its "Keep Talking" campaign. To compete with the *Stop Snitchin!* documentary and the other cultural products that shore up the code of the street, Baltimore police officers drove around in police vans labeled "Keep Talking" and handed out their own documentary DVDs and T-shirts.[89] With this "guerrilla communications" campaign,[90] the police sought to threaten local gangs and ensure that potential witnesses did not feel intimidated into silence. This struggle over urban youth's speaking subjectivity, of course, spread beyond the streets of Baltimore: federal initiatives spawned considerable research on how to keep youth talking. The NCVC, for example, urged authorities to enlist cultural figures that could compete with the likes of Carmelo Anthony, Lil' Kim, and Busta Rhymes: "Communities should enlist spokespeople who are credible to youth—hip-hop artists and DJs, trusted youth workers and faith leaders, and youth themselves—to deliver the ["Keep Talking"] message through various media."[91] This emphasis on media caught on with other seeing/saying programs—such as the "You Bet I Told" campaign in Washington, D.C.—which also used media outreach to promote snitching subjectivity among urban teens.[92]

Despite the NCVC's dreams of a star-studded cultural campaign, its naïve "Keep Talking" message has failed to gain traction in most urban communities. Opposed to the Department of Justice's ideal vision of sympathetic, seeing/speaking teenagers, local social realities push many kids to resist this speaking subjectivity. A *Washington Post* report revealed the depth of police resistance that exists in these communities: according to a seventeen-year-old student, "Around here, it's not even a question of being a snitch. . . . [Y]ou're liable to get killed."[93] A sixteen-year-old girl gave a similar response: "No matter how bad I wanted to tell . . . I feel if I snitched, I would be putting my life in danger because people with guns feel they have more power than people who don't. You just don't feel safe, no matter what. And then if those people get arrested, they'll have other people get you. That's how it is."[94] Seeing and saying, therefore, has become a dangerous civic duty in many communities, and authorities are playing with fire when they promote a spy/snitch culture among youth. Yet despite these teens' testimony, and despite the abundant evidence that snitching puts kids' lives in danger, the NCVC recommends that police develop closer relationships with youth so that they learn appropriate habits of seeing and saying. As the NCVC report concludes, "Perhaps, in the end, to assume their civic duties (including reporting crime and testifying in court), youth in high-crime urban areas require no more than any other youth—a sense that adults care about what they say and are looking out for their safety."[95] For the NCVC and its allies, getting kids to "assume their civic duties" ranks a bit higher than protecting them from retaliatory violence—and much higher, needless to say, than addressing the systemic problems of poverty and injustice that breed the conditions in which urban kids have to fear brutality from criminal gangs and the police alike.

Conclusion

Beyond the violence and threats that fuel the Stop Snitching movement, many local critics of youth/police collaboration level thought-provoking critiques against the spy/snitch culture promoted by programs like D.A.R.E. and its antecedents. Some of the students interviewed by NCVC, in fact, revealed a deeply entrenched "us vs. them" mentality in urban communities. For these kids, siding with the cops meant siding against their friends, families, and neighbors. As one student remarked: "We won't go on their side, 'cause they're not on our side. People don't trust the police."[96] So while youth/police collaboration programs attempt to bridge this divide by convincing kids to "keep talking," they face an uphill battle. In many urban communities, drug dealers and gangs work hard to keep local youth on their side—they do palpable good for their communities, for example, by financing after-school programs and conducting other outreach to youngsters. When explaining why he appeared in the *Stop Snitchin'!* video, Carmelo Anthony described why many urban teens learn to respect the drug dealers in their communities: "Drug dealers funded our programs. . . . Drug dealers bought our uniforms. . . . They just wanted to see you do good."[97] For the kids who benefit from the generosity of local dealers, that benevolence paints a stark contrast to the hostility they encounter from most cops. While some students might see a friendly D.A.R.E. officer at their schools, many urban kids, like Carmelo Anthony, grow up watching cops bully, harass, and even assault their friends. So when youth/police programs attempt to finesse a competing structure of loyalty among these kids, their efforts often fall on deaf ears.

There is another basic flaw in the logic of youth/police collaboration. Let's reflect on a statement put forward by the National Center for Victims of Crime: "Reporting illegal behavior of gang members needs to be viewed as positive action that benefits the community rather than the act of a 'snitch.' School authorities, law enforcement officers, faith leaders, and popular personalities such as radio DJs and recording artists can play important roles in bringing about this kind of change in the youth culture."[98] Of course, no matter how hard the state and its allies attempt to develop a "cool" snitching culture, we can count on young people to rebel against it. As Dick Hebdige taught us in the 1980s, breaking rules and challenging the law draws the attention that most young people crave: "When young people do these things, when they adopt these strategies, they get talked about, taken seriously, their grievances are acted upon. They get arrested harassed, admonished, disciplined, incarcerated, applauded, vilified, emulated, listened to. . . . There is a logic to transgression."[99] In its vigorous quest to turn kids into the eyes and ears of the police, the state and its allies ignore this logic of transgression. While D.A.R.E. programs will continue to convince some students to snitch on their peers, friends, and families, the police will never be able to couple their monopoly on violence with a monopoly over youth culture. With seeing/saying initiatives playing such an important role in the War on Drugs, the state, gangs, and resistance groups will continue to wage cultural battles over the speaking subjectivity of tomorrow's youth. Undoubtedly, these battles will become more intense as the state attempts to preempt Stop Snitching culture by approaching citizens at their most vulnerable and impressionable stages of life.

5

Terror Citizenship

Surveillance and Civil Defense

Make no mistake about it. We got a war here, just like we got
a war abroad.
—George W. Bush[1]

In May 2013, Talal al Rouki, a college student living in Michigan, was
invited to a dinner party in his apartment complex. Al Rouki prepared
a traditional Saudi dish, kabsah, which is made from basmati rice, veg-
etables, Middle Eastern spices, and seasoned meats. When he finished
cooking his kabsah, al Rouki carried it to his friend's apartment and the
two had dinner together. Two days later, al Rouki was awakened early
in the morning to find FBI agents surrounding his apartment block.
When they descended on al Rouki's apartment and began to question
him, al Rouki learned that one of his neighbors had alerted authorities
that he might be plotting a terrorist act. What had aroused his neighbor's
suspicion, the agents informed al Rouki, was the pressure cooker he had
carried to his friend's apartment two nights before. According to the
neighbor's police report, the pressure cooker was "bullet colored."[2] After
questioning the pudgy college student about his spare time, his political beliefs, and his major, the agents left al Rouki with a word of advice:
"You need to be more careful moving around with such things, sir."[3]

Tamal al Rouki's case illustrates the climate of vigilance and insecurity that has come to characterize American society in the wake of September 11, 2001, and subsequent terrorist attacks. To al Rouki's neighbor,
who for several weeks had been treated to nonstop media coverage of
the April 2013 Boston Marathon bombing, al Rouki's pressure cooker
was not an everyday piece of cookware: it was a weapon of mass destruc-
tion. Like the Neighborhood Watch volunteers who are instructed in
the visual semiotics of criminality, everyday Americans are thoroughly

coached in the semiotics of terror: typically unthreatening items—such as pressure cookers, automobiles,[4] lunchboxes,[5] and even toothpaste[6]—are reanimated through this new militaristic grid of intelligibility. Citizens learn how to interpret and respond to these threats from an array of authorities who remind them, in the words of former Homeland Security secretary Janet Napolitano: "Homeland security starts with hometown security, and we all have a role to play. Working together, we can all help secure our country. If you see something, say something. Always contact local law enforcement whenever you observe suspicious indicators or behaviors."[7]

While most surveillance research focuses on the post-9/11 moment—with good reason[8]—historical and comparative analyses help us ascertain what, if anything, is truly unique about citizen surveillance in the wake of September 11. Public figures routinely insist that the terrorist is a "new kind of enemy" that demands new rules of engagement.[9] However, many of this "new" enemy's essential features—and many methods of our civic response—have been promoted during previous "global" wars. This chapter focuses on one crucial element of this response, contextualizing lateral surveillance campaigns during the War on Terror within a genealogy of wartime civic mobilization strategies. Since at least World War One, the United States has repeatedly deployed a signature set of security initiatives based on the logics of total mobilization and global threat deterrence. While these have included propaganda drives aimed at urging citizens to buy war bonds, prepare food and water, provide clothes for needy soldiers, participate in emergency drills, and enter high-demand sectors of the workforce, they have also included campaigns designed to mobilize the population through suspicion, snitching, and lateral surveillance. In one "world war" after another, Americans have been reassured that they can protect the homefront by looking out for the spies, subversives, and extremists in their midst. Indeed, the Brown Scares, the Red Scares, and the "Terrorist Scare" have all included a common set of homeland security strategies: first, the rhetorical production of ambiguous and potentially omnipresent enemies,[10] and second, cultural programming that promotes seeing/saying as an essential means of protecting the homeland.

In previous chapters, this book has focused on how lateral surveillance programs have allowed American citizens to be governed through crime.[11] Discourses of crime are articulated with discourses of civic responsibility, empowering citizens to take local action against these threats through seeing, saying, and other patriotic duties. However, while Americans today are still governed through crime, they have also found themselves governed through terrorism.[12] Perhaps the most important difference between these two strategies can be seen in the discourses of terror: whereas crime has had more or less intelligible signifiers, terrorism is *by definition* looming, spontaneous, and aimed toward the targeting and disruption of everyday life. Because terrorists can be foreign-born or "homegrown," because terrorism can strike anywhere and anytime, and because its traditional weapons are typically harmless, ordinary items—such as trucks, airplanes, and pressure cookers—terrorism cannot be easily translated into coherent local discourses of risk, responsibility, and prevention.[13] Thus as with previous wartime "scares," the DHS and its allies mobilize citizens against the softly ubiquitous terrorist threat by circulating ambiguous rhetorics of terrorism: as Jacqueline Best puts it, those who govern through terrorism must "govern through ambiguity."[14]

Given the ambiguous signs of terrorism that circulate among the public, the intelligence value of lateral surveillance is more dubious than ever. As investigative journalist Brian Palmer observes, the sheer amount of antiterrorism tips received each year—which number in the millions—prevents law enforcement agencies from processing and synthesizing them in any meaningful way.[15] As citizens are encouraged to report innocuous everyday activities that under typical circumstances could never be considered threats—e.g., a college student walking through an apartment complex with a pressure cooker—these tips provide very little in the way of actionable intelligence. As Laura K. Donahue has argued about programs like the "If You See Something, Say Something" initiative: "While at one extreme, some of these [programs] help spread suspicion throughout the fabric of social life, at the other, many of them appear to have little real impact on terrorism."[16] Donohue is undoubtedly right on both accounts: while these public initiatives have had little success in deterring terrorism, participation statistics suggest that they are highly successful at getting Americans to take an active role in the War on Terror by seeing and saying. These programs, however, have elicited a vocal backlash from a broad cross-section of the public; and, of course, new and creative forms of autonomous citizen engagement have risen to the surface. Hacker collectives, whistleblowers, and other explicitly faceless seeing/saying resistance groups are using methods of anonymous enemyship to level blows against the security apparatus. So while DHS and its allies circulate specters of the ambiguous terrorist throughout the public, unidentifiable enemies of a different kind are posing legitimate threats to the state's ability to keep its secrets.

Global Wars and the Ubiquitous Enemy

When Armand Mattelart observed the anxious efforts of the United States to mobilize its population against the emerging terrorist threat, he was reminded of the national security theory of twentieth-century Brazilian general Golbery do Couto e Silva. Describing General Golbery's national security doctrine, which was highly influential following Brazil's 1964 military coup, Mattelart discusses how the new authoritarian state strove to cultivate its subjects in the everyday life of total war. According to Mattelart, these efforts sought to mobilize the populace through collective struggle: "It was a total strategy because it concerned individuals in all parts of the country, of every race, age, profession, and belief. It erased the longstanding distinction between civilian and military, between interior (homeland) and exterior. It was total because the fronts on which the struggle took place and the weapons it used belonged to every level of individual and collective life and penetrated all its interstices."[17] As Mattelart points out, the Brazilian social order was entirely renovated by the logics of total war—the population was formed into a mobile citizen army, blurring the bounds between peace time and war time, and between peace space and war space. Mattelart observes that, in General Golbery's grand civic mobilization, "The weapons were of all types. . . . Total war demanded a total response. To meet this requirement, it was necessary to mobilize the lifeblood of the nation, incorporating into the struggle the potential that Golbery called 'national power': all the physical and human resources available to each country, all of its spiritual and material capability and the whole of its economic, political, psycho-social, and military resources."[18] Analyzing this generalized state of war, Mattelart adopts the conceptual vocabulary of Carl Schmitt to argue that we are today witnessing a "'total mobilization' within the framework of 'state pedagogy.' . . . All these political, economic, cultural, and military efforts demanded that the entire population, who were all subject to the same dangers, agree to the same sacrifices."[19]

During the Global War on Terror, certain elements of this total mobilization have become familiar to citizens of the West. Yet these tactics of total mobilization have emerged under a largely liberal guise. While many local, state, and especially federal police agencies have been transformed by military tactics and technologies, the U.S. population itself has escaped the authoritarian mobilization strategies of universal conscription and compulsory military training. Rather, a uniquely liberal brand of total mobilization has surfaced under the guidance of cultural technologies that urge good citizens to do their part in the domestic war effort. A key element of this cultural strategy has been the construction of what Jordan Crandall calls "a productive economy of fear: the fear of an omnipresent enemy who could be anywhere, strike at any time and who in fact could be 'among us.' . . . It's a powerful rhetorical frame and machine of . . . indoctrination and recruitment."[20] Indeed, this economy of soft, omnipresent anxiety has proven effective at recruiting citizens to take an active, seeing/saying role in the security apparatus.

And this productive economy of fear is not unique to the Global War on Terror. Similar mobilization techniques can be seen at a number of points during the twentieth century: during World War One, for example, the production of unidentifiable domestic enemies played an important role in recruiting and deploying lateral surveillance crews like the Boy Spies of America and the American Protective League. Their target: German spies. Even before America had officially entered the war, German agents had infiltrated American industry and intelligence networks. Seeking to crack the façade of American neutrality, in July 1916 a crew of these German agents in New York Harbor detonated more than a half-ton of ammunition scheduled for delivery to Great Britain. Although the "Black Tom" attack killed only five people, it fueled the establishment of a domestic spy apparatus as well as a propaganda campaign that gave rise to America's first Brown Scare. Not long after the attack, in 1917 U.S. attorney general Timothy Gregory bragged: "I have today several hundred thousand private citizens—some as individuals, most of them as members of patriotic bodies, engaged in . . . assisting the heavily overworked Federal authorities in keeping an eye on disloyal individuals and making reports of disloyal utterances."[21] For the attorney general and other federal authorities, an important element of civil defense was the cultivation of seeing/saying subjects on the homefront.

To aid these efforts, the Committee on Public Information (CPI) and its allies built a propaganda campaign directed toward encouraging surveillance and building vigilance among the general public. For example, the New Hampshire Committee on Public Safety used familiar seeing/saying rhetoric to urge citizens to adopt "promptness in recognizing and reporting suspicious or disloyal actions to your local authorities or to us."[22] The nature of the German enemy during World War One, however, struck American propagandists with a unique opportunity: unlike Native Americans and Chicanos during the frontier wars—and unlike Turks and America's other enemies of color during the world war—the German spy was often presented as a deracialized, "unidentifiable"[23] enemy that could circulate unnoticed throughout the European American public. According to Celia Kingsbury, the emergence of this ubiquitous, unidentifiable enemy during World War One fueled a "paranoid" culture of lateral surveillance: "the ensuing paranoia pertaining to the ubiquity and evil of the enemy undoubtedly paved the way for the Orwellian impulse to spy."[24] Capitalizing on the specter of the unidentifiable enemy, American propagandists used posters, public address, films like *The Claws of the Hun* and *The Kaiser's Shadow*, and other propaganda technologies to sustain an atmosphere of suspicion, mistrust, and lateral surveillance. In fact, the frame of the unidentifiable enemy has proven so familiar to twenty-first-century Americans that Howard Blum recently referred to these German spies as "the first terrorist cell in America."[25]

While American infantrymen overseas were outfitted with rifles and bayonets, Americans back home were being equipped to carry out the right kinds of seeing/saying civic duty. Teaching citizens how to discipline their speech, domestic propaganda posters warned that because German spies could be anywhere, citizens should refrain from speaking about potentially sensitive matters in public. One poster, featuring a lurid sketch of Kaiser Wilhelm's head on a spider's body, instructed citizens: "Don't talk. The web is spun for you with invisible threads. Keep out of it. Help destroy it. . . . Ask yourself if what you were about to say might help the enemy. Spies are listening." Absent from this poster, of course, are any identifiable signs or characteristics of the spy—all the audience knows is that the spy is out there, "listening," trying to draw careless Americans into its invisible web. This poster, and many others like it, illustrate two of the main themes of domestic propaganda during World War One: (1) that the Germans had brought the war to American shores—and hence, that everyday Americans were being forced into auxiliary combat roles, and (2) that the enemy's *modus operandi* was clandestine and pervasive infiltration.

As the war progressed, speeches and other forms of public address also brought this message to the American people. In 1917, the CPI organized a band of several million propaganda orators known as the Four Minute Men. Focusing mainly on theatergoers and other captive audiences, the Four Minute Men drummed up support for the war and "urged Americans to keep track of one another and report on suspect utterances."[26] In October 1917, a contingent of Four Minute Men gave a speech warning about the German spies in their midst: "Ladies and gentlemen: I have just received the information that there is a German spy among us—a Germany spy watching *us*. He is around, here somewhere, reporting upon you and me—sending reports about us to Berlin. . . . From every section of the country these spies have been getting reports over to Potsdam. . . . Do not let the German spy hear and report that you are a slacker."[27] In this and similar four-minute speeches, American propagandists instructed their fellow citizens to closely guard their conversations from the domestic enemy. Rather than teach citizens about the typical characteristics of the spies in their midst, this propaganda suggested that Americans should modify their behavior at all times in order to safeguard the homeland from German subversion. As with the Kaiser Wilhelm "spider" poster, the Four Minute Men instructed Americans that the spy was "around," "somewhere," in "every section of the country." Embedded within this reminder that the spy is everywhere, of course, is the implication that responsible wartime citizenship requires its own brand of vigilant spy-work.

This cultivation of the citizen-spy was recycled during World War Two, when U.S. propaganda incessantly warned Americans to beware of German infiltration. The propaganda campaigns associated with domestic Operations Security (OPSEC), in particular, fueled the preemp-

Figure 5.1. A U.S. propaganda poster warns Americans of Kaiser Wilhelm's "invisible threads."

tive logic of the pervasive, unidentifiable enemy. As a domestic branch of intelligence security, OPSEC aimed to prevent America's enemies from obtaining information about the nation's military strategy, critical infrastructure, and security vulnerabilities. During the war, OPSEC's propaganda efforts centered on communications security campaigns like the "Silence Means Security" program.[28] Some of these propaganda technologies promoted citizen surveillance, such as an Office of War Information poster that urged: "Listen! The Enemy May Be Talking. Don't Talk! The Enemy May Be Listening!" Most anti-Axis propaganda, however, was less explicit in its calls for lateral surveillance. In fact, in an interesting twist on the "see something, say something" motif, a majority of these campaigns promoted information security through *silence*. The social implications, however, remained the same: because spies could be anywhere, citizens should always be vigilant about the strangers—and even friends—in their midst. Reminding citizens that they were on the frontlines of a covert battle, the "Silence Means Security" program released propaganda posters with messages such as "Loose Lips Might Sink Ships!" (with a sinking battle ship), "He's Watching You" (with an eerie set of eyes peering from beneath a soldier's helmet), "Closed for the Duration—Loose Talk Can Cost Lives" (with a man's mouth taped shut), "Award: For Careless Talk" (with a hand holding a swastika-adorned military medal), and "A Careless Word . . . Another Cross" (with a white cross sitting atop a soldier's grave).[29] Coupled with state propaganda films like *Why We Fight*, as well as fictional films like *Confessions of a Nazi Spy*,[30] these state efforts brought the war into the homeland by recruiting citizens to fight the enemy in their everyday lives.

When the U.S. government and its corporate allies rekindled the national propaganda apparatus during the Cold War, the "Silence Means Security" campaign regained prominence. One poster, which instructed citizens "How and What to Tell a Communist," informed readers that because Communist subversion is in essence deceptive, it is impossible to glean reliable signs of the Red spy: "Don't look for physical differences when you try to spot a Communist. Communists are all kinds of people in all walks of life and of all races."[31] Indeed, this theme reverberated throughout the early years of the Cold War, when national figures like J. Edgar Hoover and Joseph McCarthy hammered the "spy craze"[32] into the depths of the American political imagination. In 1950, for ex-

Figure 5.2. An American World War Two propaganda poster. See "Powers of Persuasion—Poster Art of World War II," *National Archives*, http://www.archives.gov/ education/lessons.

ample, a Department of Defense propaganda outfit called the Armed Forces Information Films released a short film entitled *Recognizing a Communist*, which warned: "When recognizing a Communist, physical appearance means nothing. . . . There are [many] Communists who don't share their real faces, who work more silently."[33] While this propaganda of the "silent" and unspecifiable enemy encouraged citizens to be cautious and vigilant, it also warned them that they could not afford to read at the level of the sign when it came to enemy detection.[34] Presaging the contemporary genre of "securitainment,"[35] Cold War–era popular entertainment taught Americans the importance of being on guard against the invisible Red enemy. For example, the English-language spy film genre exploded in the 1960s, with the rise of pop culture staples like *I Led Three Lives, Mission: Impossible, The Spy Who Came in from the Cold*, and the James Bond franchise. Films like *I Married a Communist* went so far as to teach domestic Cold Warriors that Communist subterfuge is sometimes so good that one can be married to a Communist without even knowing it. As Michael Kackman has argued, "Spies were everywhere in 1950s American media culture. . . . Books, magazines, film, radio, and television were filled with the exploits of secret agents, real and imagined. . . . The Red Scare of the late 1940s and early 1950s insisted that Communist spies lurked behind every curtained window and at the corners of every film set, as Senator Joseph McCarthy and the House of Un-American Activities Committee proclaimed that a vast Communist conspiracy threatened to undo American democracy."[36] A fixture of state propaganda and corporate entertainment, the Communist spy reminded citizens that the Cold War was, after all, a *war*, and that the enemy had reached our shores.

While it is difficult to know the direct effect these campaigns had on the public, it is undeniable that America's domestic propaganda efforts fueled a climate of often hysterical suspicion. This climate allowed authorities to repeatedly invoke the Espionage Act of 1917 to persecute German Americans during the world wars, and then alleged "Communist spies" in the 1940s and 1950s.[37] Anti-German rioting and violence was rampant in American cities during World War One, and thousands of German Americans were held in internment camps during World War Two. The Cold War, of course, cast a shadow across much of American society, prompting diverse programs designed to ferret out and marginalize the unidentifiable Communist menace. When citizens refused to join the fight, the federal government often turned to the judicial system to enforce compliance with this regime of domestic mobilization. In an interesting twist on seeing/saying citizenship, federal authorities used the interrogation chamber and the courtroom to manipulate spies and dissidents into marginalizing and denouncing the state's own internal enemies. By compelling spies to speak the truth of their crimes—as well as the alleged crimes of others—the authorities cultivated a form of speaking subjectivity that gave legitimacy to their homeland defense campaigns. Spy "rings" were prosecuted, and their agents convicted, based on the sworn testimony of double agents, co-conspirators, and faithful citizens who were serving their country by seeing something and saying something.

While these methods resulted in the breakup of sabotage operations like the Duquesne Spy Ring and Operation Pastorius during World War Two, perhaps the most interesting and best-known campaign to cultivate this speaking subjectivity was directed at American citizens during the second Red Scare in the 1940s and 1950s. When dozens of film professionals received subpoenas to appear before the House Committee on Un-American Activities in 1947, nineteen declared that they would not cooperate. Eleven of these dissenters were summoned before the committee, ten of whom—the now celebrated "Hollywood Ten"—refused to testify and invoked the First Amendment. The eleventh, eminent German playwright Bertolt Brecht, also resisted the demands on his seeing/saying subjectivity: although he agreed to testify, Brecht made a mockery of the proceedings. When he tried to read a prepared statement before the committee, he was refused—the committee hoped to use the interrogational format to maintain tight control over the content of Brecht's testimony. So throughout his half-hour appearance, he redirected, made jokes, and sent the audience into repeated bouts of laughter. Along with his comrades in the Hollywood Ten—who used silence to short-circuit the state's witch hunt against its domestic enemies—Brecht demonstrated how activists and radicals can manipulate these mechanisms of seeing/saying citizenship.[38] Yet of course, while Brecht was able to safely flee to Germany, the Hollywood Ten were forced into professional exile in the United States. And while their courageous silence dissuaded the court from filing criminal charges, their refusal to speak also fueled further campaigns to expose the unidentifiable Red menace that was busy subverting the nation's government and mass media. While some of these campaigns explicitly asked citizens to see something and say something, many simply promoted a general climate of social suspicion that fostered lateral surveillance. Perhaps these efforts' most remarkable (and, as we will see, reproducible) feature, however, was bringing a murky, omnipresent enemy into the social reality of the American public.

Domestic Terror and "Invisible Enemies"

In the eyes of authority—and maybe rightly so—nothing
looks more like a terrorist than the ordinary man.
—Giorgio Agamben[39]

Almost immediately after the Cold War, American politicians, propagandists, and their allies brought the battle back to the homeland. Dusting off a discourse that had dissipated since the 1960s, in the 1990s "terrorist" replaced "spy" as the unidentifiable enemy *du jour*. Occasional outbursts of "domestic extremism" fueled panics about the terrorists among us—especially in the wake of the Oklahoma City bombing, when countless commentators fretted about the emergence of blue-eyed, All-American terrorists like Timothy McVeigh.[40] The media response to the Oklahoma City bombing, of course, hardly had the effect of marginalizing young white men in the United States, as we had seen with previous wartime persecutions of German Americans, Japanese Americans, and citizens of the left; it did, however, rekindle the discourse of the unidentifiable enemy (or, as Daniel Levitas put it, "the terrorist next door").[41]

Of course, this legacy of "radical ambiguity"[42] found its most pernicious expression after the September 11 attacks. Solidifying the homeland's role in the Global War on Terror, in June 2002 President George W. Bush proposed the establishment of the Department of Homeland Security. According to Bush, this massive overhaul of the federal government—which he boasted would be "the most significant transformation of the U.S. government in over a half-century"[43]—was necessary to combat new threats against the homeland: "The changing nature of the threats facing America requires a new government structure to protect against invisible enemies that can strike with a wide variety of weapons."[44] While Bush's rhetoric of the "invisible enemy" wasn't new, his transformation of the federal government was truly historic: since its founding in 2003, the Department of Homeland Security (DHS) has become the nation's third-largest Cabinet department. With more than 240,000 employees and an annual budget of more than sixty billion dollars, the DHS has slowly engulfed more than twenty other federal agencies, including the Immigration and Naturalization Service, the Federal Emergency Management Agency, the Transportation Security Administration, the U.S. Coast Guard, and the U.S. Customs Service. The consolidation of these agencies under the banner of the DHS—which was founded to fight the enemies in our midst—contributed to a militarization of the homeland not seen since the previous world wars.

Under the George W. Bush administration, these rhetorics of the invisible enemy fueled the hasty development of lateral surveillance programs and intelligence analysis systems designed to process citizens' tips. In the summer of 2002, Bush launched Operation TIPS (Terrorism Information and Prevention System), in which American professionals with routine access to others' homes—such as cable installers and delivery personnel—were instructed to be on the lookout for the symptoms of terrorist activity. Soon after the TIPS program was initiated, Vermont senator Patrick Leahy condemned it as "a nationwide program giving millions of American truckers, letter carriers, train conductors, ship captains, utility employees, and others a formal way to report suspicious terrorist activity. . . . Nor would this program start small: the Administration planned a pilot program that along would have enlisted one million Americans."[45] While Operation TIPS lived a short life as the Homeland Security Act was debated and revised, it was eventually killed by a bipartisan congressional coalition led by Republican Dick Armey, the House majority leader, who insisted: "Citizens will not become informants. Citizens will not be spying on one another."[46] Thus when the Homeland Security Act was passed in late 2002, the Operation TIPS provision was stricken and the program—which called for the development of a nationwide system of federally trained citizen-spies—died in its infancy.[47]

Over the course of the next decade, however, Americans would see the rapid rise and fall of several other domestic surveillance initiatives. In 2003, the Total Information Awareness program—whose Orwellian name was quickly softened to *Terrorist* Information Awareness—gathered indiscriminate data about citizens' drug prescriptions, credit card purchases, emails, bank deposits, plane travel, academic grades, and online habits. DARPA's LifeLog program, also begun in 2003, used pervasive technical surveillance to create profiles of citizens and their associates, as did the ADVISE system (Analysis, Dissemination, Visualization, Insight, and Semantic Environment) until its official demise in 2007.[48] Although these programs were formally short-lived, Edward Snowden's 2013 leaks demonstrate that their methods continued more or less unabated under the aegis of the National Security Agency (NSA) throughout the Bush and Obama presidencies. These programs, of course, relied in part on citizen intelligence initiatives that demanded lateral surveillance from the public. The TALON (Threat and Local Observation Notice) system, for example, emerged in 2003 as part of a Department of Defense initiative to "capture non-validated domestic threat information, flow that information to analysts, and incorporate it into the DoD terrorism threat warning process."[49] According to a leaked classified memorandum issued in May 2003 by then deputy defense secretary Paul Wolfowitz, a TALON report "consists of raw information reported by concerned citizens and military members regarding suspicious incidents."[50] These reports, produced by civilians or military personnel, were directed into the Counterintelligence Field Activity agency (CIFA), a massive Department of Defense intelligence analysis program whose budget and size remain classified. Like TALON, an allied DoD program, the Air Force's post-9/11 Eagle Eyes initiative was created to serve as "the Department of Defense's 'Neighborhood Watch' program."[51] The still-extant program, which urges civilians and DoD employees to "Watch. Report. Protect," has promoted a familiar range of seeing/saying activities in the fight against terror. In 2003 a DoD spokesperson, Sergeant First Class Doug Sample, encouraged citizens to be vigilant in reporting suspicious activities as part of the fledgling Eagle Eyes program: "You don't know it's innocent until you report it. . . . We're much less concerned about too much reporting than too little. When lives are at stake, it's better to be safe than sorry."[52] These reports would be filed alongside other surveillance data, allowing security officials to discover patterns, build profiles, and eventually share this intelligence with other agencies.

In 2006, future Obama advisor Stephen E. Flynn and a colleague of his in the Department of Defense, Daniel B. Prieto, argued that citizen mobilization schemes like TIPS, TALON, and Eagle Eyes were essential to tackling the problem of terror in the twenty-first century. In fact, Flynn and Prieto's frame of intelligibility relies on a historical analogy of wartime civic mobilization: "In the fifth year of this long war, the nation's state of preparedness should be much higher. It is long past the time when we truly engage our private industry and private citizens in this struggle. In his first budget message after 9/11, President George W. Bush reminded the nation that not since World War II have our values and our way of life been so threatened. But in that war that ended half a century ago, it was not just the military that was called upon to fight."[53] In the shadow of World War Two, they argued, the state called on all citizens to take action. Today we should all follow this sense of shared responsibility, Flynn and Prieto argued, by reforming our lives in order to contribute to the war effort: "Gray-haired executives traded in pinstripe suits for uniforms to organize our defenses at home; factories stopped making cars and started making weapons and munitions; and mothers left their children in the care of neighbors and relatives so that they could work the assembly lines."[54] During the war against the Axis powers, everyone played a part by getting active in the fight. No effort was too small or too insignificant—the important thing was that the population got actively involved. This collective mobilization, Flynn and Prieto argued, drew the nation together during its time of war and crisis. Thus our victory in World War Two, they maintained, can teach us a model of citizenship based in collective mobilization against the terrorist threat: "As a nation, we were forever changed by the experience [of World War Two]. Recognizing this parallel, the president has called homeland security 'our new national calling.' Sadly, national efforts to date on homeland security are nowhere near the kind of effort this nation can produce when called to service."[55] Flynn and Prieto argued that, just as our homefront mobilization helped us triumph during the World War Two, we are at risk of losing the War on Terror because we have yet to develop effective strategies for mobilizing the domestic population against its enemies. Judging from the massive opposition to the Bush administration's lateral surveillance campaigns that emerged in 2002 and 2003, there appears to be a kernel of truth in Flynn and Prieto's critiques.

While the administration used programs like TIPS, TALON, and Eagle Eyes to fill the intelligence databases of defense and security agencies, public outrage prevented lateral surveillance programs from becoming a prominent intelligence fixture during the Bush era: TALON and Eagle Eyes remained mostly confined to the Department of Defense, and Operation TIPS was quickly shut down by civil libertarians in Congress. While citizens still registered antiterror tips with local and federal authorities, the Bush administration never developed a robust, nationwide seeing/saying campaign that integrated citizens into the war effort.

Yet after more than eight years of war, the civil libertarians were finally defeated when President Obama's Department of Homeland Security launched its ambitious "If You See Something, Say Something" program. Modeled on the New York City Metropolitan Transportation Authority campaign of the same name, the "If You See Something, Say Something" initiative stressed the "invisible enemy" theme touted nearly ten years earlier in the Bush administration's Homeland Security Act. Launched in July 2010, the federal "If You See Something, Say Something" program was founded as "a national campaign that raises public awareness of the indicators of terrorism and terrorism-related crime, as well as the importance of reporting suspicious activity to state and local law enforcement."[56] The program has become so successful, in part, because of its partnerships with the private sector and local law enforcement agencies. These DHS partners help the campaign distribute its message throughout the country at retail stores, sports stadiums, music venues, and transportation centers.

Upon its launch in 2010, the "If You See Something, Say Something" campaign produced a series of propaganda posters and videos aimed at teaching the American public how to respond to suspicious activities. The pedagogical voice narrating the initiative's major 2011 propaganda film begins by encouraging citizens to report activities that exceed their faculties of interpretation: "It's not easy to put all the pieces [of a terrorist threat] together, and we don't expect you to. That's the job of law enforcement and intelligence analysts. But homeland security is a shared effort and responsibility for each of us. When you see things that just don't seem right, that seem somehow out of the ordinary, reporting what you've observed can be invaluable to the work of law enforcement and intelligence analysts in this shared effort. Acts of terrorism against the United States can be large or small."[57] Citizens are thus encouraged to report "unusual" activities—of whatever scale—that defy their expectations of the ordinary. Illustrating a number of these ostensibly unusual, terrorist-signifying activities, the video presents a European American man who appears to be in his late teens recording video under an overpass. The narrator informs viewers that, "before they strike, many terrorists watch and study their targets." He then lists a number of supposedly suspicious situations that warrant contacting authorities—warning that terrorists "gather information," the scene shifts to an outdoor café, where a young, blonde European American woman is speaking to a cop. According to the video, potential terrorists also "test security" (a middle-aged African American man in a red sweatshirt leaves something in his pocket as he goes through airport security); "acquire funds and supplies, often through criminal activities" (two white vans are parked next to each other, as two men transfer barely visible items between the vans); and "rehearse their plans" (a middle-aged European American woman leaves her purse under a bench in a bus station). After this lesson in the semiotics of terror, the narrator instructs the viewer, "Any of what we call these 'precursor activities' might be observable and reportable by a vigilant member of the public. You are in the best position to spot these precursor activities as you go about your everyday activities in your community." Operating on this preemptive security logic, virtually anything can be a "precursor" to terrorist acts—as the video shows, taking photographs and speaking with cops can be precursor activities; and now, since the 2013 Boston Marathon attacks, walking across a college apartment complex with a pressure cooker has become a precursor activity that warrants the scrutiny of "vigilant members of the public." The video then reminds us of the preemptive logic that governs antiterrorist outreach strategy. After fostering ambiguity under the guise of a boilerplate anti-discrimination statement, the narrator instructs the viewer how to respond to suspicious activities: "It's important to carefully consider what you observe. Reporting suspicious activity should not be based on a person's race, religion, or gender, but rather on behaviors that seem suspicious. . . . So if you see something that just isn't right, report your observations to your state or local authorities."[58] Although this statement is the sort of bland, patronizing fare that one would expect from a federal outreach campaign, it is part and parcel of a recurrent wartime rhetorical strategy that governs the population by circulating ambiguous, unidentifiable threats.

Suspicious Activity Reports in the Obama Era

Condemning the role of this unidentifiable threat in Obama's surveillance programs, the American Civil Liberties Union (ACLU) has observed that in the War on Terror "everyone—our neighbors, public employees, storekeepers, local police—are encouraged to help spy on us."[59] Recognizing these ambiguous signs of terror, many seeing/saying Americans have produced mountains of tips that illustrate just how deep social suspicion runs in the national security era. Antiterrorism agencies in the U.S. receive between eight and ten thousand tips per day from seeing/saying citizens. These tips include information about forty alleged terrorist plots—*every single day*.[60] In 2013, when the ACLU procured a number of suspicious activity reports (SARs) from the Los Angeles Joint Regional Intelligence Center, they found that the reports were overwhelmingly useless for—if not counterproductive to—the gathering of antiterrorist intelligence. Some of the more interesting examples include:

- "Female subject taking photos of Folsom Office."
- "Suspicious ME [Middle Eastern] males buy several large pallets of water . . ."
- "An identified subject was reported to be taking photographs of a bridge crossing the American River Bike Trail."
- "I observed a male nonchalantly taking numerous pictures inside a purple line train [in Los Angeles County]. . . . The male said he was taking pictures because they were going to film the television show 24 on the train next week."
- "The words 'Tax Government' were found painted on the roadway on the Sacramento International Airport Perimeter . . ."
- "Reporting party received an e-mail that describes a scheduled protest by an unknown number of individuals on July 7, 2012. The information indicates the protestors are concerned about the use of excessive force by law enforcement officers."

- ". . . a female subject taking pictures of the outside of the post office in Folsom on Riley Street [in Sacramento] this morning. The female departed as a passenter [*sic*] in a silver Mazda 5."
- "A suspicious subject . . . at the Sacramento Amtrak station . . . was wearing Army fatigues and was acting suspicious."
- ". . . a cell search was conducted on [an unnamed prison inmate]. A search of the cell found a copy of the book titled *Blood in My Eye* by George L. Jackson. This book is considered contraband . . ." (This SAR was filed under "Inmate Radicalization.")
- "A private citizen reported an identified subject who requests a change of units often and asks frequently about security at the storage facility."
- "I was called out to the above address regarding a male who was taking photographs of the [name of facility blacked out] [in Commerce, California]. The male stated, he is an artist and enjoys photographing building[s] in industrial areas . . . [and] stated he is a professor at San Diego State private college, and takes the photos for his art class."

And finally, a sergeant from the Elk Grove Police Department reported "a suspicious individual in his neighborhood"; according to Intelligence Center records, the sergeant had "long been concerned about a residence in his neighborhood occupied by a Middle Eastern male adult physician who is very unfriendly."[61] Judging from these representative examples, it is no surprise that the ACLU concludes that the Nationwide Suspicious Activity Reporting Initiative database has never helped thwart a single terrorist attack.[62]

This small sampling of citizen intelligence suggests that, while certain practices (photography, for example) and types of individuals (Middle Eastern and Asian males, as well as men dressed in military attire) attract special attention, since 9/11 there has been a radical diffusion of what constitutes suspicious activity. In the words of civil liberties attorney Julia Harumi Mass, "With such a broad and vague standard, no wonder we are seeing innocent activities reported as 'suspicious,' especially when they involve community groups against whom we still see significant governmental bias."[63] This "broad and vague" rhetoric routinely infects the discourse of the Obama administration, whose officials have recycled earlier tropes of the looming, unidentifiable threat of the internal enemy. In 2010, Obama's first attorney general, Eric Holder, sol-

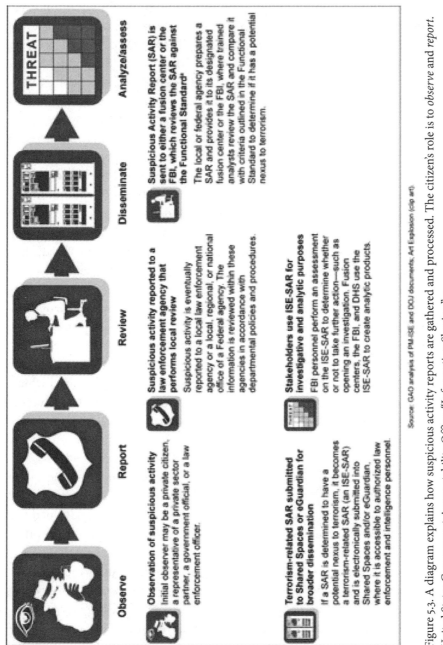

Figure 5.3. A diagram explains how suspicious activity reports are gathered and processed. The citizen's role is to *observe* and *report*. United States Government Accountability Office, "Information Sharing," 7.

emnly warned the American public "to be prepared for potentially bad news. . . . What I'm trying to do is to make people aware of the fact that the threat is real, the threat is different, the threat is constant."[64] Trying to characterize this "different" terrorism of today, Holder argues that we must turn our attention to our neighbors, colleagues, and other American citizens. The ambiguity of the terrorist threat, Holder sighed, is "one of the things that keeps me up at night. . . . You didn't worry about this even two years ago—about individuals, about Americans, to the extent that we now do. . . . The threat has changed from simply worrying about foreigners coming here, to worrying about people in the United States, American citizens—raised here, born here, and who for whatever reason have decided that they are going to become radicalized and take up arms against the nation in which they were born."[65] The War on Terror, therefore, is a war on an enemy that has an average face, an average job, and an average bourgeois lifestyle. Unfortunately, Holder is not the only American that is kept up at night worrying about citizen-terrorists. As the proliferation of antiterrorism tips suggest, terrifying visions of water pallets, army fatigues, and "female photographers" have apparently disturbed a distressing portion of Holder's constituency.

With such ambiguous signs of terror, the terrorist threat takes on a form that can potentially infect any public or private space (and which, therefore, could potentially impact any citizen at anytime). As the lines of the global battlefield have been blurred, homeland security thus demands the sacrifice and mobilization of the whole society. As Janet Napolitano argued in her 2011 State of America's Homeland Security Address, "The kinds of threats we now face demonstrate that our homeland security is a shared responsibility. Only a 'whole of nation approach' will bring us to the level of security and resilience we require."[66] Napolitano framed this state of exception in the rhetoric of collective mobilization—as she put it, a "whole of nation approach." Drawing on familiar neoliberal rhetorics of citizen responsibility and security through personal initiative, Napolitano argued that the federal government is powerless to ensure security on its own: "our approach has acknowledged that the Department of Homeland Security—indeed, the whole federal government and the military—cannot, itself, deliver security. Real security requires the engagement of our entire society, with government, law enforcement, the private sector, and the public all playing their respective roles. . . . Let us strive for more partnerships; a bigger team; and an even greater willingness from our citizens to share responsibility for our collective security."[67] Although Napolitano's "whole of nation" approach is an unachievable ideal, it informs the security apparatus's production of ubiquitous enemies as well as its programs of community response. So while we have an ever-greater number of U.S. citizens submitting tips and registering suspicion about terrorism, their collective participation in the homeland security apparatus serves a broader sociopolitical function than simple intelligence gathering. It is not especially important, therefore, that these citizens generate millions of paranoid and bogus tips every year. What is crucial, however, is that these citizens get active in the war effort. That is why, as Lyn Hinds and Peter Grabosky argue, "the targets of the state's responsibilization strategy are you and I. Its objective is transformative: to encourage us to change the everyday, normal pattern/s of our lives."[68] What counts most, in other words, is that the social patterns of our lives are transformed and retrained—that we learn to act out the raw habits of seeing and saying that comprise the citizen's predominant duties in the War on Terror.

See Something, Say Something Reborn

When Obama's second Homeland Security secretary, Jeh Johnson, relaunched the "If You See Something, Say Something" campaign in January 2015, he regrounded this civic mobilization in disciplined practices of surveillance and communication. With a revamped online and social media presence, the "If You See Something, Say Something" program provides its corporate "partners" and the general public with a host of public service announcements, fliers, and other promotional materials. With Johnson's energetic promotion of the program, "If You See Something, Say Something" has expanded to more than nine thousand federal, state, and local government buildings, and has partnered with the National Football League, Major League Soccer, Major League Baseball, National Basketball Association, National Collegiate Athletic Association, National Hockey League, NASCAR, U.S. Golf Association, and U.S. Tennis Association. Johnson boasts, in fact, that the program has become a routine feature of the Super Bowl, the NBA All-Star Game, and other major sporting events.[69] In the press release announcing the program's revival, Johnson remarked: "Public awareness, support, and participation in our homeland security efforts are essential. . . . As I've said before 'if you see something, say something' is more than just a slogan. Whether you are on the plains of Iowa, the streets of Manhattan, or a fan at the Super Bowl, we all play a role in keeping our neighborhoods and communities safe."[70]

Using the 2015 Super Bowl as the staging ground for the relaunched program, DHS plastered the Phoenix area with the "See Something, Say Something" message: billboards, magazines, visitor guides, posters at public transportation depots, telescreens at hotels, and even commercials on the video board during the game reminded citizens to be vigilant about suspicious activities. According to Johnson, these materials were designed to remind citizens that their civic duty calls for "recognizing" and "reporting": "The newly revamped materials highlight the individual role of everyday citizens to protect their neighbors and the communities they call home, by recognizing and reporting suspicious activity."[71] In the campaign's new outreach materials, some of these calls to recognize and report are peppered with stark appeals to collective sacrifice for homeland security. As a poster promoting citizen vigilance at the University of Michigan implores, "We must protect the community. Report suspicious activity."[72] Others use cartoonish outreach methods that appear to be designed for children, such as the mouse pad given out at 2014 Baltimore Ravens football games that featured a large, animated eye with a detective's hat and a magnifying glass.[73] A constant reminder to "Keep Your Good Eye Open: If You See Something, Say Something" now sits next to these lucky attendees' computer monitors.

The campaign's 2015 public service announcement, a ninety-second video entitled *Protect Your Every Day*, begins by scanning across a broad spectrum of Americans that represent diverse professions, ethnic groups, physical abilities, and genders. This promotional video, however, forwards a different representational politics than its 2011 predecessor. Just as the 2011 campaign shows a diverse assortment of characters carrying out "suspicious" activities, the 2015 video displays a similar diversity of Americans—yet in the new video these diverse citizens unite together through the common civic rituals of seeing and saying. The 2015 *Protect Your Every Day* film features a male African American firefighter, a female Asian American teacher, a European American male barber, a female "manager" in a wheel chair, a "mom" watching her kids at the park—these are the diverse Americans, the video argues, who should take their part in the antiterrorist apparatus. Despite this diversity, however, the video emphasizes: "We're all part of your community."[74]

Playing on the video's title, the audience is then shown a varied series of "everyday" environments that make up the collective American experience: morning walks, car engines starting, bus stops, and cups of coffee. Amid the whir of everyday life, however, sometimes things appear to be out of place: "There's always something unexpected. And honestly, that's fine. It's when you experience a moment of uncertainty. Something you know shouldn't be there. Or someone's behavior that doesn't seem quite right. These are the moments to take a pause. Because if something doesn't feel right, it's probably not." If we see something that just isn't "right," then it is our duty, as Americans, to say something. "It's not about paranoia. Or being afraid," the video reassures us: "It's about standing up and protecting our communities. One detail at a time. Because a lot of little details can become a pattern." While one's contribution might seem small, that "detail" becomes much more significant amid the collective intelligence of other vigilant, "everyday" Americans. Thus in the name of community protection, citizens are called on to collectively mobilize through seeing/saying action. As the video continues, the diverse characters appear on screen, in succession, to make a pledge of unity: "We. We. We. We trust our instincts. Just like you should. Because only you know what's not supposed to be in your every day. We all play a role in keeping our communities safe. So protect your every day. If you see something suspicious, say something local authorities." Despite the diversity of America—despite the broad range of ethnicities, genders, professions, abilities, and regions represented in the video— "we" are all united in a common civic sacrifice. This hypnotic emphasis on "we" forges a mythic union out of America's bustling pluralism: while we might be divided by class, sex, race, and ability in our "everyday" lives, we can overcome these divisions by joining together in the War on Terror.

Invisible Citizens, Invisible Agents

While the security apparatus asks us to join together and fight the invisible enemies in our midst, a number of domestic dissidents and resistance groups have learned how to profit from their own mixtures of invisibility, surveillance, and communicative action. The hacker collective Anonymous, for example, routinely monitors and publicizes the abuses of American intelligence and security agencies. As its name implies, invisible enemyship forms the essence of Anonymous's strategy: as a manifesto for one of Anonymous's affiliate hacking programs instructs, "Blend in. Get trusted. Trust no one. Own everyone. Disclose nothing. . . . Get in as anonymous. Leave with no trace."[75] Under the cover of this anonymity, in early 2012 Anonymous hackers crashed the websites of the FBI and the DHS for several hours, demonstrating to the security apparatus that terrorists are not the state's only invisible enemies. And this was not the first time that Anonymous had attacked the federal government. In 2011 and 2012, the group routinely released sensitive federal documents and attacked dozens of police websites as part of its #FuckFBIFriday, #ShootingSheriffsSaturday, and #MilitaryMeltdownMonday campaigns. During the same time period, Anonymous participated in Operation Anti-Security (or Operation Antisec), which targeted politicians and the security apparatuses of countries such as China, Brazil, and the United States. One especially interesting example is when hackers from Anonymous and Lulzsec (another high-profile hacking collective) attacked confidential files held by the Arizona Department of Public Safety. Angered by Arizona's borderland immigrant crackdowns, the hackers took the provocative step of publicizing the names, phone numbers, home addresses, passwords, and personal correspondence of several Arizona cops. In recent years, these efforts appear to have only escalated: police hacks have racked departments across the country, especially those where notorious brutality or police shooting cases had taken place. Following this lead, in February 2016 pro-Palestinian hackers spearheaded one of the largest police hacks in American history: in successive days, they released the names, titles, phone numbers, and email addresses of twenty thousand FBI employees and nine thousand Homeland Security personnel.[76] Disrupting the police's monopoly on systematic technological surveillance—as well as the police's monopoly over expected personal privacy—Lulzsec, Anonymous, and allied hackers often succeed in enforcing a regime of visibility upon a security apparatus that so often thrives on anonymity and the circulation of invisible enemies.

The security apparatus, however, is becoming quite adept at legally and culturally curbing the reach of these internal enemies. While Anonymous hackers like Jeremy Hammond have received stiff prison sentences, the Obama Administration has ruthlessly carried out what *The Nation* called an "unprecedented crackdown" on leakers, whistle-blowers, and other seeing/saying citizens.[77] One of the best-known examples of this crackdown is the persecution of Private First Class Chelsea Manning, the Army intelligence analyst and whistleblower who had received accolades such as the Global War on Terrorism Service Medal during her service in Iraq. Frustrated with the atrocities and corruption she saw as a soldier in the Global War on Terror, Manning supplied WikiLeaks with the notorious "Iraq War Logs"—a trove of several hundred thousand files that documented murder, backroom diplomatic deals, and other abuses by military brass and the political class. Although Manning initially operated as an invisible enemy embedded within the antiterrorism apparatus, a duplicitous confidant and fellow analyst named Adrian Lamo eventually informed the Army's counterintelligence authorities that Manning had been passing sensitive information to media outlets. Rather than protecting Manning as a whistleblower, the U.S. government court-martialed her, charging her with dozens of crimes including espionage, embezzlement, fraud, theft, and aiding the enemy (the last of which carried a potential death sentence). After Manning's conviction on twenty-one of the noncapital charges, the federal government issued a stark warning that her brand of seeing and saying would not be tolerated: Manning, who was twenty-six years old at the time, was given a thirty-five-year jail sentence. At sentencing, the prosecution had asked for an even heftier penalty for this internal enemy: "This court must send a message to any soldier contemplating stealing classified information."[78] This threatening "message," however, was accompanied by the emergence of additional surveillance technologies and security protocols in military intelligence centers: as an Obama administration memorandum instructed, "The recent irresponsible disclosure by WikiLeaks has resulted in significant damage to our national security. Any failure by agencies to safeguard classified information pursuant to relevant laws . . . is unacceptable and will not be tolerated."[79] In addition to a whole host of new oversight technologies, the military and security apparatus uses the law and its violence to regulate the seeing/saying habits of its agents.

Yet of course, whistleblowers like Chelsea Manning are not homeland security's only internal enemies. Facing invisible adversaries from within and without, the security and defense apparatus has begun to monitor and regulate its agents' standards of public visibility. When the Islamic State catapulted into the American popular imagination in mid-2014, antiterrorist agencies like the Pentagon Force Protection Agency responded to this new threat by urging military and security personnel to adopt the public guise of everyday bourgeois civilians. In a return to the tactics of World War One, agents were urged to "use OPSEC (Operations Security) at work and at home."[80] To guard against the surveillance of the terrorists next door, on October 24, 2014, the DoD gave its personnel a list of commands designed to help them blend in with other Americans. These commands included: "Remove any DoD/military/law enforcement decals or identifiers from clothing and vehicles • Vary your travel routes to and from work • *If You See Something, Say Something* . . . report suspicious activity • Be careful of information shared on social media (Twitter, Facebook, etc.) • Do not post anything on social media that affiliates you with DoD/the military or law enforcement • Do not post anything on social media opposing terrorist groups or organization."[81] While emphasizing the importance of "situational awareness" and lateral surveillance, the DoD memo also emphasized the importance of collective mobilization during this time of war: "It is important that you ensure all members of your family are made aware of this valuable information so they not only protect themselves, but also become an integral part of the overall community antiterrorism effort."[82] While these efforts might minimize terrorists' ability to identify security and defense agents, they also ensure that these agents—like the terrorists themselves—circulate unnoticed among civilians, diminishing citizens' capacity to identify them and thus place them on an appropriate plane of political intelligibility. Cops' and defense contractors' attempts to prevent rogue counter-surveillance tactics, therefore, give them an excuse to go invisible. Ironically, in doing so they adopt a social *modus vivendi* that is reminiscent of their terrorist enemies'.

In many cases, these tactics of invisibility have begun to blur the lines between terrorism and national security operations. As scholars like Amitava Kumar have demonstrated, many of these plots have been instigated and funded by undercover FBI agents and other partisans of the federal government.[83] Since September 11, 2001, almost fifty percent of the more than five hundred federal counterterrorism convictions have involved government infiltrators. As counterterrorism has become the FBI's top priority, its undercover ranks have swollen to over fifteen thousand—more than ten times their number in 1975.[84] Posing as businesspeople, welfare recipients, church and mosque members, doctors, ministers, protestors, Klansmen, and journalists, undercover FBI agents operate in a zone of indistinction in which they often find themselves fighting terrorism by creating terrorists that they can monitor and control. In nearly half of the FBI's counterterrorism cases, agents and their paid informants recruit "terrorists," fund plots, suggest targets, design and organize attacks, and often even procure weapons. Some of the best-known terror attacks of the past ten years, in fact, have been FBI sting operations: the 2006 "Liberty City Seven" plot against the Sears Tower in Chicago, the 2007 Kennedy Airport plot, the 2009 New York City Subway plot, the 2010 Washington Metro bombing plot, the 2010 Portland Christmas tree bombing plot, the 2012 Tampa Bay bombing plot, the 2015 Capitol bombing plot, and the 2015 Islamic State cell plot in Brooklyn were all instigated to varying degrees by federal informants and agents.[85] Describing how agents cultivate this predisposition to terrorism, a former federal prosecutor, David Raski, remarked: "You're not going to be able to go to a street corner and find somebody who's already blown something up. . . . [So the typical goal is not] to find somebody who's already engaged in terrorism but find somebody who would jump at the opportunity if a real terrorist showed up in town."[86] In other words, the FBI literally produces terrorists: they find impressionable subjects who are not "already engaged in terrorism," but through varying degrees of coaxing, cajoling, compensation, and compulsion can be persuaded to contribute to what they think will be an attack. But of course, these targets are never actually complicit in terrorism, because the "terrorist" event—which was closely monitored, controlled, and often even hatched by the security apparatus—was never going to be carried out.[87]

This domestic production of terrorists illustrates how traditional rules of engagement can be easily set aside during times of war. In an astonishing proportion of cases, federal agents produce the very terrorist enemies that remain invisible to the general population. While training the rest of us to see something and say something, the FBI and allied police agencies guide and provoke vulnerable subjects into creating the terrorized atmosphere from which the security apparatus draws its financial and political sustenance.

Conclusion: See, Say, Mobilize

We are the soldiers in this war to defend freedom. The real fight for freedom isn't a military struggle. It's a war to defend our free societies. All of us must fight in this war, or we will certainly lose.
—Neoconservative commentator Pamela Geller[88]

In September 2014, DHS Secretary Johnson dismissed the "police state" reputation of the American security apparatus by celebrating the liberal orientation of homeland security initiatives. According to Johnson, "In the name of national security, I can build you a perfectly safe city, but it will be a prison. I can build more fences, install more invasive screening devices, ask more intrusive questions, demand more answers, and make everybody suspicious of each other, but it will cost us who we are as a nation of people who respect the law, cherish privacy, freedom and fair play, celebrate our diversity, and who are not afraid."[89] Of course, there is a remarkable irony in Secretary Johnson's statement. While in its short existence the DHS has hardly made the U.S. a perfectly safe place, it has certainly overseen the construction of more security fences, the installation of terribly invasive screening and monitoring technologies, and the emergence of nationwide seeing/saying campaigns that make many citizens suspicious of one another (and many more citizens distrustful of the government and its increasingly juvenile, brazen propaganda). Johnson may be right, however, when he says that it has not "cost us who we are as a nation," because the foundations of this vigilance had been set long before September 11, 2001. This vigilance, indeed, runs deep into the fabric of who we are as a nation. Long before the emergence of naked body scanners and razor wire border fences, lateral surveillance programs were used to cultivate citizen-spies and foster identification between citizens and the state. Though we might agree that the DHS's current propaganda seems uniquely "Orwellian,"[90] it nevertheless corresponds to a political impulse that has often reared its head throughout American history.

As this book has demonstrated, these lateral surveillance initiatives are hardly new; yet the War on Terror's logics of total engagement have overhauled the traditional methods and rationalities of these programs. Because of the diffuseness of the terrorist threat, the call to spy on one's peers is always active.[91] Today's security discourses and citizen action programs cultivate a surveillance and snitching ethic that contributes not only to widespread suspicion and ambivalence among neighbors, but also to the insinuation of the techniques and mentalities of policing into citizens' everyday lives. "See Something, Say Something," therefore, is not just an isolated campaign by which Americans are being persuaded to watch one another; it is also a pithy statement of the domestic political demands of a society riven by rituals of preemptive security and "categorical" suspicion.[92] Because the post-9/11 Terrorist Scare has led to all people—such as the cookware-wielding Talal al Rouki, with whom we began this chapter—being declared potential walking/driving/flying/cooking bombs, this vigilance against terror translates into vigilance against one another.[93] And this strategy of cultivated suspicion has little chance of being amended in the future: following the San Bernardino terrorist attack in December 2015, Secretary Johnson responded with renewed pleas for us all to see more and say more.[94]

There are some, like Lucia Zedner, who are optimistic about DHS and other police agencies recruiting citizens to watch one another. Zedner argues that, while the state apparatus cannot claim a monopoly over policing practices, it can play a positive role in upholding reasonable standards of civility, ensuring a more equitable distribution of public resources, and protecting the marginalized and vulnerable. According to Zedner, "Defending policing as a public good accords strongly with the eighteenth-century neoclassical belief in policing as an integral aspect of civic virtue and a necessary precondition of liberty. According to this ideal, active engagement in the maintenance of liberty was a duty laid upon every citizen. Contemporary calls for 'community engagement,' 'active civic participation,' and 'local capacity building' might just signal a renaissance of this classical notion of civic virtue."[95] Despite whatever democratic veneer these initiatives might possess, it is clear that the DHS's rhetorics of "community engagement" and "active participation" have not produced the engaged, altruistic citizen, but have rather reintroduced the logics of global war into the homeland. In this war of all against all, we have to ensure that our "civic virtues" are not turned into weapons.

Conclusion

Looking the Other Way

[I]f the community is a source of power, then it could exercise this power for its own ends, rather than those of the state.
—Kristian Williams[1]

This book has traced the historical development of a number of lateral surveillance initiatives. The story I shared about police crowdsourcing, for example, examined how it developed from its origins in oral "cries" to its current manifestations in social media. My analysis of 911 technologies, too, traced them from the telegraph private boxes of the nineteenth century to today's crime-reporting smartphone apps. Likewise, I traced the development of Neighborhood Watch in order to explore the ambivalent, uneasy relationship that citizens' patrols have had with violence, surveillance, and communicative action. In Chapter Four, I turned to the development of youth police initiatives, emphasizing that the good neoliberal subject isn't always an adult. The final case study, Chapter Five, re-centers our attention upon the state's apparatuses of terror production and citizen mobilization. I decided to end with antiterrorist surveillance because it sheds unique light on "where we are" at the present cultural moment. While each of the chapters illustrates a unique present of citizen-surveillance campaigns, I think there is something uniquely contemporary—and uniquely troubling—about the trends we see in the War on Terror. As such, in my attempt to provide a history of our complex and contradictory present—with all its clashes over resistance and control—this particular slice of contemporary life seems like the best resting place for us to reflect on the cultural and political implications of current trends in seeing and saying. As the most visible, threatening, and controversial of today's spy-and-snitch culture, it gives us a clear and specific object of critique—we can dispute its truth claims, rethink its constant production of internal and external enemies, resist the citizen-policing mentality on which it thrives, and anchor our response in coordinated acts of withdrawal and resistance. Therefore, while the "If You See Something, Say Something" campaign and allied initiatives do not provide a unified telos for the diverse practices of surveillance and communication detailed in the book, by placing them alongside an extensive history of citizen responsibilization campaigns we can map these programs' points of convergence. Most of all, by epitomizing the inherent political danger of lateral surveillance practices, current antiterrorist initiatives allow us to reorient our story toward how we can recapture our sight and speech in the service of a more promising future.

From this perspective, then, the question of the future converges with the question of resistance. These stories, situated within new historical networks and placed upon new planes of intelligibility, are meant to reassemble the past in such a way that the present is recognized for all its contingency. In an interview on his "genealogical" method of historical analysis, Foucault remarked, "[T]he question I start off with is: what are we and what are we today? What is this instant that is ours? Therefore, if you like, it is a history that starts off from this present day actuality."[2] The represented past is the terrain on which we battle to better understand the challenges of this "present day actuality." Thus throughout the book I have taken pains to show how resistance movements, hackers, prankers, activists, criminals, and rebellious kids have complicated the state's regimes of citizen responsibilization. These points of misfire, struggle, and compromise illustrate the contingency and fragility of present citizen-surveillance programs. Reconfiguring how the past gave way to the present, therefore, helps us design new ejection seats as we find ourselves gliding along toward troubling futures. Surveillance scholars, for their part, have done a pretty impressive job of outlining ways to subvert the surveillance rituals demanded by the state and by digital capitalism. Disabling surveillance cameras,[3] participating in effective anti-surveillance groups like the ACLU,[4] and even "turning off all media"[5] have been proposed as worthwhile ways to resist the surveillance and datafication of our everyday lives. While these ideas provide some useful and provocative suggestions for how to resist becoming the *objects* of surveillance, they do not give us much guidance in how to resist becoming the *subjects* of surveillance. Yet in the present cultural climate, not only do we need to learn how to resist abusive surveillance practices, we also need to examine how to look the other way—that is, how to turn our eyes away from our peers and, in so doing, reenvision how we fit into the world around us.

Toward this purpose, I would like to discuss three political possibilities opened up by my analysis (although I hope there are many others, only some of which have been detailed in earlier chapters). While I find all three to be legitimate in certain social conditions, they are rooted in different theoretical and political commitments. Because of these differences, they offer somewhat opposed, and perhaps even contradictory, visions of political action. Thus in lieu of outlining a coherent, normative project of resistant action, I will reflect on how these three different responses offer potentially valuable ways to resist the pervasive call to police our peers through surveillance and communication.

Silence

This book has explored a key way in which power circulates in a liberal society like the United States: through the programs and schemes by which citizens are finessed into policing themselves and others. In order for the liberal project to function, therefore, it doesn't just need our consent—it needs our *participation*. This complicated liberal mixture of atomism and civic responsibility thrives on vigilance and suspicion— they are, in fact, two of its essential ingredients. So if we find that our seeing/saying bodies have been activated in these struggles for the production of vigilance and suspicion, perhaps the best way to resist is to find means of productive disengagement—that is, to short-circuit these demands on our surveillance and communication through *silence*.

Let me emphasize at the outset, though, that this cannot be a politically debilitated silence, as if one had been forced into shutting up and shutting down.[6] Rather, the silence we might seek is an affirmative quietude—in the words of Nick Dyer-Witheford and Greig de Peuter, "a defection that is not just negative but a project of reconstruction"[7]— that deprives liberal police power of its means of sustenance. If we are commanded to call the cops on our neighbors and family members, to send anonymous text messages that snitch on our fellow students, to scour our gated communities with little two-way radios, to rat out our parents for smoking pot, or to report every suspicious activity in sight, perhaps shutting up is the most radical and socially responsible course of action available to us. As I've argued throughout this book, in order for us to be governed through crime and terror, we have to be converted into speaking subjects. Thus if we remain silent when we encounter difference among our neighbors, colleagues, friends, and family—i.e., if we learn to look the other way—this sort of social regulation simply can't take place.

A number of theorists have proposed this very solution to capitalist demands on communicative labor. But as communicative labor has become a central demand of liberal citizenship, the autonomists' traditional critique can apply just as well to civic political relations. When Maurizio Lazzaratto writes, "Capital wants a situation where command resides within the subject him- or herself, and within the communicative process,"[8] we can extend this analysis to the processes by which private and civil authorities profit by instilling into everyday citizens this disciplined impulse to say something. For Lazzaratto, this capture of communicative labor thrives on an "authoritarian discourse" that demands we speak: "we have here a discourse that is authoritarian: one *has* to express oneself, one *has* to speak, communicate, cooperate, and so forth."[9] For the good of the homeland, for the good of the community, for the good of the children, for the good of the vulnerable—we are urged everyday to speak and to speak. Yet if we wish to be governed differently, we need to recognize that, in the words of Ronald Greene, "the political dimension of communicative labor is built into bio-political production's attempt to harness and capture the constitutive power of communication."[10] In the face of this ongoing capture, Greene advocates a "generalized refusal or defection from the commands of money/speech."[11] Greene, therefore, urges us to withhold our communicative labor in order to throw a monkey wrench into liberal capitalism's intensive machinery of capture.

Armand Mattelart, too, has voiced sympathies with this view, suggesting that we withdraw our communicative labor from apparatuses of citizen production: "the key thing may be to create spaces of non-communication, circuit breakers, so we can elude control."[12] Creating affirmative spaces of noncommunication, therefore, forestalls the conversion of our seeing/saying bodies into sheer biopower for the countless authorities and institutions who foster social regulation through casual, ongoing expressions of suspicion, intolerance, and ostracism. Now that we are trained to see all activities and everyday items as suspicious and potentially threatening to the very social order, when you see something, don't say anything. Create what Gilles Deleuze called "vacuoles of noncommunication":[13] refuse to police your neighbors, your coworkers, and even strangers whose behavior you might not understand. In a society where we are more than three times as likely to die from a lightning bolt than a terrorist attack, we need to rediscover our comfort with the "unknown unknown," as former secretary of defense Donald Rumsfeld put it.[14] We need to learn to look the other way, without fear or opportunistic suspicion. In a security society that demands our communicative labor for its very political sustenance, silence is often a radical move.

Solidarity

As it is popularly told, the infamous 1964 Kitty Genovese murder story might seem to contradict my findings about the cultural impulse to see something and say something. The original news account, as published in the *New York Times*, reported that thirty-eight bystanders looked on as Kitty Genovese, a twenty-nine-year-old Queens woman, was raped and murdered nearby. The *Times* described, "For more than half an hour thirty-eight respectable, law-abiding citizens in Queens watched a killer stalk and stab a woman in three separate attacks in Kew Gardens. . . . Not one person telephoned the police during the assault; one witness called after the woman was dead."[15] Yet as journalists and researchers have recently discovered, this popular narrative was more fiction than fact.[16] Indeed, one of Genovese's neighbors, Robert Mozer, yelled at the attacker and momentarily scared him away. A neighbor and friend of Genovese, Karl Ross, opened his apartment door just in time to see the stabbing; instead of assisting the dying woman, Ross fled his apartment through a window but *did* call the police. Genovese eventually died in the arms of a young woman who, after listening to Genovese being attacked for half an hour, finally walked outside to soothe her as she died.

A. M. Rosenthal, an executive editor of the *Times*, later authored a book about the murder in which he diagnoses the social ills that led to Genovese's death. Rosenthal essentially repeats the description in his newspaper's original report: "thirty-eight of her neighbors had seen her stabbed or heard her cries, and that not one of them, during that hideous half-hour, had lifted the telephone in the safety of his own apartment to call the police and try to save her life."[17] Waxing philosophical on the bigger picture of American alienation and atomism, Rosenthal suggests, "[I]n dying she gave every human being . . . an opportunity to examine some truths about the nature of apathy."[18] Yet when Rosenthal alleges that Genovese's "neighbors heard her scream her last half hour away and did nothing, nothing at all, to give her succor or even cry alarm,"[19] he is only half right. Her neighbors did, in fact, cry alarm—several of them called the cops and yelled at the attacker. But that's all they did. They associated neighborly duty with calling the police. Their neighborly responsibility, therefore, had been successfully transformed into civic responsibility, placing the state in the center of their social obligations. So they called the police and waited inside their comfortable homes, listening to their young neighbor scream until an ambulance and the police arrived in just enough time to cart off Genovese on a stretcher.

Contrary to Rosenthal's claims, then, the Genovese case is less indicative of social apathy than of the cultivation of a very particular sort of community responsibility. Rather than take direct action to save their friend and neighbor—whose attacker had a knife, not a gun—they did the civically responsible thing by calling the cops and hoping that the police would confront the attacker and save Genovese. What this illustrates, then, is not that citizens are apathetic or that they're "bad Samaritans"; rather, it demonstrates how the introduction of the home telephone allowed citizens' social responsibility to be rerouted through the police. The phone and allied media technologies provide the technical conditions in which citizens can be *passively* engaged in the safety and well being of their neighbors by deferring direct action to a centralized police force. In fact, as *New Yorker* journalist Nicholas Lemann remarked in his 2014 reflection on the Genovese case, the city's response was to institute 911 as the nationally standardized emergency number.[20] The city's response, then, was to make it easier for citizens to call the cops. (Despite the fact, of course, that Genovese's neighbors *had* called the local police department, but the cops were simply too slow to save Genovese.)

While the telephone and other media devices have allowed us to more easily see something and say something, the Genovese case provides an unsettling example of how these technologies have helped transform our social responsibility into civic responsibility. Accordingly, it demonstrates how the phone and other technologies have distanced us from our neighbors by discouraging direct local action. While Sherry Turkle[21] and other critics have recognized that today these technologies separate us from one another by making screens and distractions ubiquitous, I am describing a different sort of separation—a separation by which these devices have allowed the police apparatus to colonize our social responsibility, such that our first impulse is not to help our neighbors when they're in trouble, but to call the cops. But there are times when our communities demand social action that is not filtered through the state, when we should participate in local acts of what Paolo Virno calls "nonservile virtuosity."[22] We should cultivate direct forms of community solidarity—not vigilant, suspicious ones that involve scouring our communities for petty criminals (à la George Zimmerman), but an openness to and care for our neighbors that would make it unthinkable to sit indoors while they were being murdered right outside. As Harvey Molotch has argued, we need to develop forms of solidarity that are not rooted in the vigilance of Neighborhood Watch and homeland security initiatives: "Very often . . . the need is to be *proactive*, but in a different direction than is ordinarily undertaken in the realm of official security. One should move forward to relax, assist, and to set up ways for people to make good on their inclination to come to one another's support and rescue."[23] Indeed, our mission to find new forms of direct communal action that eschew suspicion, vigilance, and the state's rechanneling of our social responsibility confronts us with a difficult task. But it is a task that must be carried out.

Knowing When to Say When: Sousveillance

Despite the social and political dangers inherent in any seeing/saying initiative, the present confluence of preemptive security logics, lateral surveillance culture, and mobile technologies allows for productive avenues of resistance. There are ways in which the technologization of the American citizenry can be used to actively counter the abuses of the police and other individuals in positions of power. New trends in "sousveillance"—the methods by which individuals carry out "bottom-up" surveillance, typically through new technologies—have freed citizens to turn their gaze against the state, allowing them to capture and publicize police brutality and other offenses.[24] In fact, the widespread popularity of mobile surveillance devices has empowered citizens while it has simultaneously disciplined their conduct: nowadays everyone, including police officers, is under threat of constant surveillance by mobile phones and other devices equipped with video and audio recording capabilities.[25]

When CIA contractor Edward Snowden released several million intelligence files to *Guardian* journalist Glenn Greenwald, he forced the issue of pervasive surveillance into the open. In the wake of Snowden's revelations, polls found that a majority of the American public approved of the NSA's dragnet surveillance measures. As time has progressed, however, the American consensus has evolved significantly: a Pew Research study released in 2015 showed that a majority of Americans, fifty-seven percent vs. forty percent, disapproved of the massive federal surveillance of U.S. citizens.[26] As the Snowden revelations have sunken deeply into political discourse, Americans have become increasingly wary of the state's shadowy data collection programs. Despite President Obama's attempts to ensure the American people that "their rights are being protected, even as our intelligence and law enforcement agencies maintain the tools they need to keep us safe,"[27] most Americans simply aren't buying it. Combined with the growing arrogance and invasiveness of DHS surveillance programs and the TSA's humiliating security theater, the "Snowden Revolution"[28] has helped make possible a political sea change. Conservative Republicans like senators Rand Paul (KY) and Ted Cruz (TX) are joining with progressive Democrats like Mark Udall (CO), Ron Wyden (OR), and Martin Heinrich (NM) in order to haul in the out-of-control and unaccountable domestic surveillance apparatus. While their efforts have not had a significant impact on the U.S.'s domestic surveillance policy, Snowden's own brand of seeing and saying has once again made opposing state surveillance a politically profitable stance.

The Snowden revelations present us with an opportunity to clarify a positive political vision of seeing and saying in the contemporary American moment. Snowden's recording and transmission of classified American intelligence files was not a product of the kind of citizen-to-citizen lateral surveillance I've outlined in this book. On the contrary, his activities illustrate how citizens can turn their trained and technologized bodies against corrupt authorities. Like Snowden, many courageous whistleblowers, investigative journalists, and other citizens investigate and publicize the abuses of capital and the state. Rather than aiming a suspicious eye at their fellow citizens, whistleblowers like Snowden demonstrate how vigilant citizenship need not be translated into the kinds of lateral surveillance hysteria we see with Neighborhood Watch, D.A.R.E., and the "If You See Something, Say Something" campaign. This, I argue, forms an important line of distinction between lateral surveillance and sousveillance: while lateral surveillance turns citizens against one another, sousveillance—at least in theory—allows citizens to unite against power.

Although there are countless politically diverse organizations and professional communities that carry out innovative sousveillance work—such as the previously discussed Cop Block and the Huey P. Newton Gun Club—Copwatch provides an especially interesting grassroots example. Founded in 1990 in Berkeley, Copwatch began by organizing street patrols to document police abuses.[29] Within months, the group was holding "Know Your Rights" training seminars that instructed citizens in the legal limits of police power (and, of course, in legal methods for carrying out sousveillance of police officers). In addition to frequent protests, national conferences, and community events, Copwatch released a training video, *These Streets Are Watching*, in 2003, which was accompanied by lesson plans for school children that covered the Bill of Rights and civil liberties.[30] These innovative activities not only succeeded in raising awareness of police brutality, they also publicized legislative efforts to suppress sousveillance of police officers. As Copwatch and other activists point out, officers routinely confiscate video cameras, phones, and other recording devices that are being used to document police abuses. The right to record cops has thus become a serious bone of legal contention, as a number of jurisdictions (such as Atlanta and New Haven, Connecticut) have declared citizens' rights

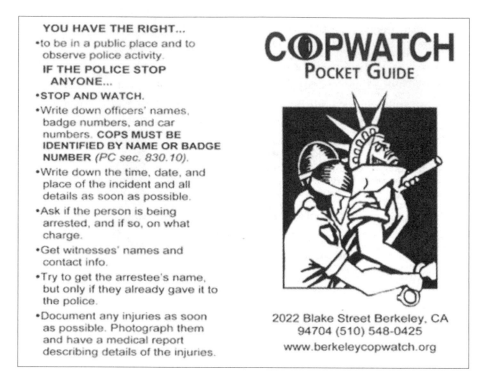

Figure C.1. Taking on police brutality with surveillance and communication. *Copwatch Pocket Guide*, www.berkeleycopwatch.org.

to capture footage of the police. Yet some states, such as Illinois, Maryland, and Massachusetts, have reinterpreted the law in order to prevent citizens from monitoring cops. (Some have even invoked "homeland security" in doing so.)[31]

Despite these legal controversies, Copwatch and likeminded citizens have effectively used cutting-edge media technologies to record and publicize police brutality. As the late Jim Aune reminded us, we shouldn't lose sight of the positive political potential of new media: "every technology simultaneously opens up possibilities of emancipation and domination."[32] Although much of this book has focused on the dangers and political ambivalence of new surveillance and communication technologies, this emancipatory potential is clear in the many ways that citizens have used mobile media to carry out important acts of sousveillance: from the Rodney King beating in 1991 to the 2009 Oscar Grant shooting, and in countless episodes since the widespread emergence of the smartphone, cop watchers have used their technologized bodies to bring legal accountability to an increasingly violent and repressive police apparatus.[33] This trend in sousveillance, in fact, is gaining significant cultural ground: the ACLU, for example, has developed a smartphone app that lets citizens secretly record traffic stops.[34] In addition, the ACLU's New York branch has developed a Stop and Frisk Watch app, which allows New Yorkers to record abuses of New York's controversial anti-firearm stop-and-frisk policy.[35] After an app user records a stop and frisk, s/he is immediately sent a survey that allows ACLU officials to monitor patterns and assess for illegalities. Most interesting, the app automatically alerts other app users of the location of the stop and frisk, so that activists can crowdsource sousveillance and attempt to prevent the escalation of police brutality.

Yet as this book has taken pains to show, power and its abuses do not simply emanate from what Foucault called the "mythicized abstraction"[36] of the state. Without the assistance of a diverse assortment of citizens and private institutions, liberal police power simply could not thrive. So by advocating sousveillance against cops and other state authorities, I risk sending an ambivalent message about power, its transmission, and its resistance. Despite this ambivalence, our current stage of surveillance culture begs for a line in the sand. While acknowledging the multipolarity of power, we should recognize above all that our seeing/saying bodies are cultivated to bring continuity and social cohesion to the present political order. A top priority of concerned citizens, activists, and critical scholars, then, should be disrupting that process, which means rejecting suspicion and overlooking our peers' petty infractions in favor of turning our collective vigilance toward the more fundamental and far-reaching abuses of the agents of state power.

* * *

All of these suggestions, in one way or another, urge us to avoid getting pulled into lateral surveillance efforts. When we are pushed to become the "eyes and ears" of the security apparatus or the local police department, we can resist by rejecting those demands on our sight and speech—by refusing to look at our neighbors with suspicion, by sidestepping the state's colonization of our social responsibility, and by turning our eyes toward reckless and abusive figures of authority. Yet trends in security politics and digital culture suggest that in the coming years we will be increasingly expected to police one another using the communication and surveillance technologies we have on hand. As Copwatch helps demonstrate, there is liberatory potential inherent in this "empowerment." But to truly embrace the political potential of that empowerment, we have to avoid buying into the climate of pervasive suspicion to which the "If You See Something, Say Something" campaign and its corollaries contribute. Instead, we need to learn to *look the other way*. Ultimately, citizen-policing initiatives—no matter how well-intentioned—simply gloss over the U.S.'s myriad structural maladies (such as neoliberal economic policies and unbridled military interventionism) that ensure the reproduction of crime and fan the flames of terrorist rage. Thus in a very important sense, the impulse to police our peers threatens to be more depoliticizing and socially destructive than the merely symptomatic threats of crime, petty immorality, and terrorism. The problem is not that we don't live in a radically homogenized social order free of moral and criminal transgressions, it's that we are being mobilized against one another in endless battles for more security, more safety, more comfort, and more moral conformity.

Yet in order to thrive, these citizen-policing projects demand our consent.[37] As Barbara Cruikshank reminds us, "citizens must be made—which says to me that citizens can be remade, and that the social construction of citizenship is both a promise and a constraint upon the will to empower."[38] Keeping this promise in mind, we can use our eyes and mouths to learn from others, remake ourselves, and build creative new forms of community and solidarity. If any cause is worth going vigilant for, surely that is it.

NOTES

INTRODUCTION

1 Anthea Butler, "The Zimmerman Acquittal: America's Racist God," *Religion Dispatches Magazine*, July 14, 2013. www.religiondispatches.org.

2 In particular, civil rights attorney Lisa Bloom has argued that we can trace George Zimmerman's violence to the rise of the U.S. as a "suspicion nation." See Bloom, *Suspicion Nation*.

3 Ted Nugent, "Nugent: Zimmerman Verdict Vindicates Citizen Patrols, Self-Defense," *Rare Magazine*, July 18, 2013. http://rare.us.

4 Nugent, "Nugent."

5 For different perspectives on this tension, see Shain, *The Myth of American Individualism*. For a more general view of the myth's contradictions, also see Dorsey, *We Are All Americans*.

6 See Engels, *Enemyship*.

7 National Sheriffs' Association, *Neighborhood Watch Manual: USAonWatch— National Neighborhood Watch Program* (Alexandria, VA: National Sheriffs' Association, 2011), 25.

8 Weber, "Religious Rejections," 334. Also see Amoore, "Vigilant Visualities," 223.

9 Campbell, Sahid, and Stang, *Law and Order Reconsidered*, 424.

10 For an earlier answer to this question, see Redden, *Snitch Culture*.

11 U.S. Homeland Security, "Walmart Public Service Announcement," *YouTube*, October 16, 2011. www.youtube.com.

12 NASCO, "NASCO Endorses 'See Something, Say Something' Act to Protect Citizens Who Report Suspicious Activity," *PRNewsWire.com*, September 14, 2011. www.prnewswire.com.

13 NASCO, "NASCO Endorses 'See Something, Say Something' Act."

14 Ericson and Haggerty, *Policing the Risk Society*, 267.

15 In a speech before the Council on Foreign Relations in September 2014, newly tapped DHS Secretary Jeh Johnson emphasized that "'If You See Something, Say Something' is more than a slogan." Jeh Johnson, "Remarks by Secretary of Homeland Security Jen Johnson at the Council on Foreign Relations—as Delivered." *U.S. Department of Homeland Security*, September 10, 2014. www.dhs.gov.

16 Magnet and Gates, *The New Media of Surveillance*.

17 Gates and Magnet, "Communication Research and the Study of Surveillance," 278.

18 See Greene, "Rhetorical Materialism."

19 Greene, "Rhetorical Materialism," 44.

20 Greene, "Rhetorical Materialism," 51.

21 Greene, "Orator Communist," 91.

22 Greene and Hicks, "Lost Convictions," 101.

23 See, e.g., Haggerty and Ericson, "The Surveillant Assemblage"; and Lyon, *Surveillance Society*, 2.

24 Lyon, *The Electronic Eye*.

25 See Marnie Ritchie's take on "feeling for the state," in Ritchie, "Feeling for the State."

26 Mattelart, *The Globalization of Surveillance*, 138.

27 Michael Hayden, "Ex-CIA Chief: What Edward Snowden Did," *CNN.com*, July 19, 2013. www.cnn.com.

28 See especially Foucault, *Security, Territory, Population*.

29 Cruikshank, *The Will to Empower*, 4.

30 Foucault, *Security, Territory, Population*.

31 Miller, *The Well-Tempered Self*, xiii.

32 Bennett, *The Birth of the Museum*, 95.

33 Foucault, *The History of Sexuality, Volume I: An Introduction*, 105. Also see O'Malley and Palmer, "Post-Keynesian Policing"; and Garland, "The Limits of the Sovereign State."

34 Rose, "Government and Control," 329.

35 See Rose, "Governing 'Advanced' Liberal Democracies," 48, 57. Also see Dean, "Culture Governance and Individualization," 130.

36 See Johnston, "What Is Vigilantism?"

37 Johnston, "What Is Vigilantism?," 226.

38 See especially Andrejevic, *iSpy*. Also refer to Larsen and Piché, "Public Vigilance Campaigns"; and Smith, "Surveillance Workers."

39 Andrejevic, *iSpy*, 163. Kristy Hess and Lisa Waller have referred to digitally equipped lateral surveillance as "isurveillance," which transforms "the ordinary citizen into an embodied surveillance system with the power to alert the world to acts of immoral/illegal behavior." See Hess and Waller, "The Digital Pillory: Media Shaming of 'Ordinary' People for Minor Crimes."

40 See especially Walsh, "Community, Surveillance, and Border Control"; and Chavez, "Spectacle in the Desert." Also see Hasian and McHendry, "The Attempted Legitimation of the Vigilante Civil Border Patrols."

41 Although I engage these programs briefly in chapter 5, much closer attention could be (and has been) paid. See Kackman, *Citizen Spy*; Helen Laville, *Cold War Women: The International Activities of American Women's Organizations* (Manchester, UK: Manchester University Press, 2002), 96–123; and Sirgiovanni, *An Undercurrent of Suspicion*.

42 See Ross, *Manning the Race*.

43 See especially Chauncey, *Gay New York*. Also see Kinsman, "Constructing Gay Men and Lesbians as National Security Risks"; and, more generally, Feinberg, *Transgender Warriors*.

44 Treichler, *How to Have Theory in an Epidemic.*

45 Bratich, "Sovereign Networks, Pre-emptive Transgression," 226.

46 Rose, "Government and Control."

47 Lyon, *Surveillance Studies,* 77.

48 See, for example, John Whitehead, "Janet Napolitano's Orwellian Legacy," *FoxNews.com*, July 17, 2013. www.foxnews.com.

CHAPTER 1. THE POWER OF THE CROWD

1 McLuhan and Fiore, *The Medium Is the Massage,* 24.

2 David Freed and Carol McGraw, "Police Identify Stalker Suspect: 25-Year-Old L.A. Man Named in Seven-Month Spree of Killings," *Los Angeles Times* (August 31, 1985): 1.

3 Hall, *Wanted,* 6.

4 Scranton Police Department, "Be Part of the Solution: Scranton Police PSA," *YouTube*, January 20, 2011. www.youtube.com.

5 As most critical/cultural scholars and social scientists agree, *America's Most Wanted* and similar police crowdsourcing programs function simultaneously through the production of suspicion, fear, and insecurity as well as through ideals of community responsibility. For a review, see Arthur J. Lurigio, "Victimology," in *Violent Crime: Clinical and Social Implications,* ed. Christopher J. Ferguson (Thousand Oaks, CA: SAGE, 2010), 338–39. Also see David Prior, "Civil Renewal and Community Safety: Virtuous Policy Spiral or Dynamic of Exclusion?," *Social Policy and Society* 4.4 (2005): 357–67.

6 Marx, "Soft Surveillance," 43.

7 Brabham, "Crowdsourcing as a Model for Problem Solving."

8 Howe, *Crowdsourcing,* 14.

9 See Gabriele Paolacci, Jesse Chandler, and Panagiotis G. Ipeirotis, "Running Experiments on Amazon Mechanical Turk," *Judgment and Decision Making* 5.5 (2010): 411–19.

10 Shirky, *Here Comes Everybody.*

11 Trottier, "Vigilantism and Power Users," 218.

12 For a different take on crowdsourced surveillance, see Monahan and Mokos, "Crowdsourcing Urban Surveillance."

13 Agamben, "Sovereign Police"; Foucault, "Omnes et Singulatim."

14 Zedner, "Policing before and after the Police."

15 Trojanowicz and Bucqueroux, *Community Policing,* 43.

16 A long line of English scholars have characterized this shift in policing culture as a defining element of the "Norman Yoke"—that is, the colonizing apparatus by which the Normans exploited the native Anglo-Saxons. While—as Foucault points out in *Society Must Be Defended*—the "Norman Yoke" legend tends to exaggerate the severity of the Norman Conquest, it is clear that the Normans made a number of essential reforms to Anglo-Saxon civil society. See Chibnall, *The Debate on the Norman Conquest,* as well as Foucault, *Society Must Be Defended,* 105–7.

17 Morris, *The Frankpledge System,* 1–8.

18 Morris, *The Frankpledge System*, 2.
19 Bonnie S. Fisher and Steven P. Lab, *Encyclopedia of Victimology and Crime Prevention, Vol. I* (Thousand Oaks, CA: Sage, 2010), 198–99.
20 Roth and Olson, "Hue and Cry," 63.
21 Pollock and Maitland, *The History of English Law*, 577.
22 Burn, *The Justice of the Peace*, 553.
23 Burn, *The Justice of the Peace*, 554. The horn—as the "hue" in *hue and cry*—can be traced in the English policing tradition at least as far back the Middle Ages; and we do know, moreover, that the horn, which has long been used to herd flocks, was used by the Romans as a method of patrol and troop coordination. See Baines, *Brass Instruments*, 37–66. The horn provided important new capacities for managing people's behavior across space, making a significant impact on the organization of roving police patrols. As we see in Monelle's account, patterns of repetition, tone, and emphasis allowed patrols in disparate communities to announce a criminal's presence and direct the dispersal of a number of civilian patrols. At least by 1302, horns were employed to alert neighboring towns of a criminal's movement during hue and cry campaigns. See DeWindt and DeWindt, *Ramsey*. During the following century horns were given to England's night watchman, who would patrol the town on foot. These watchmen, however, were soon moved to bell towers, where they could (either with trumpets or bells) customize their alerts based upon the threat posed to the community. See Thomas Dudley Fosbroke, *Encyclopedia of Antiquities: and Elements of Archaeology, Ancient and Medieval, Vol. 1* (London: John Nichols and Son, 1825), 472.
24 Critchley, *A History of Police in England*, 2–6.
25 Costello, *Our Police Protectors*, 12.
26 Bruce L. Berg, *Policing in Modern Society* (Butterworth-Heinemann: Woburn, MA, 1999), 30–32.
27 See, for example, John Fauchereaud Grimké, "Hue and Cry," in *The South-Carolina Justice of the Peace; Containing All the Duties, Powers, and Authorities of That Office, as Regulated by the Laws Now of Force in This State* (New York: T. & J. Swords, 1810), 227–32.
28 Costello, *Our Police Protectors*, 45–46.
29 See Wirt, *The Life of Patrick Henry*, 147.
30 See Foucault, *Society Must Be Defended*, 82.
31 In order to broaden the gaze against theft, the gazettes also allowed citizens to advertise rewards for stolen goods. For an early discussion of this, see Colquhoun, *A Treatise on the Police of the Metropolis*, 210. This method of distribution was hotly debated among nineteenth-century police officials. See, for instance, Clarkson and Richardson, *Police!*, 280–85.
32 Battles, *Calling All Cars*, 147–86. Also see Glynn, *Tabloid Culture*, 1–45.
33 Hall, *Wanted*, 111. Also see Jessica M. Fishman, "The Populace and the Police: Models of Social Control in Reality-Based Crime Television," *Critical Studies in Mass Communication* 16.3 (1999): 268–88.

34 See the show's official Facebook page, https://www.facebook.com/1800crimetv/ info?ref= page_internal.

35 Claire Martin, "The End of *America's Most Wanted*: Good News for Criminals, Bad News for the FBI," *Time*, July 29, 2011. http://content.time.com.

36 Martin, "The End of *America's Most Wanted*."

37 Martin, "The End of *America's Most Wanted*."

38 Alejandro Martínez-Cabrera, "Social Media a Police Weapon That Can Backfire," *San Francisco Chronicle*, September 25, 2010. www.sfgate.com.

39 Krainik, "Amber Alert."

40 Devon Glenn, "Google Brings AMBER Alerts for Missing Children to Search and Maps," *SocialTimes.com*, November 1, 2012. http://socialtimes.com.

41 Office of Juvenile Justice and Delinquency Prevention, "AMBER Alerts for Abducted Children Now Available on Facebook," *OJJDP News*, January/February 2011. www.ncjrs.gov.

42 Associated Press, "Amber Alerts Hit Cellphones, Aggravate Users," *OregonLive. com*, February 1, 2013. www.oregonlive.com.

43 Amber Alert, "Bringing Abducted Children Home," *Office of Juvenile Justice and Delinquency Prevention*, April 2005. www.ojjdp.gov.

44 See Trottier, "Policing Social Media." In addition, an article in *Police Chief* magazine outlines suggested protocols for police departments' social media development. See Lauri Stevens, "Social Media in Policing: Nine Steps for Success." *The Police Chief: The Professional Voice of Law Enforcement*, February 2010. www.policechiefmagazine.org.

45 IACP Center for Social Media, "2015 Survey Results," *IACPSocialMedia.org*, October 2015. www.iacpsocialmedia.org.

46 Hank Silverberg, "Police Turn to Social Media to Combat Crime," *WTOP*, April 25 2013. www.wtop.com.

47 Heather Kelly, "Police Embrace Social Media as Crime-Fighting Tool," *CNN.com*, August 30, 2012. www.cnn.com.

48 "Twitter Transparency Report," *Twitter.com*, July 2, 2012. http://blog.twitter.com.

49 Renee C. Lee, "DWI Suspects to Have Names Plastered on Twitter," *Houston Chronicle*, January 6, 2010. www.chron.com.

50 Joseph Master, "Philadelphia Police Department—Version 2.0," *Market Street*, Fall 2012. www2.lebow.drexel.edu.

51 Master, "Philadelphia Police Department." Also see Police Social Media, "1-Day Progressive Training for Police Leaders and Spokespersons," *PoliceSocialMedia. com*, 2013. www.policesocialmedia.com.

52 Frank Domizio, "Social Media in Law Enforcement," *SocialMediaToday.com*, January 28, 2012. http://socialmediatoday.com.

53 Master, "Philadelphia Police Department."

54 Troy Graham. 2013. "Philly in 2012: Killings Rise, Overall Crime Falls," *Philly.com*, January 1, 2013. http://articles.philly.com.

55 Aubrey Whelan, "Homicides on the Rise in Philadelphia; Fewer Cases Solved," *Philly.com*, January 4, 2016. http://articles.philly.com.

56 Pottstown Police Department, "Wanted by Police," *Pinterest.com.* http://pinterest. com.

57 Robert J. Moore, "Pinners Be Pinnin': How to Justify Pinterest's $3.8B Valuation," *RJ Metrics Blog,* May 7, 2014. https://blog.rjmetrics.com.

58 Government Technology, "Pinterest Helps Police Catch Criminals," *Governing. com,* January 3, 2013. www.governing.com.

59 Emma Jacobs, "To Catch a Suspect—on Pinterest," *NPR.org,* December 7, 2012. http://m.npr.org.

60 Jacobs, "To Catch a Suspect."

61 Bob Moffitt, "Crime Down as Nextdoor Sign-Ups Hit Ten-Thousand Mark," *Capital Public Radio,* November 20, 2013. www.capradio.org.

62 Ashley Knight, "Next Door App a Virtual Neighborhood Watch.," *WKRG.org,* August 14, 2014. www.wkrg.com.

63 Gary Rotstein, "*America's Most Wanted* Leads to the Wrong Man," *Pittsburgh Post-Gazette,* September 30, 1993.

64 Skolnick and Bayley, *The New Blue Line.* Quoted in Ericson and Haggerty, *Policing the Risk Society,* 78.

65 Roberto Baldwin, "How a Facebook Joke Made One Guy San Francisco's Public Enemy No. 1," *Wired.com,* October 30, 2012. www.wired.com.

66 Baldwin, "How a Facebook Joke."

67 Tara Murtha, "Administrator of 'Kensington Stranger' Facebook Page Threatened," *Philadelphia Weekly,* December 22, 2010. http://blogs.philadelphiaweekly.com.

68 Richard DesLauriers, "Remarks of Special Agent in Charge Richard DesLauriers at Press Conference on Bombing Investigation," *FBI.gov,* April 18, 2013. www.fbi.gov.

69 See Marx, "The Public as Partner?"

70 Michael Walsh, "Reddit Apologizes for Online 'Witch Hunt' for Boston Marathon Bombers," *New York Daily News,* April 24, 2013. www.nydailynews.com.

71 David Montgomery, Sari Horwitz, and Marc Fisher, "Police, Citizens, and Technology Factor into Boston Bombing Probe," *Washington Post,* April 20, 2013. www.washingtonpost.com.

72 See Trottier, "Vigilantism and Power Users," 219.

73 Montgomery, Horwitz, and Fisher, "Police, Citizens, and Technology."

74 DesLauriers, "Remarks of Special Agent in Charge."

75 Manuel Valdes, "In Boston Manhunt, Online Detectives Flourish," *NBC Bay Area,* April 20, 2013. www.nbcbayarea.com.

76 See LEEDIR (Large Emergency Event Digital Information Repository) at www. leedir.com.

77 Valdes, "In Boston Manhunt, Online Detectives Flourish."

78 See, for example, Della Porta and Mattoni, "Social Networking Sites in Pro-Democracy and Anti-Austerity Protests."

79 Schneider, "Police 'Image Work' in an Era of Social Media," 228.

80 Schneider, "Police 'Image Work,'" 229. Also see Carlos Miller's excellent website, Photography Is Not a Crime, at https://photographyisnotacrime.com.

81 Kevin Fagan, "How Viral Video Put Occupy UC Davis on the Map," *San Francisco Chronicle*, November 23, 2011, www.sfgate.com.

82 Fagan, "How Viral Video Put UC Davis on the Map."

83 Reuters, "Occupy Pepper-Spray Cop John Pike Banks $38,000 for 'Psychiatric' Trauma," *New York Daily News*, October 24, 2013. www.nydailynews.com.

84 Kathleen Hickey, "Crowdsourcing Video Surveillance Can Work Both Ways," *GCN.com*, May 15, 2013, http://gcn.com.

85 Daniel Pérez, "Bill Restricting Rights of Citizens to Videotape Police Introduced in Texas House," *Houston Chronicle*, March 12, 2015. www.chron.com.

86 Brian X. Chen, "Smartphones Embracing Theft Defense," *New York Times* (June 20, 2014): B1.

87 See "I Am Mike Brown Live from Ferguson, MO," *LiveStream.com*, August 19, 2014. http://new.livestream.com.

88 Jenkins, *Convergence Culture*, 219.

89 For example, see CrimeMapping.com at www.crimemapping.com.

90 See, just for example, the coordination between the Miami University Police Department and a company called e2Campus: http://miamioh.edu/police/services/etms/index.html. Text message crime alerts are particularly popular on college campuses.

CHAPTER 2. CITIZEN EQUIPMENT

1 Kieran Nicholson, "Denver Police Looking at Lag Time between 911 Call, Body's Discovery," *Denver Post.*, November 11, 2012. www.denverpost.com.

2 Sadie Gurman, "Loretta Barela's Husband Told 911 He Might Have Killed Wife," *Denver Post*, November 21, 2012. www.denverpost.com.

3 Nicholson, "Denver Police Looking at Lag Time."

4 Miller and Rose, "Governing Economic Life."

5 Moskos, *Cop in the Hood*, 93.

6 Nicholson, "Denver Police Looking at Lag Time."

7 See, for example, Greene, "Y Movies"; Ouellette and Hay, *Better Living through Reality TV*; and Pepper, "Subscribing to Governmental Rationality."

8 In general, see Manning, *The Technology of Policing*.

9 Packer, *Mobility without Mayhem*, 163.

10 In the late twentieth and early twenty-first centuries, as media technologies became more mobile and popular, policing strategies have been constantly refined in accordance with these technological changes. In the words of Gary T. Marx, informing has been increasingly seen "as an element of good citizenship, commanding growing institutional and technical support." Marx, *Undercover*, 207.

11 Barry, "Lines of Communication and Spaces of Rule," 124.

12 Sprogle, *The Philadelphia Police*, iv.

13 DeWindt and DeWindt, *Ramsey*, 76.

14 Reiss, *The Police and the Public*, 64.

15 In fact, critical criminologists like Richard Ericson and Kevin Haggerty have recognized "the organized incapacity of the police to detect and risk-manage crime

and other troubles on their own." Ericson and Haggerty, *Policing the Risk Society*, 76.

16 Moskos, *Cop in the Hood*, 92.
17 See, for example, Wald, "Keynote Address," 86.
18 Lee P. Brown, *Policing in the 21st Century: Community Policing* (Bloomington, IN: AuthorHouse), 150.
19 Of course, police officials had long required citizens to use media technologies to carry out lateral surveillance and to record evidence of potentially criminal activities. Carriage operators and hoteliers in the eighteenth and nineteenth centuries, for example, were required to keep meticulous written records of their mobile clientele so that police could scour their notes for evidence. See Reeves and Packer, "Police Media," 364.
20 Marvin, *When Old Technologies Were New*, 92.
21 Sprogle, *The Philadelphia Police*, 396.
22 See Philips and Robinson, *Philips' and Robinson's Municipal Telegraph*, 18–19.
23 See Folsom (ed.), *Our Police*, 464.
24 Prescott, *Bell's Electric Speaking Telephone*, 309.
25 Carey, "Technology and Ideology," 210.
26 Pope, *Modern Practice of the Electric Telegraph*, 162.
27 See Ewald, "Norms, Discipline, and the Law."
28 For more on the importance of eliminating "noise" in high-intensity communication scenarios, see Kittler, "Media Stars."
29 Philips and Robinson, *Philips' and Robinson's Municipal Telegraph*, 13.
30 United States Department of Commerce and Labor, *Special Reports*, 146.
31 United States Department of Commerce and Labor, *Special Reports*, 143–45. One of the first police telephones was introduced in 1880 by J. P. Barrett, who was then superintendent of Chicago's electrical department. This phone was so successful that by 1893 several hundred private boxes had been installed in the city. See U.S. Department of Commerce and Labor, *Special Reports*, 146.
32 Prescott, *Bell's Electric Speaking Telegraph*, 312.
33 Prescott, *Bell's Electric Speaking Telegraph*, 312.
34 United States Department of Commerce, *Special Reports*, 147.
35 United States War Department, *Telephone Switchboard Operating Procedure*, 1.
36 United States War Department, *Telephone Switchboard Operating Procedure*, 2.
37 United States War Department, *Telephone Switchboard Operating Procedure*, 2.
38 *The Challenge of Crime in a Free Society*, 116.
39 *The Challenge of Crime in a Free Society*, 246.
40 *The Challenge of Crime in a Free Society*, vi.
41 *The Challenge of Crime in a Free Society*, 250
42 *The Challenge of Crime in a Free Society*, 250.
43 *The Challenge of Crime in a Free Society*, 250.
44 *The Challenge of Crime in a Free Society*, 250.

45 *The Challenge of Crime in a Free Society*, 250.

46 Manning, *The Technology of Policing*, 52.

47 Manning, *The Technology of Policing*, 52.

48 See Sherman, "Patrol Strategies for Police."

49 For more information, see Platt, "Crime Rave."

50 As an example of this research, see Bickman, "Bystander Intervention in a Crime."

51 National Institute of Justice, *Calling the Police*, 137.

52 National Institute of Justice, *Calling the Police*, 181.

53 National Institute of Justice, *Calling the Police*, 190.

54 National Institute of Justice, *Calling the Police*, 194. For more about this classifica-
tion, see Farmer (ed.), *Differential Police Response Strategies*, 1981.

55 National Institute of Justice, *Calling the Police*, 194.

56 Gow and Ihnat, "Prepaid Mobile Phone Service and the Anonymous Caller."

57 Department of Homeland Security, *A Resource Guide to Improve Your Community's Awareness*, 13.

58 Federal Communications Commission, "What You Need to Know about Text-
to-911," *FCC.gov*, December 22, 2015. www.fcc.gov.

59 John Cook, "iWitness: This iPhone App Fights Crime by Recording Incidents and
Dialing 911," *Geekwire: Dispatches from the Digital Frontier*, March 14, 2012. www.
geekwire.com.

60 Cook, "iWitness."

61 Anushay Hossain, "Downloading Empowerment: Application Gives Citizens
Control over Crime," *Forbes*, February 1, 2012. www.forbes.com.

62 For a farsighted political analysis of anonymous tips and 911 technologies, see
Marx, "Commentary," 516.

63 Heather Tomlinson, "Ky. Police Unveil Texting Program Targeting Students," *Of-
ficer.com*, January 21, 2013. www.officer.com.

64 Tomlinson, "Ky. Police Unveil Texting Program."

65 Lyon, "Why Where You Are Matters."

66 Phillips, "Texas 9-1-1," 843.

67 Lindberg, *To Serve and Collect*, 23.

68 For a very early example, see United States Department of Commerce and Labor,
Investigation of Telephone Companies, 339.

69 CBS News, "Texting: Can We Pull the Plug on Our Obsession?," *CBSNews.com*,
September 30, 2012. www.cbsnews.com.

70 Juan Gonzalez, "Report Concludes That City's $2 Billion 911 Modernization is Re-
dundant and Inefficient," *New York Daily News*, May 10, 2012. www.nydailynews.
com.

71 "Dealing with Anonymous Drug Tip Lines," *CopBlock.org*, December 31, 2011.
www.copblock.org.

72 Tracy and Tracy, "Emotion Labor at 911," 396-97.

73 Tracy and Tracy, "Emotion Labor at 911," 396-97.

74 Simpson, *Misuse and Abuse of 911*, 1.

75 Simpson, *Misuse and Abuse of 911*, 21.

76 Danielle Paquette, "Miley Cyrus Gets a Swatting: Police Lights Are One, Nobody's Home," *Los Angeles Times*, August 2, 2012. http://articles.latimes.com.

77 Irving Oala, "Miley Cyrus Swatted for Second Time as Police Arrive at Her Home Following Hoax Call of Shots Fired Inside the House," *Daily Mail*, May 18, 2013. www.dailymail.co.uk.

78 Maria Elena Fernandez, "Ashton Kutcher, Miley Cyrus, and Others Terrorized in Dangerous 'Swatting' Prank," *Daily Beast*, October 5, 2012. www.thedailybeast.com.

79 Don Lemon and Erick Erickson, "SWATting Prank Could Be Deadly," *CNN Newsroom*, June 8, 2012. http://newsroom.blogs.cnn.com.

80 Fernandez, "Ashton Kutcher, Miley Cyrus, and Others Terrorized."

81 Dave Kinchen, "Police Respond to 'Swatting' Prank Call in Upper Uwchlan Township," *My Fox Detroit*, June 9, 2014. www.myfoxdetroit.com.

82 Adrianne Jeffries, "Meet 'Swatting,' the Dangerous Prank That Could Get Someone Killed," *The Verge*, April 23, 2013. www.theverge.com.

83 Erick Erickson, "The 911 Call and 80+ Members of Congress," *RedState.com*, June 11, 2012. www.redstate.com.

84 Lyon, *Surveillance Studies*, 52.

85 See Brian Krebs, "Swatting Incidents Tied to ID Theft Sites?," *KrebsOnSecurity.com*, April 13, 2013. http://krebsonsecurity.com.

86 Federal Communications Commission, "IP Relay Fraud," *FCC.gov*, www.fcc.gov.

87 Jeff Black, "California Governor Signs Bill to Crack Down on Celebrity 'Swatting,'" *NBC News*, September 10, 2013. www.nbcnews.com.

88 Erickson, "The 911 Call."

89 Erickson, "The 911 Call."

90 David Clarke, "Sheriff David Clarke PSA for Milwaukee County," *YouTube*, January 26, 2013. www.youtube.com.

91 David Schaper, "Milwaukee County Sheriff: 'You Have a Duty to Protect Yourself,'" *NPR.org*, January 31, 2013. www.npr.org.

92 Bruce Vielmetti, Steve Schultze, and Don Walker, "Sheriff David Clarke's Radio Ad Says 911 Not Best Option, Urges Residents to Take Firearms Classes," *Milwaukee Journal-Sentinel*, January 25, 2013. www.jsonline.com.

93 Vielmetti, Schultze, and Walker, "Sheriff David Clarke's Radio Ad."

94 Don Walker, "David Clarke, Tom Barrett Square Off Over Guns on CNN," *Milwaukee Journal-Sentinel*, January 19, 2013. www.jsonline.com.

95 iWatchLA, "iWatchLA Report," *iWatchLA.org*, 2012. www.iWatchLA.org.

96 See the features and local program advertisements in Department of Homeland Security, *A Resource Guide*.

97 Foucault, "Two Lectures," 98.

98 Monahan, *Surveillance in the Time of Insecurity*, 29.

CHAPTER 3. NEIGHBORHOOD WATCHING

1 Isabelle Zehnder, "George Zimmerman's 911 Call Transcribed," *Examiner.com*, March 24, 2012. www.examiner.com.

2 Zehnder, "George Zimmerman's 911 Call Transcribed."

3 Michael Thompson, "George Zimmerman Doesn't Reflect True Neighborhood Watch," *Yahoo! News*, April 24, 2012. http://news.yahoo.com.

4 Michael Thompson, "George Zimmerman Doesn't Reflect True Neighborhood Watch."

5 National Crime Prevention Council, "Strategy: Starting Neighborhood Watch Groups," *NCPC.org*, 2013. www.ncpc.org.

6 National Sheriff's Association, "National Sheriff's Association Releases Statement on Florida Neighborhood Watch Tragedy," *Law Officer: Police and Law Enforcement*, March 21, 2012. www.lawofficer.com.

7 See, in particular, Greenberg, *Citizens Defending America*. Williams's *Our Enemies in Blue* also contains a valuable parallel history of citizen participation in policing.

8 Johnson and Wolfe, *History of Criminal Justice*, 79. Quoted in Greenberg, *Citizens Defending America*, 21–22.

9 Greenberg, *Citizens Defending America*, 23–25.

10 Trojanowicz and Bucqueroux, *Community Policing*, 46.

11 Williams, *Our Enemies in Blue*, 121–48.

12 Pfeifer, "Introduction," 3.

13 See Klein, *Unification of a Slave State*, 47–77.

14 Brown, *Strain of Violence*, 96.

15 Abrahams, *Vigilant Citizens*, 3–4.

16 Chriss, *Beyond Community Policing*, 55–65.

17 See Brown, *Strain of Violence*, 162; and Thelen, *Paths of Resistance*, 95–96.

18 David J. Brewer, "The Right of Appeal," *Independent*, October 29, Volume 55.2865 (1903): 2547–50.

19 Greenberg, *Citizens Defending America*, 6.

20 For more on neoliberal policing and responsibilization, see O'Mally and Palmer, "Post-Keynesian Policing"; and Garland, "The Limits of the Sovereign State."

21 Campbell, Sahid, and Stang, *Law and Order Reconsidered*, 416.

22 Greenberg, *Citizens Defending America*, 9.

23 Brown, *Strain of Violence*, 132.

24 See Aaron Major's excellent analysis of how U.S. economic policy of the 1950s and 1960s sowed the seeds of neoliberal austerity in the 1970s and 1980s. Major, *Architects of Austerity*.

25 See Fox, "Demographics and U.S. Homicide."

26 Justice Kennedy Commission, *Reports with Recommendations*, 18.

27 Campbell, Sahid, and Stang, *Law and Order Reconsidered*, 422.

28 Campbell, Sahid, and Stang, *Law and Order Reconsidered*, 413. Also see Marx, "Commentary," 513.

29 Yin et al., *Patrolling the Neighborhood Beat*, 193–96.
30 Yin et al., *Patrolling the Neighborhood Beat*, 204.
31 Yin et al., *Patrolling the Neighborhood Beat*, 253.
32 .Yin et al., *Patrolling the Neighborhood Beat*, 126.
33 Yin et al., *Patrolling the Neighborhood Beat*, 124.
34 Yin et al., *Patrolling the Neighborhood Beat*, 126.
35 Yin et al., *Patrolling the Neighborhood Beat*, 127.
36 Yin et al., *Patrolling the Neighborhood Beat*, 128.
37 Yin et al., *Patrolling the Neighborhood Beat*, 253.
38 Hollander et al., *Reducing Residential Crime and Fear*, 2.
39 Hollander et al., *Reducing Residential Crime and Fear*, 153.
40 Hollander et al., *Reducing Residential Crime and Fear*, 11.
41 Hollander et al., *Reducing Residential Crime and Fear*, 5–6, 122.
42 Mesa Police Department, *Neighborhood Block Captains Guide* (Mesa, AZ, 1999), 4.
43 National Sheriffs' Association, *National Neighborhood Watch Program Review*, 2.
44 National Sheriffs' Association, *National Neighborhood Watch Program Manual*, 19.
45 William H. Petersen, *National Neighborhood Watch Program Discretionary Grant Progress Report*, 1.
46 Midwest Research Institute, *Evaluation of the National Sheriffs' Association*, 1.
47 Midwest Research Institute, *Evaluation of the National Sheriffs' Association*, 1–2.
48 Midwest Research Institute, *Evaluation of the National Sheriffs' Association*, 24.
49 Midwest Research Institute, *Evaluation of the National Sheriffs' Association*, 52.
50 Midwest Research Institute, *Evaluation of the National Sheriffs' Association*, 52.
51 Midwest Research Institute, *Evaluation of the National Sheriffs' Association*, 52.
52 Office of Crime Prevention, *Program Guide*, 3.
53 See Beth Kassab, "Trayvon Martin Would Be Alive if Neighborhood Watch Rules Followed," *Orlando Sentinel*, March 14, 2012, http://articles.orlandosentinel.com; and Jane Morse, "Neighborhood Watch Programs Help Build Citizen-Police Trust: Communities Find Fighting Residential Crime Requires Cooperation," *America.Gov*, March 10, 2009. www.america.gov.
54 Campbell Robertson and John Schwartz, "Shooting Focuses Attention on a Program That Seeks to Avoid Guns," *New York Times* (March 23, 2012): A12.
55 Robertson and Schwartz, "Shooting Focuses Attention," A12.
56 Robertson and Schwartz, "Shooting Focuses Attention," A12.
57 Robertson and Schwartz, "Shooting Focuses Attention," A12.
58 Robertson and Schwartz, "Shooting Focuses Attention," A12.
59 Yin et al., *Patrolling the Neighborhood Beat*, iii.
60 Virginia Division of Justice and Crime Prevention, *Neighborhood Watch Guide*, 1.
61 Virginia Division of Justice and Crime Prevention, *Neighborhood Watch Guide*, 2.
62 Virginia Division of Justice and Crime Prevention, *Neighborhood Watch Guide*, 6.
63 Virginia Division of Justice and Crime Prevention, *Neighborhood Watch Guide*, 6.
64 National Institute of Justice, *Calling the Police*, xxxii.

65 Sanford Police Department, "History of Neighborhood Watch," *Trayvon Martin Killing: Neighborhood Watch 2* (n.d.): 3. Available at http://documents.latimes.com/trayvon-martin-and-george-zimmerman.

66 Bureau of Justice Assistance, *Neighborhood Watch Manual: USAonWatch— National Neighborhood Watch Program* (Washington, DC: Bureau of Justice Assistance, 2010), 7. Available at www.usaonwatch.org.

67 Bureau of Justice Assistance, *Neighborhood Watch Manual*, 7.

68 Sanford Police Department, "Crime Prevention Tips," *Trayvon Martin Killing: Neighborhood Watch 2* (n.d.): 7. Available at http://documents.latimes.com/trayvon-martin-and-george-zimmerman.

69 Bureau of Justice Assistance, *Neighborhood Watch Manual*, 21.

70 Bureau of Justice Assistance, *Neighborhood Watch Manual*, 24.

71 Bureau of Justice Assistance, *Neighborhood Watch Manual*, 25.

72 Bureau of Justice Assistance, *Neighborhood Watch Manual*, 22.

73 See http://neighborhoodwatchradio.org.

74 Morgan Whitaker, "Sanford Police Chief Flips on Gun Ban for Neighborhood Watch," *MSNBC.com*, November 6, 2013. www.msnbc.com.

75 Kim Clare, "Sanford Bans Guns for Neighborhood Watch Volunteers," *MSNBC.com*, October 31, 2013. www.msnbc.com.

76 Clare, "Sanford Bans Guns."

77 Whitaker, "Sanford Police Chief Flips on Gun Ban," and Susan Jacobson and Arelis R. Hernández, "Sanford Police Chief Clarifies Gun Rules for Neighborhood Watch Volunteers," *Orlando Sentinel*, November 5, 2013. http://articles.orlandosentinel.com.

78 Jacobson and Hernández, "Sanford Police Chief Clarifies Gun Rules."

79 Whitaker, "Sanford Police Chief Flips on Gun Ban."

80 Whitaker, "Sanford Police Chief Flips on Gun Ban."

81 Clare, "Sanford Bans Guns."

82 Jacobson and Hernández, "Sanford Police Chief Clarifies Gun Rules."

83 Garofalo and McLeod, "The Structure and Operation of Neighborhood Watch," 338–39.

84 Marx and Archer, "Citizen Involvement in the Law Enforcement Process."

85 Yin et al., *Patrolling the Neighborhood Beat*, 215–16.

86 Yin et al., *Patrolling the Neighborhood Beat*, 216.

87 Yin et al., *Patrolling the Neighborhood Beat*, 219.

88 Cicchini and Kushner, *But They Didn't Read Me My Rights*, 83.

89 Pennell, Curtis, and Henderson, *Guardian Angels*, 61.

90 For more on this conflict, see Pennell, Curtis, and Henderson, *Guardian Angels*, 110–13; and Susan Pennell, Christine Curtis, Joel Henderson, and Jeff Tayman, "Guardian Angels: A Unique Approach to Crime Prevention," *Crime and Delinquency* 35.3 (1989): 378–400. Partly as a result of these cultural, legal, and violent methods of conduct regulation, citizen's arrests are exceedingly rare. Indeed, this has been the case for decades. Soon after the Guardian Angels helped introduce

the term "citizen's arrest" into the popular lexicon, in 1984 a Department of Justice task force found that victims and witnesses chased and restrained suspects in too few cases to generate reliable statistics about the phenomenon. See National Institute of Justice, *Calling the Police*, 136.

91 Berkowitz, *Local Heroes*, 158.

92 Berkowitz, *Local Heroes*, 156.

93 Berkowitz, *Local Heroes*, 157.

94 Berkowitz, *Local Heroes*, 157.

95 Nicholas Pileggi, "The Guardian Angels: Help—or Hype?," *New York* (November 24, 1980): 14–19.

96 Pileggi, "The Guardian Angels," 19.

97 Breslin, *The World According to Breslin*, 98.

98 Pennell, Curtis, and Henderson, *Guardian Angels*, 114.

99 Pileggi, "The Guardian Angels," 16.

100 Pennell, Curtis, and Henderson, *Guardian Angels*, 69.

101 Berkowitz, *Local Heroes*, 157–58.

102 Pileggi, "The Guardian Angels," 16.

103 Jay Maeder, "Citizens on Patrol Guardian Angels December 1980–February 1981 Chapter 442," *New York Daily News*, October 15, 2001. www.nydailynews.com.

104 "A Way to Remember Frank Melvin," *New York Times*, January 5, 1982. www. nytimes.com.

105 Maeder, "Citizens on Patrol."

106 Breslin, *The World According to Breslin*, 98.

107 Breslin, *The World According to Breslin*, 100.

108 Jennifer N. Grimes, "Guardian Angels," in *Encyclopedia of Street Crime in America* (Thousand Oaks, CA: SAGE, 2013), 183–86.

109 Berkowitz, *Local Heroes*, 158.

110 "Curtis Sliwa: Zimmerman Was 'Mad Dogging,'" *CNN.com*, March 30, 2012. http://cnnpressroom.blogs.cnn.com.

111 Associated Press, "Hazy Statistics Deter Firm Analysis of Officer-Involved Deaths," *San Francisco Chronicle*, December 7, 2014. www.sfgate.com.

112 Kimberly Kindy, Marc Fisher, Julie Tate, and Jennifer Jenkins, "A Year of Reckoning: Police Fatally Shoot Nearly 1,000," *Washington Post*, December 26, 2015. www. washingtonpost.com.

113 Rebecca Lopez, "Inner-City Gun Club Takes Issue with Dallas Police," *WFAA/ ABC News*, January 30, 2015. www.wfaa.com.

114 Huey P. Newton Gun Club, Press Release, August 17, 2014. See "Video: The Texas Based Huey P. Newton Gun Club Participates in Serious Show of Resistance," *Black Talk Radio Network*, August 21, 2014. www.blacktalkradionetwork.com.

115 Aaron Lake Smith, "Revolutionary Gun Clubs Patrolling the Black Neighborhoods of Dallas," *Vice.com*, January 5, 2015. www.vice.com.

116 Smith, "Revolutionary Gun Clubs."

117 Smith, "Revolutionary Gun Clubs."

118 Brandy Zadrozny, "Texas Gun Slingers Police the Police—With a Black Panthers Tactic," *Daily Beast*, January 2, 2015. www.thedailybeast.com.

119 Howard Zinn, *A People's History of the United States* (New York: HarperCollins, 2010), 63–65.

120 Stevens, "Urban Communities and Homicide."

121 Pepinsky, "Issues of Citizen Involvement in Policing," 461.

122 Pepinsky, "Issues of Citizen Involvement in Policing," 461.

123 Andrejevic, *iSpy*, 178.

124 See Reeves, "License to Kill."

125 Patrik Jonsson, "Trayvon Martin 911 Tapes: Who Screamed for Help before Shot Rang Out?," *Christian Science Monitor*, March 17, 2012. www.csmonitor.com.

CHAPTER 4. RECOGNIZE, RESIST, REPORT

1 *Crystal Grendell v. James Gillway, et al.*, United States District Court, District of Maine (July 11, 1997), 3.

2 *Grendell v. Gillway*, 4.

3 Joseph Periera, "The Informants: In a Drug Program, Some Kids Turn in Their Own Parents," *Wall Street Journal* (April 20, 1992): 1, A4.

4 *Grendell v. Gillway*, 7.

5 See Giroux, "Doing Cultural Studies."

6 See Hebdige, *Hiding in the Light*, 19–26.

7 Hall et al., *Policing the Crisis*, 111.

8 See, for example, Kidd, *Making American Boys*; and Kwon, *Uncivil Youth*.

9 "Juvenile Coppettes," 1731.

10 Grant, *The Boy Problem*.

11 Brace, *The Dangerous Classes of New York*, 316–24.

12 Brace, *The Dangerous Classes*, 418.

13 Brace, *The Dangerous Classes*, 28.

14 Brace, *The Dangerous Classes*, 78.

15 Brace, *The Dangerous Classes*, 78–81.

16 Brace, *The Dangerous Classes*, 91.

17 See Donzelot, *The Policing of Families*; Boyer, *Urban Masses and Moral Order*; and Hunt, *Governing Morals*, 110–39.

18 For a more general history of boy police programs, see Greenberg, *Citizens Defending America*, 133–43.

19 "Boy Police," in *The Americana Supplement*, ed. Frederick Converse Beach (New York: Scientific American Compiling Department, 1911), 189.

20 "Boy Police," 189.

21 "Boy Police," 189.

22 "Boy Police for the Fourth?"

23 "Boy Police of New York," 1258.

24 "New York's Campaign of Crime Prevention," 296.

25 Mason, "Boy Police of New York," 708.

26 "The Junior Police of New York City," 653.

27 "Boy Police of New York," 1258.

28 "Boy Police of New York," 1259.

29 "Juvenile Coppettes," 1732.

30 "Juvenile Coppettes," 1732.

31 "Juvenile Coppettes," 1732.

32 "Juvenile Coppettes," 1732.

33 "Juvenile Coppettes," 1731.

34 Goosman, *Group Harmony*, 54.

35 Sealander, *The Failed Century of the Child*, 33; see, more generally, 19–52.

36 Lindquist, *Race, Social Science, and the Crisis of Manhood*, 158–60.

37 Macleod, *Building Character in the American Boy*, 67–71.

38 Washington, "A Study of the Program and Activities of the Junior Police," 1.

39 Butterfield, "Our Kids Are in Trouble," 108.

40 Maxine Davis, "The Cop Appeals to the Kids,"97. Also see Martin Alan Greenberg, "A Short History of Junior Police," *Police Chief Magazine*, April 2008. www.policechiefmagazine.org.

41 Davis, "The Cop Appeals," 28.

42 Ness, "The Participation of Boys," 338.

43 Juttee T. Garth, "Juvenile Delinquency and Suggested Treatment," 16.

44 Davis, "The Cop Appeals," 96.

45 Woltman, "Town Up in Arms."

46 New York Times News Service, "U.S. Drug Czar Urges Teens to Just Say Snitch," *Chicago Tribune*, May 19, 1989. http://articles.chicagotribune.com.

47 For an excellent analysis of our society's panic about youth violence during the 1990s, see Franklin E. Zimring, *American Youth Violence* (New York: Oxford University Press, 1998).

48 Yin et al., *Patrolling the Neighborhood Beat*, 296.

49 Yin et al., *Patrolling the Neighborhood Beat*, 297.

50 Yin et al., *Patrolling the Neighborhood Beat*, 300.

51 Campbell, Sahid, and Stang, *Law and Order Reconsidered*, 416.

52 Gottfredson, "School-Based Crime Prevention," 381.

53 For example, see Foucault, *Discipline and Punish*, 135–69; Giroux, *The Abandoned Generation*, 71–102; Matthew, "Reading, Writing, and Readiness"; and Simmons, "The Docile Body in School Space."

54 Klein, *Street Gang Patterns and Policies*, 97. See Patrick Boyle, "A D.A.R.E.ing Rescue: How an Intervention by Critics and Federal Officials Brought the Anti-Drug Program into Rehab," *Youth Today* 10.4 (2001): 16.

55 See Gard and Pluim, *Schools and Public Health*, 87–112.

56 See "About," *DARE.org*. www.dare.org.

57 Stoil and Hill, *Preventing Substance Abuse*, 59.

58 "D.A.R.E. Program Celebrates Twenty-Five Years," *DARE.org*, August 18, 2014. www.dare.org.

59 Jennifer Gonnerman, "Truth or D.A.R.E.: The Dubious Drug-Education Program Takes New York," *Village Voice*, April 6, 1999. www.villagevoice.com. Others, however, disagree that D.A.R.E. is effective at reaching youth. As Ryan Grim has pointed out, 1996 was the first year that high school drug use rose, after declines through the 1980s and early 1990s. The class of 1996 was the first cohort to have received D.A.R.E. all throughout their public school years, as the program was founded in 1983. See Grim, *This Is Your Country on Drugs*, 91–92.

60 Kevin Sapp, "Florida Law Enforcement Teaching New D.A.R.E. Program," *F.D.O.A. e-Times* 1.2 (December 21, 2005): 3–4.

61 See, for example, "Father & Son in Kindergarten D.A.R.E. Class," *DARE.org*, February 16, 2014. www.dare.org.

62 *Child Safety Coloring and Activity Book: Safety at Home, at School, and with Friends* (Lansing: Michigan Legislature, 2011), 30. Available at www.legislature. mi.gov/publications/childsafety coloring.pdf.

63 *Child Safety Coloring and Activity Book*, 16.

64 D.A.R.E. America, *Elementary and Middle School Curriculum*, 2. Available at http://darealaska.com/download/teachers/Elementary%20and%20Middle%20 School%20Curriculum%20Design.pdf.

65 *Child Safety Coloring and Activity Book*, 40.

66 Katrina B., "Kids' Essays," *DareAlaska.com*. http://darealaska.com.

67 Taylor D., "Kids' Essays," *DareAlaska.com*. http://darealaska.com.

68 Steve, "Kids' Essays," *DareAlaska.com*. http://darealaska.com.

69 Bureau of Justice Assistance, *Implementing Project DARE*, 72.

70 Bureau of Justice Assistance, *Implementing Project DARE*, 34.

71 Bureau of Justice Assistance, *Implementing Project DARE*, 72.

72 Marx, *Undercover*, 207.

73 Periera, "The Informants."

74 Ericson and Haggerty, *Policing the Risk Society*, 267.

75 James Bovard, "DARE Scare: Turning Children into Informants?," *Washington Post* (January 30, 1994): C3.

76 Jeff Rivenbark and Tom Roussey, "Elementary Student Brings Pot to School to Turn in His Parents," *WBTV.com*, October 15, 2010. www.wbtv.com.

77 *Safe City Commission Campus Crime Stoppers: 2010–2011 School Year End Report* (Fort Worth, TX: Safe City Commission, 2011).

78 See, for example, Benjamin Alexander-Bloch, "Two Belle Chasse Middle School Students Arrested on Drug Charges," *Times-Picayune*, October 22, 2014. www. nola.com; and "Safe Schools Hotline–Youth Program," *Crimestoppers Greater New Orleans*. www.crimestoppersgno.org.

79 Gonnerman, "Truth or D.A.R.E."

80 See Gonnerman, "Truth or D.A.R.E."

81 Anderson, *Code of the Street*.

82 Natapoff, *Snitching*, 135–38.

83 Woldoff and Weiss, "Stop Snitchin'," 189.

84 See Police Executive Research Forum, *The Stop Snitching Phenomenon*, 10–11, 19–26.

85 Police Executive Research Forum, *The Stop Snitching Phenomenon*, 10.

86 Whitman and Davis, *Snitches Get Stitches*, 9.

87 "Police: Juveniles Laughed after Setting 15-Year-Old on Fire," *CNN.com*, October 14, 2009. www.cnn.com.

88 Whitman and Davis, *Snitches Get Stitches*, 7.

89 See "Baltimore City Cops Response to Stop Snitching 1 DVD," *YouTube*, December 29, 2007. www.youtube.com.

90 Ryan Davis, "Police Hit Streets with Their Answer to 'Snitch' DVD," *Baltimore Sun*, May 11, 2005. www.baltimoresun.

91 Whitman and Davis, *Snitches Get Stitches*, 11.

92 See Police Executive Research Forum, *The Stop Snitching Phenomenon*, 28–30.

93 Merida, "Fearful Kids Maintain a Code of Silence," *Washington Post* (April 27, 1999): C8.

94 Merida, "Fearful Kids Maintain a Code of Silence."

95 Whitman and Davis, *Snitches Get Stitches*, 47.

96 Whitman and Davis, *Snitches Get Stitches*, 41.

97 Tom Farrey, "'Melo Looks Past Hoops to Streets," *ESPN.com*, December 17, 2006. http://insider.espn.go.com.

98 Whitman and Davis, *Snitches Get Stitches*, 32.

99 Hebdige, *Hiding in the Light*, 18.

CHAPTER 5. TERROR CITIZENSHIP

1 Quoted in "CNN Live Event/Special: Sessions, Murphy Debate Use of Military Tribunals; Willis, Frederick Discuss U.S. Recession; Frank, Hitchens Talk about Military Efforts," *CNN.com*, December 1, 2001. http://transcripts.cnn.com.

2 Martin Jay, "FBI Surrounds House of Saudi Student after Sightings of Him with Pressure Cooker Pot—Only to Discover He Was Cooking Rice," *Daily Mail*, May 12, 2013. www.dailymail.co.uk.

3 Jay, "FBI Surrounds House."

4 Packer, "Becoming Bombs."

5 "Bomb Squad Called in for Old Metal Luncbox," *WFMZ-TV News*, September 22, 2014. www.wfmz.com.

6 Sean Alfano, "Toothpaste Terror in the Skies," *CBSNews.com*, August 24, 2006. www.cbsnews.com.

7 U.S. Department of Homeland Security, "Walmart Public Service Announcement," *YouTube*, December 6, 2010. www.youtube.com.

8 Kelly Gates, for example, questions "whether the post-9/11 moment represents a decisive transformation in the configuration of state power. Are the U.S. 'homeland security' policies ushering in a new era of state sovereignty with potential authoritarian tendencies?" Gates, "Biometrics and Post-9/11 Technostalgia," 49.

9   For a description of the discourses and programs that have characterized this "new" enemy and the state of exception that has accompanied it, see Ralph, *America's War on Terror.*

10 Rutherford, "At War," 632. Also see Hay and Andrejevic, "Toward an Analytic of Governmental Experiments," 340.

11 See Monahan, "Identity Theft Vulnerability"; and Simon, *Governing through Crime.*

12 Mythen and Walklate, "Communicating the Terrorist Risk."

13 See Beck, "Living in the World Risk Society."

14 Best, "Ambiguity, Uncertainty, and Risk," 356.

15 Brian Palmer, "10,000 Potential Maniacs," *Slate,* November 8, 2010. www.slate.com.

16 Donohue, *The Cost of Counterterrorism,* 254.

17 Mattelart, *The Globalization of Surveillance,* 72.

18 Mattelart, *The Globalization of Surveillance,* 72.

19 Mattelart, *The Globalization of Surveillance,* 72. For a related account of this transformation, see Jack Bratich's discussion of the evolution from the *polis* to the *polemos,* from the government of citizens to the control of combatants. Bratich, "User-Generated Discontent."

20 Crandall, "Envisioning the Homefront," 20.

21 Kennedy, *Over Here,* 82.

22 Capozzola, *Uncle Sam Wants You,* 122.

23 For more on unidentifiable enemies in the War on Terror, see Gates, *Our Biometric Future,* 98–99.

24 Celia Malone Kingsbury, *For Home and Country: World War I Propaganda on the Home Front* (Lincoln: University of Nebraska Press, 2010), 177.

25 Blum, *Dark Invasion.*

26 Gary, *The Nervous Liberals,* 19.

27 Cornebise, *War as Advertised,* 72.

28 For how the "Silence Means Security" program took hold in American life, see Hales, *Atomic Spaces,* 243–72.

29 See the U.S. National Archives' World War Two propaganda archive for examples of many of these posters: http://www.archives.gov/exhibits/powers_of_persuasion/powers_of_persuasion_home.html#.

30 See Birdwell, *Celluloid Soldiers.*

31 See the poster archived at http://users.humboldt.edu/ogayle/HowtotellaCommunist.png.

32 For analyses, see Bennett and Woollacott, *Bond and Beyond*; and Miller, *Spyscreen.*

33 See "Armed Forces Information Film: Recognizing a Communist," *YouTube.* www.youtube.com.

34 See Biesecker, "No Time for Mourning," 158.

35 Andrejevic, "'Securitainment' in the Post-9/11 Era."

36 Kackman, *Citizen Spy*, 1.

37 See, in particular, Moynihan, *Secrecy*.

38 Dick, *Radical Innocence*, 6–9.

39 Agamben, "What Is an Apparatus?," 23.

40 See, for example, Robert L. Snow, *Terrorists among Us: The Militia Threat* (Cambridge, MA: Perseus Publishing, 1999).

41 Levitas, *The Terrorist Next Door*.

42 Molotch, *Against Security*, 192.

43 George W. Bush, *Proposal to Create the Department of Homeland Security*, *DHS.gov*, June 2002, 2. www.dhs.gov.

44 Bush, *Proposal to Create the Department of Homeland Security*, 2.

45 Patrick Leahy, "Congressional Record—Senate, November 19, 2002," *Congressional Record: Proceedings and Debates of the 107th Congress, Second Session* (Washington, DC: U.S. Government Printing Office, 2002), 23012.

46 See Nat Hentoff, "Ashcroft's Master Play to Spy on Us," *Village Voice*, August 6, 2002. www.villagevoice.com.

47 Important elements of the TIPS program, however, have survived under other guises. Consider, just for example, how employees of Walt Disney World and Sea-World have been trained by the Transportation Security Administration (TSA) to keep an eye out for terrorists. Jana Winter, "TSA Trained Disney, SeaWorld to SPOT Terrorists," *The Intercept*, April 16, 2015, https://theintercept.com.

48 "Homeland Security Revives Supersnoop," *Washington Times*, March 8, 2007. www.washingtontimes.com.

49 Paul Wolfowitz, "Memorandum: Collection, Reporting, and Analysis of Terrorist Threats to DoD Within the United States," May 2, 2003. Available at https://wikileaks.org/wiki/Paul_Wolfowitz_TALON_memo.

50 Wolfowitz, "Memorandum."

51 Doug Sample, "'Eagle Eyes' Teaches Pentagon Personnel to Be on the Lookout," *DOD News*, January 24, 2003, www.defense.gov.

52 Sample, "'Eagle Eyes' Teaches Pentagon Personnel."

53 Flynn and Prieto, *Neglected Defense*, 43.

54 Flynn and Pietro, *Neglected Defense*, 43.

55 Flynn and Pietro, *Neglected Defense*, 43.

56 See Department of Homeland Security, "If You See Something, Say Something: About the Campaign," *DHS.gov*, http://www.dhs.gov/see-something-say-something/about-campaign.

57 U.S. Department of Homeland Security, "'If You See Something, Say Something (TM)' Public Awareness Video," *YouTube*, March 15, 2011. www.youtube.com.

58 U.S. Department of Homeland Security, "If You See Something."

59 "Buying Water Is Not a Suspicious Activity," *ACLU.org*. www.aclu.org.

60 Laura Muth, "How Many Terror Threats Does the U.S. Get Every Day?," *PolicyMic*, August 8, 2013. www.policymic.com. Also see Palmer, "10,000 Potential Maniacs."

61 Julia Harumi Mass, "The Government Is Spying on You: ACLU Releases New Evidence of Overly Broad Surveillance of Everyday Activities," *ACLU.org*, September 19, 2013. www.aclu.org.

62 "Buying Water Is Not a Suspicious Activity," *ACLU.org*.

63 Mass, "The Government Is Spying on You."

64 Jack Cloherty and Pierre Thomas, "Attorney General Eric Holder's Blunt Warning on Terror Attacks," *ABCNews.com*, December 21, 2010. http://abcnews.go.com.

65 Cloherty and Thomas, "Attorney General Eric Holder's Blunt Warning."

66 Janet Napolitano, "State of America's Homeland Security Address," *DHS.gov*, January 27, 2011. www.dhs.gov.

67 Napolitano, "State of America's Homeland Security Address."

68 Hinds and Grabosky, "Responsibilisation Revisited," 95.

69 Robert Jensen, "Written Testimony of DHS Office of Public Affairs Principal Deputy Assistant Secretary Robert Jensen," *DHS.gov*, June 14, 2013. www.dhs.gov.

70 Jeh Johnson, "Secretary Johnson Highlights Super Bowl XLIX Security Operations," *DHS.gov*, January 28, 2015. www.dhs.gov .

71 Johnson, "Secretary Johnson Highlights Super Bowl."

72 See "Campaign Print Materials," *DHS.gov*. www.dhs.gov.

73 See Mikael Thalen, "'See Something, Say Something' Promotional Items Handed out at NFL Games," *Infowars.com*, November 11, 2014. www.infowars.com.

74 "'If You See Something, Say Something' Video: Protect Your Every Day Public Service Announcement," *DHS.gov*, January 21, 2015. www.dhs.gov.

75 Coleman, *Hacker, Hoaxer, Whistleblower, Spy*, n.p.

76 Brian Barrett, "Hack Brief: Hacker Leaks the Info of Thousands of FBI and DHS Employees," *Wired.com*, February 8, 2016. www.wired.com.

77 Tim Shorrock, "Obama's Crackdown on Whistleblowers," *Nation*, March 26, 2013. www.thenation.com.

78 Amy Davidson, "Manning's Sentence, Miranda's Detention," *New Yorker*, August 21, 2013. www.newyorker.com.

79 Jacob L. Lew, "M-11-06: Memorandum for the Heads of Executive Departments and Agencies," November 28, 2010. Available at www.fas.org/sgp/obama/wh-wikileaks.pdf.

80 Pentagon Force Protection Agency, "Security Advisory No. 14-01: Subject: Recent Threats and Individual Protective Measures," October 24, 2014. Available at projects.militarytimes.com/pdfs/PFPA-102914.pdf.

81 Pentagon Force Protection Agency, "Security Advisory No. 14-01." Emphasis in original.

82 Pentagon Force Protection Agency, "Security Advisory No. 14-01."

83 See Kumar, *A Foreigner Carrying in the Crook of His Arm a Tiny Bomb*; and Human Rights Watch, *Illusions of Justice: Human Rights Abuses in US Terrorism Prosecutions* (New York: Human Rights Institute at Columbia Law School, 2014).

84 Trevor Aaronson, "The Informants," *Mother Jones*, September/October 2011. www.motherjones.com.

85 In 2012, the *New York Times* claimed: "Of the twenty-two most frightening terror-
    ist plots on American soil since 9/11, fourteen were organized during sting opera-
    tions." David K. Shipler, "Terrorist Plots, Hatched by the F.B.I.," *New York Times*
    (April 29, 2012): SR4.

86 Shipler, "Terrorist Plots."

87 Perhaps the most notorious example of this is the case of the Newburgh Four,
    a group of poor African American Muslims who were set up by an ex-convict-
    turned-FBI informant named Shahed Hussain. See Human Rights Watch, *Illu-
    sions of Justice*.

88 Pamela Geller, "Can American Stop Paris-Style Terror from Coming Here?,"
    WND.com, January 10, 2015. www.wnd.com.

89 Jeh Johnson, "Remarks by Secretary of Homeland Security Jeh Johnson at the
    Council on Foreign Relations—As Delivered," *DHS.gov*, September 10, 2014.
    www.dhs.gov.

90 See, especially, Andrew Rubin's nuanced commentary in *Archives of Authority*,
    24–46.

91 And as Rachel Hall has pointed out, this has the complementary effect of turning
    us into "citizen-suspects." See Hall, "Of Ziploc Bags and Black Holes."

92 See Gary T. Marx's classic *Undercover*.

93 See Packer, "Becoming Bombs."

94 Jeh Johnson, "Remarks by Secretary of Homeland Security Jeh C. Johnson at the
    Adams Center—as Prepared for Delivery," *DHS.gov*, December 7, 2015. www.dhs.
    gov.

95 Zedner, "Policing before and after the Police," 92–93.

CONCLUSION

1 Williams, *Our Enemies in Blue*, 223.

2 Berten and Foucault, "What Our Present Is," 136–37.

3 Monahan, *Surveillance in the Time of Insecurity*, 128.

4 Lyon, *Surveillance after September 11*, 157.

5 Packer, "Epistemology Not Ideology."

6 See Lyotard, *The Differend*.

7 Dyer-Witheford and De Peuter, *Games of Empire*, 218.

8 Lazzaratto, "Immaterial Labor," 135.

9 Lazzaratto, "Immaterial Labor," 134.

10 Greene, "Rhetoric and Capitalism," 203. Also see Galloway and Thacker's discus-
    sion of "life-resistance" in *The Exploit*, 78–81.

11 Greene, "Orator Communist," 87. Also see May, "Orator-Machine," 440–42.

12 Mattelart, *The Globalization of Surveillance*, 184.

13 Deleuze, "Control and Becoming," 175.

14 See Massumi, "Potential Politics and the Primacy of Preemption."

15 Martin Gansberg, "Thirty-Eight Who Saw Murder Didn't Call the Police," *New
    York Times*, March 27, 1964. Quoted in Rosenthal, *Thirty-Eight Witnesses*, 19–20.

16 For more information on this controversy, see Nicholas Lemann, "A Call for Help: What the Kitty Genovese Story Really Means," *New Yorker*, March 10, 2014. www. newyorker.com.

17 Rosenthal, *Thirty-Eight Witnesses*, 64. Quoted in Lemann, "A Call for Help."

18 Rosenthal, *Thirty-Eight Witnesses*, 67–68.

19 Rosenthal, *Thirty-Eight Witnesses*, viii. Quoted in Lemann, "A Call for Help."

20 Lemann, "A Call for Help."

21 See Turkle, *Alone Together*.

22 Virno, "Virtuosity and Revolution," 199.

23 Molotch, *Against Security*, 194.

24 See especially Mann, Nolan, and Wellman, "Sousveillance."

25 For more on the importance of this development, see Wilson and Serisier, "Video Activism."

26 Lee Rainie and Mary Madden, "Americans' Privacy Strategies Post-Snowden," *Pew Research Center*, March 16, 2015. www.pewinternet.org.

27 Jack A. Smith, "Obama Defends NSA Spying on Americans," *Foreign Policy Journal*, January 27, 2014. www.foreignpolicyjournal.com.

28 Andrew Leonard, "Edward Snowden's Unintended Internet Revolution," *Salon*, October 15, 2013. www.salon.com.

29 See "History," *Berkeley Copwatch*. www.berkeleycopwatch.org.

30 "History," *Berkeley Copwatch*.

31 See Andrea Pritchett and Annie Paradise, *The Criminalization of Copwatching: Berkeley Copwatch Report on State Violence, Police Repression, and Attacks on Direct Monitoring*. (Berkeley, CA: Copwatch, 2011), 6. http://berkeleycopwatch.org.

32 Aune, "The Work of Rhetoric in the Age of Digital Dissemination," 240.

33 See user-generated YouTube footage of the shooting at https://www.youtube.com/watch?v=Q2LDw5l_yMI.

34 "ACLU-NJ Launches Smartphone App That Lets Users Secretly Record Police Stops," *CBS New York*, July 3, 2012. http://newyork.cbslocal.com.

35 See "Stop and Frisk Watch App," *NYCLU.org*. www.nyclu.org.

36 Michel Foucault, *Security, Territory, Population*, 144.

37 See Hall et al., *Policing the Crisis*, 202.

38 Cruikshank, *The Will to Empower*, 123.

REFERENCES

Abrahams, Ray. 1998. *Vigilant Citizens: Vigilantism and the State*. Malden, MA: Polity.

Agamben, Giorgio. 2000. "Sovereign Police." In *Means without Ends: Notes on Politics*, 103–8. Trans. Vincenzo Binetti and Cesare Casarino. Minneapolis: University of Minnesota Press.

———. 2007. "What Is an Apparatus?" In *What Is an Apparatus and Other Essays*, 1–24. Ed. Werner Hamacher. Trans. David Kishik and Stefan Pedatella. Stanford, CA: Stanford University Press.

Amoore, Louise. 2007. "Vigilant Visualities: The Watchful Politics of the War on Terror." *Security Dialogue* 38 (2): 215–32.

Anderson, Elijah. 1999. *Code of the Street: Decency, Violence, and the Moral Life of the Inner City*. New York: W.W. Norton and Co.

Andrejevic, Mark. 2007. *iSpy: Surveillance and Power in the Interactive Era*. Lawrence: University of Kansas Press.

———. 2011. "'Securitainment' in the Post-9/11 Era." *Continuum: Journal of Media and Cultural Studies* 25 (2): 165–75.

Aune, James Arnt. 1997. "The Work of Rhetoric in the Age of Digital Dissemination." *Quarterly Journal of Speech* 83: 230–68.

Baines, Anthony. 1993. *Brass Instruments: Their History and Development*. Mineola, NY: Dover.

Barry, Andrew. 1996. "Lines of Communication and Spaces of Rule." In *Foucault and Political Reason: Liberalism, Neo-Liberalism, and Rationalities of Government*, 123–42. Ed. Andrew Barry, Thomas Osborne, and Nikolas S. Rose. Chicago: University of Chicago Press.

Battles, Kathleen. 2010. *Calling All Cars: Radio Dragnets and the Technology of Policing*. Minneapolis: University of Minnesota Press.

Beck, Ulrich. 2006. "Living in the World Risk Society." *Economy and Society* 35 (3): 329–45.

Bennett, Tony. 1995. *The Birth of the Museum: History, Theory, Politics*. London: Routledge.

Bennett, Tony, and Janet Woollacott. 1987. *Bond and Beyond: The Political Career of a Popular Hero*. London: Methuen.

Berkowitz, Bill, 1998. *Local Heroes: The Rebirth of Heroism in America*. Lanham, MD: Lexington Books.

Berten, André, and Michel Foucault. 2007. "What Our Present Is." In Michel Foucault, *The Politics of Truth*, 129–43. Ed. Sylvère Lotringer. Trans. Lysa Hochroth and Catherine Porter. Los Angeles: Semiotext(e).

Best, Jacqueline. 2008. "Ambiguity, Uncertainty, and Risk: Rethinking Indeterminacy." *International Political Sociology* 2: 355–74.

Bickman, Leonard. 1975. "Bystander Intervention in a Crime: The Effect of a Mass-Media Campaign." *Journal of Applied Social Psychology* 5 (4): 296–302.

Biesecker, Barbara A. 2007. "No Time for Mourning: The Rhetorical Production of the Melancholic Citizen-Subject in the War on Terror." *Philosophy and Rhetoric* 40 (1): 147–69.

Birdwell, Michael. 2000. *Celluloid Soldiers: The Warner Bros. Campaign against Nazism.* New York: New York University Press.

Bloom, Lisa. 2014. *Suspicion Nation: The Story of the Trayvon Martin Injustice and Why We Continue to Repeat It.* Berkeley, CA: Counterpoint.

Blum, Howard. 2015. *Dark Invasion: 1915—Germany's Secret War and the Hunt for the First Terrorist Cell in America.* New York: Harper Perennial.

Bouthoul, Gaston. 1975. "Definitions of Terrorism." In *International Terrorism and World Security*, 50–59. Ed. David Carlton and Carlo Schaerf. London: Croom Helm.

"Boy Police for the Fourth?" 1907. *Bulletin of the League of American Municipalities* 8 (2): 51.

"Boy Police of New York." 1917. *The Literary Digest, Volume 54.* New York: Funk and Wagnall's.

Boyer, Paul S. 1978. *Urban Masses and Moral Order in America, 1820–1920.* Cambridge, MA: Harvard University Press.

Brabham, Daren C. 2008. "Crowdsourcing as a Model for Problem Solving: An Introduction and Cases." *Convergence: The International Journal of Research into New Media Technologies* 14 (1): 75–90.

Brace, Charles Loring. 1872. *The Dangerous Classes of New York, and Twenty Years Among Them.* New York: Wynbeck and Hallenbeck.

Bratich, Jack. 2007. "Apocryphal Now Redux." In *Contesting Empire, Globalizing Dissent: Cultural Studies after 9/11*, 264–79. Ed. Norman K. Denzin and Michael D. Giardina. Boulder, CO: Paradigm Press.

———. 2008. *Conspiracy Panics: Political Rationality and Popular Culture.* Albany: State University of New York Press.

———. 2011. "Sovereign Networks, Pre-emptive Transgression, Communications Warfare: Case Studies in Social Movement Media." In *Transgression 2.0: Media, Culture, and the Politics of a Digital Age*, 224–39. Ed. Ted Gournelos and David J. Gunkel. New York: Continuum.

———. 2011. "User-Generated Discontent." *Cultural Studies* 25 (4–5): 621–40.

Breslin, Jimmy. 1984. *The World According to Breslin.* New York: Ticknor and Fields.

Brown, Richard Maxwell. 1975. *Strain of Violence: Historical Studies of American Violence and Vigilantism.* New York: Oxford University Press.

Bureau of Justice Assistance. 2010. *Final Report: Information Sharing Environment (ISE)-Suspicious Activity Reporting (SAR) Evaluation Environment.* Washington, DC: U.S. Department of Justice.

———. 1988. *Implementing Project DARE: Drug Abuse Resistance Education.* Washington, DC: U.S. Department of Justice.

Burn, Richard. 1785. *The Justice of the Peace and Parish Officer, Volume Two.* London: W. Strahan and W. Woodfall.

Butterfield, Roger. 1943. "Our Kids Are in Trouble." *Life.* December 20.

Campbell, James S., Joseph R. Sahid, and David P. Stang. 1972. *Law and Order Reconsidered: A Staff Report to the National Commission on the Causes and Prevention of Violence.* Washington, DC: National Commission on the Causes and Prevention of Violence.

Capozzolla, Christopher. 2010. *Uncle Sam Wants You: World War I and the Making of the Modern American Citizen.* New York: Oxford University Press.

Carey, James W. 1989. "Technology and Ideology: The Case of the Telegraph." In *Communication as Culture: Essays on Media and Society,* 201–29. New York: Routledge.

The Challenge of Crime in a Free Society: A Report by the President's Commission on Law Enforcement and Administration of Justice. 1967. Washington, DC: Government Printing Office.

Chan, Janet. 2007. "Dangerous Art and Suspicious Packages." *Law Text Culture* 11 (1): 51–69.

Chauncey, George. 1994. *Gay New York: Gender, Urban Culture, and the Marking of the Gay Male World, 1890–1940.* New York: Basic Books

Chavez, Leo R. 2013. "Spectacle in the Desert: The Minutemen Project on the U.S.–Mexico Border." In *Governing Immigration through Crime: A Reader,* 115–27. Ed. Julie Dowling and Jonathan Inda. Stanford, CA: Stanford University Press.

Chibnall, Marjorie. 1999. *The Debate on the Norman Conquest.* New York: Manchester University Press.

Chicago Police Department. 1882. *Report of the General Superintendent of Police of the City of Chicago.* Chicago, IL: Geo. K. Hazlitt & Co.

Chriss, James J. 2010. *Beyond Community Policing: From Early Beginnings to the 21st Century.* Boulder, CO: Paradigm Publishers.

Cicchini, Michael D., and Amy B. Kushner. 2010. *But They Didn't Read Me My Rights! Myths, Oddities, and Lies about Our Legal System.* Amherst, NY: Prometheus Books.

Clarkson, Charles Tempest, and J. Hall Richardson. 1889. *Police!* London: The Leadenhall Press.

Coleman, Gabriella. 2014. *Hacker, Hoaxer, Whistleblower, Spy: The Many Faces of Anonymous.* New York: Verso Press.

Colquhoun, Patrick. 1796. *A Treatise on the Police of the Metropolis.* London: H. Fry.

Cornebise, Alfred E. 1984. *War as Advertised: The Four Minute Men and America's Crusade, 1917–1918.* Philadelphia: American Philosophical Society.

Costello, Augustine E. 1885. *Our Police Protectors: History of the New York Police from the Earliest Period to the Present Time.* New York: Chas. F. Roper & Co., 1885.

Crandall, Jordan, with John Armitage. 2005. "Envisioning the Homefront: Militarization, Tracking, and Security Culture." *Journal of Visual Culture* 4 (1): 17–38.

Critchley, T. A. 1967. *A History of Police in England and Wales, 900–1966.* London:

Cruikshank, Barbara. 1999. *The Will to Empower: Democratic Citizens and Other Subjects*. Ithaca, NY: Cornell University Press.

Dahl, Erik J. 2011. "The Plots That Failed: Intelligence Lessons Learned from Unsuccessful Terrorist Attacks against the United States." *Studies in Conflict and Terrorism* 34: 621–48.

Davis, Maxine. 1955. "The Cop Appeals to the Kids." *Saturday Evening Post*. April 29.

Dean, Mitchell. 2003. "Culture Governance and Individualization." In *Governance as Social and Political Communication*, 117–39. Ed. Henrik P. Bang. Manchester, UK: Manchester University Press.

Deleuze, Gilles. 1995. "Control and Becoming." In *Negotiations: 1972–1990*, 169–76. Trans. Martin Joughin. New York: Columbia University Press.

Della Porta, Donatella, and Alice Mattoni. 2014. "Social Networking Sites in Pro-Democracy and Anti-Austerity protests: Some Thoughts from a Social Movement Perspective." In *Social Media, Politics, and the State: Protests, Revolutions, Riots, Crime, and Policing in the Age of Facebook, Twitter, and Facebook*, 39–66. Ed. Daniel Trottier and Christian Fuchs. New York: Routledge.

Department of Homeland Security. 2012. *A Resource Guide to Improve Your Community's Awareness and Reporting of Suspicious Activity: For Law Enforcement and Community Partners*. Washington, DC: Department of Homeland Security.

DeWindt, Anne Rieber, and Edwin Brezette DeWindt. 2006. *Ramsey: The Lives of an English Fenland Town, 1200–1600*. Washington, DC: Catholic University of America Press.

Dick, Bernard F. 1989. *Radical Innocence: A Critical Study of the Hollywood Ten*. Lexington: University of Kentucky Press.

Dohonue, Laura K. 2008. *The Cost of Counterterrorism: Power, Politics, and Liberty*. New York: Oxford University Press.

Donzelot, Jacques. 1997. *The Policing of Families*. Trans. Robert Hurley. Baltimore: Johns Hopkins University Press.

Dorsey, Leroy G. 2007. *We Are All Americans, Pure and Simple: Theodore Roosevelt and the Myth of Americanism*. Tuscaloosa: University of Alabama Press.

Dyer-Witheford, Nick, and Greig de Peuter. 2009. *Games of Empire: Global Capitalism and Video Games*. Minneapolis: University of Minnesota Press.

Easson, Joseph J., and Alex P. Schmid. 2011. "250-plus Academic, Governmental, and Intergovernmental Definitions of Terrorism." In *The Routledge Handbook of Terrorism Research*, 99–157. Ed. Alex P. Schmid. New York: Routledge.

Engels, Jeremy. 2010. *Enemyship: Democracy and Counter-Revolution in the Early Republic*. East Lansing: Michigan State University Press.

Ericson, Richard V., and Kevin D. Haggerty. 1997. *Policing the Risk Society*. Toronto: University of Toronto Press.

Ewald, Francois. 1990. "Norms, Discipline, and the Law." *Representations* 30 (2): 138–61.

Farmer, Michael T. (Ed.). 1981. *Differential Police Response Strategies*. Washington, DC: Police Executive Research Forum.

Feinberg, Leslie. 1996. *Transgender Warriors, Making History from Joan of Arc to Dennis Rodman*. Boston: Beacon Press.

Flynn, Stephen E., and Daniel B. Prieto. 2006. *Neglected Defense: Mobilizing the Private Sector to Support Homeland Security*. New York: Council on Foreign Relations.

Folsom, de Francais (Ed.). 1888. *Our Police: A History of the Baltimore Force from the First Watchman to the Latest Appointee*. Baltimore, MD.

Foucault, Michel. 1977. *Discipline and Punish: The Birth of the Prison*. Trans. Alan Sheridan. New York: Random House.

———. 1978. *The History of Sexuality, Volume I: An Introduction*. Trans. Robert Hurley. New York: Penguin Books.

———. 1994. "Omnes et Singulatim." In *The Essential Works of Foucault, Volume III: Power.*, 134–56. Ed. James D. Faubion. Trans. Robert Hurley and others. New York: New Press.

———. 2004. *Security, Territory, Population: Lectures at the Collège de France, 1977–1978*. Trans. Graham Burchell. New York: Picador.

———. 2003. *Society Must Be Defended: Lectures at the Collège de France, 1975–76*. Trans. Graham Burchell. New York: Picador.

———. 1980. "Two Lectures." In *Power/Knowledge: Selected Interviews and Other Writings, 1972–1977*, 78–108. Ed. Colin Gordon. Trans. Colin Gordon, Leo Marshall, John Mepham, and Kate Soper. New York: Pantheon Books.

Fox, James Alan. 2000. "Demographics and U.S. Homicide." In *The Crime Drop in America*, 288–318. Ed. Alfred Blumstein and Joel Wallman. New York: Cambridge University Press.

Fronc, Jennifer. 2009. *New York Undercover: Private Surveillance in the Progressive Era*. Chicago: University of Chicago Press.

Galloway, Alexander R., and Eugene Thacker. 2007. *The Exploit: A Theory of Networks*. Minneapolis: University of Minnesota Press.

Gard, Michael, and Carolyn Pluim. 2014. *Schools and Public Health: Past, Present, Future*. Lanham, MD: Lexington Books.

Garland, David. 1996. "The Limits of the Sovereign State: Strategies of Crime Control in Contemporary Society." *British Journal of Sociology* 36 (4): 445–71.

Garofalo, James, and Maureen McLeod. 1989. "The Structure and Operation of Neighborhood Watch Programs in the United States." *Crime and Delinquency* 27 (3): 326–44.

Garth, Juttee T. 1945. "Juvenile Delinquency and Suggested Treatment." *Pennsylvania Police and Parole Quarterly* 2 (4): 14–17.

Gary, Brett. 1999. *The Nervous Liberals: Propaganda Anxieties from World War I to the Cold War*. New York: Columbia University Press.

Gates, Kelly A. 2005. "Biometrics and Post-9/11 Technostalgia." *Social Text* 23 (2): 35–53.

———. 2011. *Our Biometric Future: Facial Recognition Technology and the Culture of Surveillance*. New York: New York University Press.

Gates, Kelly, and Shoshana Magnet. 2007. "Communication Research and the Study of Surveillance." *Communication Review* 10 (4): 277–93.

Giddens, Anthony. 1985. "Modernity, Totalitarianism, and Critical Theory." In *The Nation-State and Violence: Volume Two of A Contemporary Critique of Historical Materialism*, 294–341. Cambridge, UK: Polity Press.

Giroux, Henry A. 2003. *The Abandoned Generation: Democracy beyond the Culture of Fear*. New York: Palgrave MacMillan.

———. 1994. "Doing Cultural Studies: Youth and the Challenge of Pedagogy." *Harvard Educational Review* 64 (3): 278–308.

Glynn, Kevin. 2000. *Tabloid Culture: Trash Taste, Popular Power, and the Transformation of American Television*. Durham, NC: Duke University Press.

Goosman, Stuart L. 2005. *Group Harmony: The Urban Roots of Rhythm and Blues*. Philadelphia: University of Pennsylvania Press.

Gottfredson, Denise C. 1998. "School-Based Crime Prevention." In *Preventing Crime: What Works, What Doesn't, What's Promising: A Report to the United States Congress*. Washington, DC: National Institutes of Justice. www.ncjrs.gov.

Gow, Gordon, and Mark Ihnat. 2004. "Prepaid Mobile Phone Service and the Anonymous Caller: Considering Wireless E9-1-1 in Canada." *Surveillance and Society* 1 (4): 555–72.

Grant, Julia. 2014. *The Boy Problem: Educating Boys in Urban America*. Baltimore: Johns Hopkins University Press.

Greenberg, Martin Alan. 2005. *Citizens Defending America: From Colonial Times to the Age of Terrorism*. Pittsburgh: University of Pittsburgh Press.

Greene, Ronald Walter. 2006. "Orator Communist." *Philosophy and Rhetoric* 39 (1): 85–95.

———. 2004. "Rhetoric and Capitalism: Rhetorical Agency as Communicative Labor." *Philosophy and Rhetoric* 37 (3): 188–206.

———. 2009. "Rhetorical Materialism: The Rhetorical Subject and the General Intellect." In *Rhetoric, Materiality, and Politics*, 43–65. Ed. Barbara A. Biesecker and John Louis Lucaites. New York: Peter Lang.

———. 2005. "Y Movies: Film and the Modernization of Pastoral Power." *Communication and Critical/Cultural Studies* 2 (1): 20–36

Greene, Ronald Walter, and Darrin Hicks. 2005. "Lost Convictions: Debating Both Sides and the Ethical Self-Fashioning of Liberal Citizens." *Cultural Studies* 19 (1): 100–26.

Grim, Ryan. 2009. *This Is Your Country on Drugs: The Secret History of Getting High in America*. Hoboken, NJ: John Wiley and Sons.

Haggerty, Kevin D., and Richard V. Ericson. 2002. "The Surveillant Assemblage." *British Journal of Sociology* 51 (4): 605–22.

Hales, Peter Bacon. 1997. *Atomic Spaces: Living on the Manhattan Project*. Urbana: University of Illinois Press.

Hall, Rachel. 2007. "Of Ziploc Bags and Black Holes: The Aesthetics of Transparency in the War on Terror." *Communication Review* 10 (4): 319–46.

———. 2009. *Wanted: The Outlaw in American Visual Culture*. Charlottesville: University of Virginia Press.

Hall, Stuart, Chas Critcher, Tony Jefferson, John Clarke, and Brian Roberts. 1978. *Policing the Crisis: Policing, the State, and Law and Order*. London: Macmillan.

Hasian, Marouf, Jr., and George F. McHendry, Jr. 2012. "The Attempted Legitimation of Vigilante Civil Border Patrols, the Militarization of the Mexican-US Border, and the

Law of Unintended Consequences." In *Border Rhetorics: Citizenship and Identity on the US-Mexico Frontier*, 103–16. Ed. D. Robert Dechaine. Tuscaloosa: University of Alabama Press.

Hay, James, and Mark Andrejevic. 2006. "Toward an Analytic of Governmental Experiments in These Times: Homeland Security as the New Social Security." *Cultural Studies* 20 (4–5): 331–48.

Hess, Kristy, and Lisa Waller. 2013. "The Digital Pillory: Media Shaming of 'Ordinary' People for Minor Crimes." *Continuum: Journal of Media and Cultural Studies* 28 (1): 101–11.

Hebdige, Dick. 1988. *Hiding in the Light: On Images and Things*. New York: Routledge.

Hewitt, Steve. 2010. *Snitch!: A History of the Modern Intelligence Informer*. New York: Continuum.

Hinds, Lyn, and Peter Grabosky. 2010. "Responsibilisation Revisited: From Concept to Attribution in Crime Control." *Security Journal* 23 (1): 95–113.

Hollander, Brian, et al. 1979. *Reducing Residential Crime and Fear: The Hartford Neighborhood Crime Prevention Program*. Washington, DC: Department of Justice.

Horn, Eva. 2003. "Knowing the Enemy: The Epistemology of Secret Intelligence." Trans. Sara Ogger. *Grey Room* 11 (1): 58–85.

Howe, Jeff. 2008. *Crowdsourcing: Why the Power of the Crowd Is Driving the Future of Business*. New York: Random House.

Hunt, Alan. 1999. *Governing Morals: A Social History of Moral Regulation*. New York: Cambridge University Press.

Jenkins, Henry. 2006. *Convergence Culture: Where Old and New Media Collide*. New York: New York University Press.

Johnson, Herbert A., and Nancy Travis Wolfe. 1996. *History of Criminal Justice*. Cincinnati: Anderson.

Johnston, Les. 1996. "What Is Vigilantism?" *British Journal of Criminology* 36 (2): 220–36.

Jones, Benjamin R. 2007. "Comment: Virtual Neighborhood Watch: Open Source Software and Community Policing against Cybercrime." *Journal of Criminal Law and Criminology* 97 (2): 601–29.

"The Junior Police of New York City." 1915. *The Survey, Volume 33*. New York: Survey Associates.

Justice Kennedy Commission. 2004. *Reports with Recommendations to the ABA House of Delegates, August 2004*. Chicago: American Bar Association.

"Juvenile Coppettes." 1916. *The Literary Digest, Volume 52*. New York: Funk and Wagnall's.

Kackman, Michael. 2005. *Citizen Spy: Television, Espionage, and Cold War Culture* Minneapolis: University of Minnesota Press.

Kennedy, David M. 2004. *Over Here: The First World War and American Society*. New York: Oxford University Press.

Kidd, Kenneth B. 2004. *Making American Boys: Boyology and the Feral Tale*. Minneapolis: University of Minnesota Press.

Kinsman, Gary. 2000. "Constructing Gay Men and Lesbians as National Security Risks." In *Whose National Security? Canadian State Surveillance and the Creation of Enemies*, 142–53. Ed. Gary Kinsman, Dieter Buse, and Mercedes Steedman. Toronto: Between the Lines Press.

Kittler, Friedrich. 1999. *Gramophone, Film, Typewriter*. Trans. Geoffrey Winthrop-Young and Michael Wutz. Stanford, CA: Stanford University Press.

———. 1997. "Media Wars: Trenches, Lightning, Stars." In *Literature, Media, Information Systems: Essays*, 117–29. Ed. John Johnston. Amsterdam: G and B Arts International.

Klein, Malcolm W. 2006. *Street Gang Patterns and Policies*. New York: Oxford University Press.

Klein, Rachel. 1992. *Unification of a Slave State: The Rise of the Planter Class in the South Carolina Backcountry, 1760–1808*. Chapel Hill: University of North Carolina Press.

Krainik, Peggy Wilkins. 2002. "Amber Alert." *Law and Order* 50 (12): 84–85.

Kumar, Amitava. 2010. *A Foreigner Carrying in the Crook of His Arm a Tiny Bomb*. Durham, NC: Duke University Press.

Kwon, Soo Ah. 2013. *Uncivil Youth: Race, Activism, and Affirmative Governmentality*. Durham, NC: Duke University Press.

Larsen, Mike, and Justin Piché. 2010. "Public Vigilance Campaigns and Participatory Surveillance after 11 September 2001." In *Surveillance: Power, Problems, and Politics*, 187–202. Ed. Sean Patrick Hier and Joshua Greenberg. Vancouver: University of British Columbia Press.

Lazzarato, Maurizio. 1996. "Immaterial Labor." In *Radical Thought in Italy: A Potential Politics*, 133–49. Ed. Paolo Virno and Michael Hardt. Minneapolis: University of Minnesota Press.

Levitas, Daniel. 2002. *The Terrorist Next Door: The Militia Movement and the Radical Right*. New York: St. Martin's Press.

Lindberg, Richard. 2008. *To Serve and Collect: Chicago Politics and Police Corruption from the Lager Beer Riot to the Summerdale Scandal, 1855–1960*. Carbondale: Southern Illinois University Press.

Linder, Dennis. 2012. "From E-Government to We-Government: Defining a Typology for Citizen Coproduction in the Age of Social Media." *Government Information Quarterly* 29: 446–54.

Lindquist, Malinda A. 2012. *Race, Social Science, and the Crisis of Manhood*. New York: Routledge.

Los, Maria. 2006. "Looking into the Future: Surveillance, Globalization, and the Totalitarian Potential." In *Theorizing Surveillance: The Panopticon and Beyond*, 69–93. Ed. David Lyon. Portland, OR: Willan Publishing.

———. 2004. "The Technologies of Total Domination." *Surveillance & Society* 2 (1): 15–38.

Lyon, David. 1994. *The Electronic Eye: The Rise of Surveillance Society*. Minneapolis: University of Minnesota Press.

———. 2003. *Surveillance after September 11*. Malden, MA: Polity Press.

———. 2002. *Surveillance Society: Monitoring Everyday Life*. Buckingham: Open University Press.

———. 2007. *Surveillance Studies: An Overview*. Malden, MA: Polity Press.

———. 2006. "Why Where You Are Matters: Mundane Mobilities, Transparent Technologies, and Digital Discrimination." In *Surveillance and Security: Technological Politics and Power in Everyday Life*, 209–24. Ed. Torin Monahan. New York: Routledge.

Lyotard, Jean-Francois. 1988. *The Differend: Phrases in Dispute*. Trans. Georges Van Den Abbeele. Minneapolis: University of Minnesota Press.

Macleod, David. 1983. *Building Character in the American Boy: The Boy Scouts, YMCA, and their Forerunners, 1870–1920*. Madison: University of Wisconsin Press.

Maddalena, Kate, and Jeremy Packer. 2015. "The Digital Body: Telegraphy as Discourse Network." *Theory, Culture, and Society* 32 (1): 93–117.

Magnet, Shoshana, and Kelly Gates (Eds.). 2009. *The New Media of Surveillance*. New York: Routledge.

Major, Aaron. 2014. *Architects of Austerity: International Finance and the Politics of Growth*. Stanford, CA: Stanford University Press.

Mann, Steve, Jason Nolan, and Barry Wellman. 2003. "Sousveillance: Inventing and Using Wearable Computing Devices for Data Collection in Surveillance Environments." *Surveillance and Society* 1 (3): 331–55.

Manning, Peter K. 2011. *The Technology of Policing: Crime Mapping, Information Technology, and the Rationality of Crime Control*. New York: New York University Press.

Marvin, Carolyn. 1988. *When Old Technologies Were New: Thinking about Electric Communication in the Late Nineteenth Century*. New York: Oxford University Press.

Marx, Gary T. 1989. "Commentary: Some Trends and Issues in Citizen Involvement in the Law Enforcement Process." *Crime and Delinquency* 35 (3): 500–19.

———. 2013. "The Public as Partner? Technology Can Make Us Auxiliaries as Well as Vigilantes." *Security & Privacy, IEEE* 11 (5): 56–61.

———. 2006. "Soft Surveillance: The Growth of Mandatory Volunteerism in Collecting Personal Information—'Hey Buddy Can You Spare a DNA.'" In *Surveillance and Security: Technological Politics and Everyday Life*, 37–56. Ed. Torin Monahan. New York: Routledge.

———. 1988. *Undercover: Police Surveillance in America*. Berkeley: University of California Press.

Marx, Gary T., and Dane Archer. 1971. "Citizen Involvement in the Law Enforcement Process: The Case of Community Police Patrols." *American Behavioral Scientist* 15 (1): 52–72.

Mason, Gregory. 1915. "Boy Police of New York." *The Outlook: A Weekly Newspaper, Volume 150*. New York: Outlook Company.

Massumi, Brian. 2007. "Potential Politics and the Primacy of Preemption." *Theory and Event* 10 (2). http://muse.jhu.edu.

Mattelart, Armand. 2010. *The Globalization of Surveillance*. Trans. Susan Taponier and James A. Cohen. Malden, MA: Polity.

Matthew, Richard A. 2010. "Reading, Writing, and Readiness." In *Schools under Surveillance: Cultures of Control in Public Education*, 123–39. Ed. Torin Monahan and Rodolfo D. Torres. New Brunswick, NJ: Rutgers University Press.

May, Matthew S. 2012. "Orator-Machine: Autonomist Marxism and William D. 'Big Bill' Haywood's Cooper Union Address." *Philosophy and Rhetoric* 45 (4): 429–51.

McLuhan, Marshall, and Quentin Fiore. 1967. *The Medium Is the Massage: An Inventory of Effects*. New York: Bantam.

Midwest Research Institute. 1977. *Evaluation of the National Sheriffs' Association National Neighborhood Watch Program, Final Report, MRI Project No. 4321-D, August 10, 1977*. Kansas City, MO: Midwest Research Institute.

Miller, Peter, and Nikolas Rose. 1990. "Governing Economic Life." *Economy and Society* 19 (1): 1–31.

Miller, Toby. 2003. *Spyscreen: Espionage on Film and TV from the 1930s to the 1960s*. New York: Oxford University Press.

———. 1993. *The Well-Tempered Self: Citizenship, Culture, and the Postmodern Subject*. Baltimore: Johns Hopkins University Press.

Molotch, Harvey Luskin. 2012. *Against Security: How We Go Wrong at Airports, Subways, and Other Sites of Ambiguous Danger*. Princeton, NJ: Princeton University Press.

Monahan, Torin. 2009. "Identity Theft Vulnerability: Neoliberal Governance Through Crime Construction." *Theoretical Criminology* 13 (2): 155–76.

———. 2015. "The Right to Hide? Anti-Surveillance Camouflage and the Aestheticization of Resistance." *Communication and Critical/Cultural Studies* 12 (2): 159–78.

———. 2010. *Surveillance in the Time of Insecurity*. New Brunswick, NJ: Rutgers University Press.

Monahan, Torin, and Jennifer Mokos. 2013. "Crowdsourcing Urban Surveillance: The Development of Homeland Security Markets for Environmental Sensor Networks." *Geoforum* 49: 279–88.

Monelle, Raymond. 2006. *The Musical Topic: Hunt, Military, and Pastoral*. Bloomington: University of Indiana Press.

Morris, William Alfred. 1910. *The Frankpledge System*. New York: Longmans, Green, and Co.

Mosher, Clayton J., and Scott Akins. 2007. *Drugs and Drug Policy: The Control of Consciousness Alteration*. Thousand Oaks, CA: SAGE.

Moskos, Peter. 2008. *Cop in the Hood: My Year Policing Baltimore's Eastern District*. Princeton, NJ: Princeton University Press.

Moynihan, Daniel Patrick. 1999. *Secrecy: The American Experience*. New Haven, CT: Yale University Press.

Mythen, Gabe, and Sandra Walklate. 2006. "Communicating the Terrorist Risk: Harnessing a Culture of Fear?" *Crime, Media, Culture* 2: 123–42.

Natapoff, Alexandra. 2009. *Snitching: Criminal Informants and the Erosion of American Justice*. New York: New York University Press.

National Institute of Justice. 1984. *Calling the Police: Citizen Reporting of Serious Crime.* Washington, DC: U.S. Government Printing Office.

National Sheriffs' Association. 1978. *National Neighborhood Watch Program Manual: Guidelines and Suggestions for the Implementation of Local Neighborhood Watch Programs by Law Enforcement Agencies and Citizen Organizations.* Washington, DC: National Sheriffs' Association.

———. 1974. *National Neighborhood Watch Program Review.* Washington, DC: National Sheriffs' Association.

Nealon, Jeffrey Thomas. 2008. *Foucault beyond Foucault: Power and Its Intensifications since 1984.* Stanford, CA: Stanford University Press.

Ness, Eliot. 1940. "The Participation of Boys." *Phi Delta Kappan* 22 (7): 337–39.

"New York's Campaign of Crime Prevention." 1916. *Journal of the American Institute of Criminal Law and Criminology* 7 (2): 295–98.

Office of Crime Prevention. 1981. *Program Guide: New York Neighborhood Watch.* Washington, DC: National Institute of Justice.

O'Mally, Pat, and Darren Palmer. 1996. "Post-Keynesian Policing." *Economy and Society* 25: 137–55.

Ouellette, Laurie, and James Hay. 2008. *Better Living through Reality TV: Television and Post-Welfare Citizenship.* Malden, MA: Blackwell.

Packer, Jeremy. 2006. "Becoming Bombs: Mobilizing Mobility in the War of Terror." *Cultural Studies* 20 (4–5): 378–99.

———. 2013. "Epistemology Not Ideology OR Why We Need New Germans." *Communication and Critical/Cultural Studies* 10 (2–3): 295–300.

———. 2007. "Homeland Subjectivity: The Algorithmic Identity of Security." *Communication and Critical/Cultural Studies* 4 (2): 211–15.

———. 2008. *Mobility without Mayhem: Safety, Cars, and Citizenship.* Durham, NC: Duke University Press.

Packer, Jeremy, and Joshua Reeves. 2013. "Romancing the Drone: Military Desire and Anthropophobia from SAGE to Swarm." *Canadian Journal of Communication* 38 (3): 309–32.

Pennell, Susan, Christine Curtis, and Joel Henderson. 1985. *Guardian Angels: An Assessment of Citizen Response to Crime: Volume II, Technical Report.* San Diego: Association of Governments.

Pepinsky, Harold E. 1989. "Issues of Citizen Involvement in Policing." *Crime and Delinquency* 35 (3): 458–70.

Pepper, Shayne. 2014. "Subscribing to Governmental Rationality: HBO and the AIDS Epidemic." *Communication and Critical/Cultural Studies* 11 (2): 120–38.

Periera, Joseph. 1992. "The Informants: In a Drug Program, Some Kids Turn in Their Own Parents." *Wall Street Journal.* April 20.

Petersen, William H. 1976. *National Neighborhood Watch Program Discretionary Grant Progress Report.* Washington, DC: National Sheriffs' Association.

Pfeifer, Michael J. 2013. "Introduction." In *Lynching beyond Dixie: American Mob Violence Outside the South,* 1–18. Ed. Michael J. Pfeifer. Champaign: University of Illinois Press.

216 | REFERENCES

Philips, William J., and Charles Robinson. 1857. *Philips' and Robinson's Municipal Telegraph: To Which Is Invited the Attention of the Municipal Authorities, Fire Departments, Property Owners, Insurance Companies, and Citizens of All Large Cities.* Philadelphia.

Phillips, David. 2005. "Texas 9-1-1: Emergency Telecommunications and the Genesis of Surveillance Infrastructure." *Telecommunications Policy* 29: 843–56.

Platt, Anthony M. 1995. "Crime Rave." *Monthly Review* 47 (2): 35–46.

Police Executive Research Forum. 2008. *The Stop Snitching Phenomenon: Breaking the Code of Silence.* Washington, DC: Police Executive Research Forum/ U.S. Department of Justice.

Police Foundation. 1972. *Experiments in Police Improvement: A Progress Report.* Washington, DC: Police Foundation.

Pollock, Frederick, and Frederic William Maitland. 1895. *The History of English Law before the Time of King Edward, Vol. 2* London: C.J. Clay and Sons.

Pope, Franklin Leonard. 1872. *Modern Practice of the Electric Telegraph: A Handbook for Electricians and Operators.* New York: D. Van Nostrand.

Prescott, George B. 1884. *Bell's Electric Speaking Telephone: Its Invention, Construction, Application, and History.* New York: Appleton.

Ralph, Jason. 2013. *America's War on Terror: The State of the 9/11 Exception from Bush to Obama.* New York: Oxford University Press.

Redden, Jim. 2000. *Snitch Culture: How Citizens Are Turned into the Eyes and Ears of the State.* Los Angeles: Feral House.

Reeves, Joshua. 2012. "If You See Something, Say Something: Lateral Surveillance and the Uses of Responsibility." *Surveillance and Society* 10 (3/4): 235–48.

———. 2015. "License to Kill: Trayvon Martin and the Logic of Exception." *Cultural Studies <=> Critical Methodologies* 15 (4): 287–91.

Reeves, Joshua, and Jeremy Packer. 2013. "Police Media: The Governance of Territory, Speed, and Communication." *Communication and Critical/Cultural Studies* 10 (4): 359–84.

Reiss, Albert J. 1971. *The Police and the Public.* New Haven, CT: Yale University Press.

Rigakos, George S. 2002. *The New Parapolice: Risk Markets and Commodified Social Control.* Toronto: University of Toronto Press.

Ritchie, Marnie. 2015. "Feeling for the State: Affective Labor and Anti-Terrorism Training in U.S. Hotels." *Communication and Critical/Cultural Studies* 12 (2): 179–97.

Rose, Nikolas. 1996. "Governing 'Advanced' Liberal Democracies." In *Foucault and Political Reason: Liberalism, Neo-Liberalism, and Rationalities of Government*, 37–64. Ed. Andrew Barry, Thomas Osborne, and Nikolas S. Rose. University of Chicago Press.

———. 2000. "Government and Control." *British Journal of Criminology* 40 (2): 321–39.

Rose, Nikolas, and Peter Miller. 1992. "Political Power beyond the State: Problematics of Government." *British Journal of Sociology* 43 (2): 172–205.

Ross, Marlon Bryan. 2004. *Manning the Race: Reforming Black Men in the Jim Crow Era.* New York: New York University Press.

Rosenthal, A. M. 1999. *Thirty-Eight Witnesses: The Kitty Genovese Case*. Berkeley: University of California Press.

Roth, Michael P. 2001. "Hue and Cry." In *The Historical Dictionary of Law Enforcement, 163*. Westport, CT: Greenwood Press.

Rotstein, Gary. 1993. "*America's Most Wanted* Leads to the Wrong Man." *Pittsburgh Post Gazette*. September 30.

Rubin, Andrew. 2012. *Archives of Authority: Empire, Culture, and the Cold War*. Princeton, NJ: Princeton University Press.

Rubinstein, Jonathan. 1973. *City Police*. New York: Farrar, Straus and Giroux.

Rutherford, Jonathan. 2005. "At War." *Cultural Studies* 19 (5): 622–42.

Schneider, Christopher J. 2014. "Police 'Image Work' in an Era of Social Media: YouTube and the 2007 Montebello Summit Protest." In *Social Media, Politics, and the State: Protests, Revolutions, Riots, Crime, and Policing in the Age of Facebook, Twitter, and YouTube*, 227–46. Ed. Daniel Trottier and Christian Fuchs. New York: Routledge.

Schneider, Matthew C., Robert Chapman, and Amy Schapiro. 2009. "Toward the Unification of Policing Innovations under Community Policing." *Policing: An International Journal of Police Strategies & Management* 32 (4): 694–718.

Sealander, Judith. 2003. *The Failed Century of the Child: Governing America's Young in the Twentieth Century*. New York: Cambridge University Press.

Shain, Barry Alan. 1996. *The Myth of American Individualism: The Protestant Origins of American Political Thought*. Princeton, NJ: Princeton University Press.

Sherman, Lawrence W. 1983. "Patrol Strategies for Police." In *Crime and Public Policy*, 145–64. Ed. James Q. Wilson. San Francisco: Institute for Contemporary Studies.

Shirky, Clay. 2008. *Here Comes Everybody: The Power of Organizing without Organizations*. New York: Penguin Books.

Simmons, Lizbet. 2010. "The Docile Body in School Space." In *Schools under Surveillance: Cultures of Control in Public Education*, 55–72. Ed. Torin Monahan and Rodolfo D. Torres. New Brunswick, NJ: Rutgers University Press.

Simon, Jonathan. 2009. *Governing through Crime: How the War on Crime Transformed American Democracy and Created a Culture of Fear*. New York: Oxford University Press.

Simpson, Rana. 2004. *Misuse and Abuse of 911*. Washington, DC: U.S. Department of Justice.

Sirgiovanni, George. 1990. *An Undercurrent of Suspicion: Anti-Communism in America during World War II*. New Brunswick, NJ: Transaction Publishers.

Skolnick, Jerome H., and David H. Bayley. 1986. *The New Blue Line: Police Innovation in Six American Cities*. New York: Free Press.

Smith, Gavin J. D. 2012. "Surveillance Work(ers)." In *Routledge Handbook of Surveillance Studies*, 107–15. Ed. Kirstie Ball, Kevin D. Haggerty, and David Lyon. New York: Routledge.

Sprogle, Howard O. 1887. *The Philadelphia Police, Past and Present*. Philadelphia.

Steeves, Valerie. 2010. "Online Surveillance in Canadian Schools." In *Schools under Surveillance: Cultures of Control in Public Education*, 87–103. Ed. Torin Monahan and Rodolfo D. Torres. New Brunswick, NJ: Rutgers University Press.

Stenson, Kevin. 1993. "Community Policing as a Governmental Technology." *Economy and Society* 22 (3): 373–89.

Stevens, Dennis J. 1998. "Urban Communities and Homicide: Why American Blacks Resort to Murder." *Policing and Society* 8 (3): 253–67.

Stewart, R. W. 1994. "The Police Signal Box: A 100-Year History." *Engineering Science Education Journal* 3 (4): 161–68.

Stoil, Michael J., and Gary Hill. 1996. *Preventing Substance Abuse: Interventions That Work*. New York: Plenum.

Thelen, David R. 1986. *Paths of Resistance: Tradition and Dignity in Industrializing Missouri*. New York: Oxford University Press.

Tracy, Sarah J., and Karen Tracy. 1998. "Emotion Labor at 911: A Case Study and Theoretical Critique." *Journal of Applied Communication Research* 26: 390–411.

Treichler, Paula. 1999. *How to Have Theory in an Epidemic: Cultural Chronicles of AIDS*. Durham, NC: Duke University Press.

Trojanowicz, Robert C., and Bonnie Bucqueroux. 1990. *Community Policing: A Contemporary Perspective*. Cincinnati: Anderson Publishing.

Trottier, Daniel. 2012. "Policing Social Media." *Canadian Review of Sociology* 49 (4): 411–25.

———. 2014. "Vigilantism and Power Users: Police and User-Led Investigations on Social Media." In *Social Media, Politics, and the State: Protests, Revolutions, Riots, Crime, and Policing in the Age of Facebook, Twitter, and Facebook*, 209–26. Ed. Daniel Trottier and Christian Fuchs. New York: Routledge.

Turkle, Sherry. 2012. *Alone Together: Why We Expect More from Technology and Less from Each Other*. New York: Basic Books.

United States Department of Commerce and Labor. 1908. *Investigation of Telephone Companies: Letter from the Secretary of Commerce and Labor Transmitting, in Response to a Senate Resolution of May 28, 1908*. Washington, DC: Government Printing Office.

———. 1906. *Special Reports: Telephones and Telegraphs, 1902*. Washington, DC: Government Printing Office.

United States Government Accountability Office. 2013. "Information Sharing: Additional Actions Could Help Ensure That efforts to Share Terrorism-Related Suspicious Activity Reports Are Effective." Washington, DC: United States Government Accountability Office.

United States War Department. 1944. *Telephone Switchboard Operating Procedure*. Washington, DC: United States Government Printing Office.

Virginia Division of Justice and Crime Prevention. 1981. *Neighborhood Watch Guide*. Richmond: Virginia Division of Justice and Crime Prevention.

Virno, Paolo. 1996. "Virtuosity and Revolution: The Political Theory of Exodus." In *Radical Thought in Italy: A Potential Politics*, 189–211. Ed. Paolo Virno and Michael Hardt. Minneapolis: University of Minnesota Press.

Wald, Patricia. 1998. "Keynote Address: A Retrospective on the Thirty-Year War against Crime." In *The Challenge of Crime in a Free Society: Looking Back Looking*

Forward, 81–92. Ed. U.S. Department of Justice and Laurie Robinson. Washington, DC: U.S. Department of Justice.

Walsh, James. 2008. "Community, Surveillance, and Border Control: The Case of the Minuteman Project." In *Surveillance and Governance: Crime Control and Beyond*, 11–34. Ed. Mathieu Deflem. Bingley, UK: JAI Press.

Washington, Elizabeth Jean. 1945. "A Study of the Program and Activities of the Junior Police and Citizens Corps in Washington, D.C." Master's Thesis, Atlanta University School of Social Work.

Weber, Max. 1946. "Religious Rejections of the World and Their Directions." In *Max Weber: Essays in Sociology*, 323–62. Ed. Hans H. Gerth and C. Wright Mills. New York: Oxford University Press.

Whitfield, Stephen J. 1996. *The Culture of the Cold War*. Baltimore: Johns Hopkins University Press.

Whitman, Julie L., and Robert C. Davis. 2007. *Snitches Get Stitches: Youth, Gangs, and Witness Intimidation in Massachusetts*. Washington, DC: National Center for Victims of Crime.

Williams, Kristian. 2007. *Our Enemies in Blue: Police and Power in America*. Cambridge, MA: South End Press.

Wilson, Dean, and Tanya Serisier. 2010. "Video Activism and the Ambiguities of Counter-Surveillance." *Surveillance and Society* 8 (2): 166–80.

Wirt, William. 1903. *The Life of Patrick Henry*. Ed. Henry Ketcham. New York: A.L. Bert Co.

Woldoff, Rachael A., and Karen G. Weiss. 2010. "Stop Snitchin': Exploring Definitions of the Snitch and Implications for Urban Black Communities." *Journal of Criminal Justice and Popular Culture* 17 (1): 184–223.

Woltman, George. 1951. "Town Up in Arms; Four in School Boy Patrol Fired On." *Chicago Daily Tribune*. February 23.

Woodward, Bob. 2002. *Bush at War*. New York: Simon and Schuster.

Wouters, Cas. 1999. "Changing Patterns of Social Controls and Self-Controls: On the Rise of Crime since the 1950s and the Sociogenesis of a 'Third Nature.'" *British Journal of Criminology* 39 (3): 416–32.

Wuthnow, Robert. 2010. *Be Very Afraid: The Cultural Response to Terror, Pandemics, Environmental Devastation, Nuclear Annihilation, and Other Threats*. New York: Oxford University Press.

Yin, Robert K., Mary E. Vogel, Jan M. Chaiken, and Deborah Both. 1976. *Patrolling the Neighborhood Beat: Residents and Residential Security Case Studies and Profiles*. Santa Monica, CA: Rand Corporation.

Zedner, Lucia. 2006. "Policing before and after the Police: The Historical Antecedents of Contemporary Crime Control." *British Journal of Criminology* 46 (1): 78–96.

INDEX

911 Emergency, 51–76; centrality to policing strategy, 54–55; emergence of, 63–64; pranks, 68–73; surveillance of, 56, 57, 63–73

Agamben, Giorgio, 149, 183n13 ch.1
AMBER alert, 35–36
American Civil Liberties Union, 155–156, 170, 179
American Protective League, 141
America's Most Wanted, 11, 16, 22, 25, 33–34, 41, 50, 183n5 ch.1
Andrejevic, Mark, 14, 107
Anglo-Saxons, 25–26, 28, 183n16 ch.1
Anonymous (hacker collective), 162–163
Anthony, Carmelo, 132–133, 135
Arlington Police Department, 105
Armed Forces Information Films, 145, 147
Armey, Dick, 150
austerity, 23, 84, 191n24. *See also* neoliberalism
Automatic Location Identification, 69
autonomous citizenship, 13–14, 74, 80, 82, 84–85, 98, 100; compared to responsible citizenship, 17, 49, 79–80, 82–87; defined, 13; violence and, 74, 80–85

Bay Youth Courtesy Patrol, 122
Bennett, Tony, 12
Bennett, William, 122

biopolitics, 11, 36
Black Panther Party, 103
Black Tom explosion, 141
Boston Marathon Bombing, 42–45
Boston Police Department, 44–45, 129
"boy police" programs, 114–122, 195n18; compared to "girl police," 117–119; conflict with gangs, 120–121; violence against, 121
Boy Scouts of America, 111–119
Boy Spies of America, 141
Brace, Charles Loring, 110–112
Bratich, Jack, 15, 199n19
Breslin, Jimmy, 101–102
Brewer, David J., 82
Brecht, Bertolt, 148
Brown, Michael, 48, 103
Brown Scare, 2, 138, 141
Bureau of Justice Assistance, 3
Bush, George W., 19, 137, 149–153; surveillance programs of, 150–153
Busta Rhymes, 131, 133

California State Police, 21
Campus Crime Stoppers, 130
Carey, James, 57
Chicago Police Department, 59, 60, 69, 85–86
Chicago Organization of Radio Operators, 85–86
Children's Aid Society, 111–113
citizen's arrest, 98–104, 193–4n90 ch.3
citizens' patrol, 77–81, 87, 96, 102–106

221

ABOUT THE AUTHOR

Joshua Reeves is Assistant Professor of New Media Communications and Speech Communication at Oregon State University.